AFRICAN HEROES
AND HEROINES

Carter Godwin Woodson

AFRICAN HEROES AND HEROINES

Carter Godwin Woodson
Introduction by Charles H. Wesley

Black Classic Press
Baltimore

African Heroes and Heroines

Copyright © 1939, 1944, 1969 by The Associated Publishers, Inc.
Published 2016 by Black Classic Press

Library of Congress Control Number: 2015952502

Softcover ISBN: 978-1-57478-128-1
E-book ISBN: 978-1-57478-129-8
Hardcover ISBN: 978-1-57478-144-1

Cover design by Mitchell & Sennaar Communications, Inc.

Printed by BCP Digital Printing,
An affiliate company of Black Classic Press, Inc.

To review or purchase Black Classic Press books, please visit:
www.blackclassicbooks.com

You may also obtain a list of titles by writing to:
Black Classic Press
c/o List
P.O. Box 13414
Baltimore, MD 21203

Introduction to the Woodson Series

The Association for the Study of African American Life and History (ASALH) is pleased to partner with Black Classic Press to make available the works published by the Associated Publishers (AP.) Founded by Carter G. Woodson in 1921, the Associated Publishers dedicated itself to bringing to the public works by and about Africans and people of African descent that could not find a home among mainstream publishers.

For decades, Black Classic Press has distinguished itself as a company dedicated to ensuring that important works remain before the reading public. Moreover, the proprietor, Paul Coates, has been a stalwart supporter of ASALH and an exemplar of Woodson's philosophy that important knowledge about Black people must be available.

When Carter G. Woodson passed away on April 3, 1950, the Association he founded became the majority stockholder of the publishing house and continued to carry the mission forward. Over the years, the press was run by the giants of the Association, including Benjamin Quarles and Edgar Toppin. Yet, Miss W. Leona Miles was the day-to-day presence. She labored alongside of Carter G. Woodson during his last years, and continued to manage the AP until her own death in the 1990s. By the late 1990s, the publishing agenda of the Association had waned and, in 2005, the corporation was dissolved. Since then, ASALH has published directly through its own imprint, the ASALH Press.

The partnership between ASALH and Black Classic Press could not have come at a better time: the centennial of the founding of Woodson's Association in 1915. The works will appear as originally published in their final editions. The Woodson Series will not only bring "Black Classics" back to life but do so at the major milestone in the history of the study of Black life, history, and culture.

Daryl Michael Scott, Centennial President of ASALH 2013-2014

To

My Uncle George Woodson and to all other descendants of Africa, who in captivity in America manifested the African spirit of resistance to slavery and died fighting the institution.

PREFACE

The Africans, we ignorantly say, left no history of their entire continent, but no nation has recorded a history of the whole natural division of the universe in which it developed. The ancient history of certain parts of Europe is as obscure as that of areas in Africa, and the past of Asia is scarcely better known than that of Africa. As in the case of most of the other continents, we find certain parts of Africa with well kept records whereas others defy penetration of their past. Much more of the history of Africa is known, moreover, than we appreciate; and what has been made available we have permitted our bias to let us pass by unnoticed.

The record herein noted is not a history of Africa but a biographical treatment of heroes and heroines intended to show the possibilities of the field. These leaders of a despised people measure up to the full stature of the heroic in the histories of other nations. With their record the youth in quest of the dramatic in history may read with unusual interest these exploits of an all but forgotten people. The curriculum can hereby be enriched with this racial heritage which will broaden the minds of the youth and make for better citizenship in the modern world.

For the facts herein set forth the author is indebted to many sources, especially to those writers who have been sufficiently open-minded not to record traditional bias and have reported what they observed with the eye of the scientist. In an elementary work of this type these could not be cited from page to page, but somewhere in each chapter there are given sufficient references to indicate the main sources on which the author depended. A further study of Africa is possible in making use of such works with students for whom this book is intended.

The illustrations have been worked out from source materials by Miss Lois M. Jones. Dean David A. Lane, of the Louisville Municipal College, most obligingly read the galley proof.

C. G. WOODSON

PREFACE TO THE SECOND EDITION

The first edition of this book sold very slowly, as was expected. In this country there was very little interest in the study of Africa, a remote land with which the Negroes themselves in other parts scarcely realized that they had any close connection. The Second World War and the movements leading thereto, however, placed Africa in the foreground, not merely as a field of expansion for the economic imperialists, but as a land of essentials for the entire modern world. When Monrovia in Liberia became an objective to combat hostile forces at Dakar in order that the allies might use Africa as a base for dispossessing the Nazis of Europe, the public began to seek literature on the background and the present status of Africa and Africans. The second edition of this volume is an effort to meet this demand.

This book is not a new production. It is the same work revised and slightly enlarged. The revision has been mainly changes necessary to bring certain treatments up to date, and these were not numerous for the reason that the book is an historical work rather than a treatment of present-day problems.

CARTER G. WOODSON

INTRODUCTION

Africa has changed, and its tradition will change with it. Once it was regarded as "The Dark Continent," and the land of dark mystery, barbarism, slaves, animals, gold and precious stones. It was then a land from which East and West could take rather than give. Nevertheless, there were missionaries, devoted to their causes, who sacrificed themselves for that which they regarded as their goals and gave themselves in service. But they distorted Africa in their accounts and reports. They found it a land to be saved from sin, and for them it had no history nor civilization until it was entered by Asiatics, Europeans, and then Americans. Africa's history became for them a record of the deeds of the conquerors and colonizers who would make their way ultimately by might and power.

Travelers found it to be a country of beauty, savagery and dark hues, but they regarded themselves as the kindly pioneers who opened the way into Africa. Merchants followed with things to sell and to give away in deception for the exchange in human flesh that was black and brown. They bartered, they seized, they used one against the other and began the nefarious slave trade. From these sources much of what is known as African history has arisen.

So far as Europe and Africa were concerned, there were similar developments in their history. There were kingdoms in Africa as glorious and as brilliant as those of the Goths, the Vandals, the Huns, the Angles, the Saxons, the Jutes and the Franks. Europe had its Charlemagne, its Charles the Great, and its heroes and heroines, and Africa had its Askia Mohammed, its Askia the Great with its black and brown heroes and heroines. There were rulers with governments, laws, industrial and economic manifestations which rivaled the early kingdoms of Europe under its kings and emperors. At the time when European states were emerging from the period of the barbarian invasions, there were kingdoms in Africa which had gained a relatively high degree of civilization. Africa was more than a continent which gave to the western world a labor supply, while Europe reveled in the glories of its leadership. Africa had a history comparable, and in respects superior, to the histories of the other countries which had indigenous civilizations. Africa can be favorably compared with them even at the period when Europe had acquired the heritage of Greece and Rome, for upon these civilizations western Europe built its civilizations. For many centuries in the Middle Ages, African kingdoms were worthy rivals of analogous kingdoms in Europe whose civilizations are more renowned. Basil Davidson, in his *The Lost Cities of Africa* (1954) declares, "The medieval Sudan had little to fear from comparison in civilization with medieval Europe."

The continuance of the African kings and their dynasties show the value of their political organizations. These governments were carried on by kings, chiefs, and headmen of families. The plan of government by the family group was quite similar to the kinship group of the Germanic tribes. A considerable group of families belonging to clans constituted the smaller state, which sometimes embraced a single village. Then above these were clans which might constitute themselves a state under a superior chief. These small states would extend their authority over others and thus an empire or kingdom would rise as a result of conquest or political intrigue. Land was often held in common and was distributed so as to support the entire group. Either the king or the chief of the land had authority to administer it.

These kingdoms differed in government and social structure. The Kingdom of Bornu, in the south of the Sudan was described as an elective monarchy. The privilege of electing one of the sons of a deceased king was granted to three of the distinguished men of the state. This system was a direct contrast with the election of an emperor by the Seven Electors of the Holy Roman Empire, which was decreed by the well known Golden Bull of 1356. On the other hand, there was an absolute monarchy in the Songhay Empire, with appointed governors over provinces, much as one would find in the ancient and medieval empires of Europe. There were ministers who composed a kind of parliament of conference with the king.

The contentment of the people with their material life was due to an equitable distribution of wealth and not its ownership by the few. Collectivism was a characteristic of African society. The quarrels of capital and labor, unemployment, and the crimes of the surban slum were unknown to them. In agriculture and in the domestication of animals, such as sheep, swine, goats, cattle and chickens, there was much to rival the primitive life of Europeans. Africans living on the seas and rivers devoted their interest to fishing and navigation. Others occupied themselves with cattle-raising. There were workers in the metals, iron, copper, gold and silver. There were weavers and tailors and dyers.

The metal industry was found to be very extensive in early Africa in the lake region of the Nile. Arrows and war implements were made of iron and carried into Egypt and North Africa, for iron culture was discovered in this continent. The Kaffirs and Zulus were good blacksmiths and copper smelters. On the Gold Coast, rings and chains, knives, and ivory ornaments of great value were made by Negro artisans. Dutch and Portuguese travelers have described the curious bronze work of Benin during the Middle Ages—some of which now can be seen in European Museums. The market and the fair were fundamental economic institutions in the commercial life of the Negroes of the Sudan.

The extent of iron manufacture in Africa has led some observers to conclude that the blacks were the inventors of the smelting of iron. This seems to be the belief of Mortillet, Von Luschan, Schweinfurth, and others. Professor Franz Boas of Columbia University has said, "It seems likely that at a time when the European was still satisfied with rude stone tools the African had invented or adopted the art of smelting iron—it seems not unlikely that the people who made the marvelous discovery of reducing iron ores by smelting were African Negroes. Neither Europe, nor ancient western Asia, nor ancient China knew the iron and everything points to its introduction from Africa." Delafosse declared in his *Negroes of Africa—History and Civilization* that "it would perhaps be proper to attribute to the Negroes of the second wave of immigration, the local invention of working in iron."

African literature contained poetry, stories, riddles, and proverbs which are similar to the folk literature of other races. Nature speaks, the animals talk and act as human beings, and a moral follows each story. There are supernatural stories, epic poems, love songs, comic tales, and drama. Fire, water, caves, groves and animals become animated for the African as for all primitive peoples. Heroes meet demons in conflict, and the elements of the mysterious run throughout these tales. These stories remind the reader of the chivalry and the heroic episodes in Europe of the Middle Ages. For example, Samba Gana, in love with beautiful Annalja Tu Bari, conquers eighty principalities, struggles eight years with a mighty serpent, dying by suicide with his love unrequited. After his death he is acclaimed as a hero by Annalje Tu Bari who prepares to unite with him by her own death. These epics could be a basis for worthy tradition, similar to the Germanic ones brought into opera by the famed Wagner and made into folk history by the Minnisingers. The storyteller and the narrator of tribal traditions occupied a prominent place in the life of the people. The proverbs which have come down to us show the heroic as well as the folk wisdom and experiences of African life.

The facts which have come to life through recent investigations have led to the conclusion that the people of Africa who were brought as slaves to America, have a history, a culture, and abilities comparable to other poeples. Africa had intellectual and artistic tribes like the early Greeks and other Europeans. Africa had its aggressive leaders who compared favorably with the conquerors among the Romans, and it had weaker and cruder leaders like those of all lands who had only the simplest evidences of cultures.

These contributions to a continuous history and a developing civilization were checked and adversely affected by the rise and expansion of the extensive Mohammedan slave trade to the East and the more extensive slave trade to the West. Whole villages were depopulated. Kingdoms turned to slave-hunting and trading as more profitable than the slower methods of civilization building. Then came the invasions of the imperialistic nations and the division of Africa among them. The civilizations of Africa known in its ancient and medieval periods disappeared. Frobenius refers to this decline as "the decadence of Africa."

History reveals that the people of Africa whose descendants were brought as slaves and workers to America had their heroes and heroines, their culture and their talents in men and women comparable to those of other peoples. Africa had its intellectuals, artists and its warlike heroes as the Greeks, Romans and Europeans had.

In earlier years, some Negro-Americans manifested little interest in Africa, for they regarded it, as did white Americans, as a Dark Continent and a benighted land. It was somewhat in this vein that Contee Cullen asked:

What is Africa to me?
Copper sun or scarlet sea,

Jungle star or jungle track
Strong bronze men or regal black
Women from whose loins I sprang
When the birds of Eden sang.
One three centuries removed
From the scenes his fathers loved
Spicy grove, cinnamon tree
What is Africa to me?

Dr. Carter G. Woodson, in commenting upon this situation, said in 1945, "With a more sympathetic approach, a few Negroes have recently become more intelligently interested in the fate of the man of African blood in the crucible of international affairs." However, as the African peoples achieved self-government or independence and were admitted to the United Nations, their histories became factors of importance to them. Since World War II, the independent movements in Africa have been rapid and have increased in rapidity. The old colonial map of Africa has completely changed as black nationalism has spread over the entire continent either as independent governments or as governments within the Empire.

Africa has had to come a long way to achieve a recognition of its historical background. Such recognition means much for the total field of history and current acceptance of dark people as well as for all mankind. An intellectual, Leopold-Sedar Senghor, African poet of Senegal, has declared,

The more African writers are inspired by African culture, the more they will raise themselves to international ranks; the more they turn their backs on Africa the more they will degenerate and weaken.

The publication of these fact about Africa and their use in the schools, colleges and universities will cause the passing of the old tradition of Africa without a civilization or history. It is now being recognized that Africa has a place in history, not only because of the penetration of its interior by Europeans and their establishments for profit there, but also because of historical truth and its own store of the great in history.

Marked changes have been made since 1944, when Carter G. Woodson assembled these biographical sketches. Black was disdained in his time, but now black is beautiful and we seek to find the heroic in history, which can be identified with blackness. There was once a deep ignorance concerning Africa, and an unwillingness to learn anything about it. This is no longer the case. Eagerly youth and the aged read and learn of black heroes and heroines in history and they seek to know the truth about those who are called "great" of dark color. This book is a step in this direction in education, and its reading is, as it was in early editions, for white and black.

CHARLES H. WESLEY

CONTENTS

ILLUSTRATIONS AND MAPS

THE "BARGAIN"

CHAPTER I

THE AFRICAN NATIVES AND THEIR EARLY VISITORS

Neither Europeans nor Americans, as a rule, endeavor to tell the truth about Africa. Most foreign writers produce such accounts as support their religious propaganda and the program of the economic imperialists. What they have found in Africa is observed through the eye of a prejudiced mind, and the faults of the natives are played up as justification for conquest and exploitation. Less than a score of modern writers have endeavored to treat those people and their continent scientifically.[1] Earlier writers help us little because they did not know much about Africa. The annalists of our day know more than they dare publish.

According to some of our scientists there are very few Negroes in Africa. Certain European scientists claim less Negroes for Africa than are found in the United States. The reason for such a small number is that European scientists consider as a Negro only the perfectly black man with thick lips, a flat nose, and a prognathic jaw; but in the United States any white person with one drop of Negro blood is designated as a Negro and oppressed accordingly. In Europe the definition sometimes assumes also a political aspect. Backward African natives who show no evidence of yielding to the stimuli of contacts with modern culture retain the designation of "Negroes," but the progressive type exhibiting the capacity to measure arms with Europeans are con-

[1] For a more extensive treatment of the early opinions with respect to Africa consult the author's *African Background Outlined or Handbook for the Study of the Negro,* Chapter I.

veniently reclassified as ''white'' regardless of color. It would never do to record as ''history'' that blacks can defeat whites.

This difficult method, however, does do as much as to show that there is no such thing as race, not even in Africa, which has had less contact with foreigners than other continents. Yet various elements have gone into that continent although nature denied it good harbors and streams navigable from the ocean and handicapped the land with a hot climate and the all but impenetrable Sahara barrier in the north. Just as Asiatics and Africans have helped to make up the population of Europe so have Europeans and Asiatics contributed to the make-up of the African population, although in a more limited degree for lack of facilities for contacts. The less frequent the influx the better the chance for assimilating to one type the elements already on hand. Africa, then, has tended to be colored while Europe and Asia have shown only here and there those of dark hue.

What we know of the story of Africa has been all but a fairy tale spun out of the imagination of a few writers who have tried to build a narrative out of isolated facts. We have such all but legendary accounts as the voyages of the Phoenicians, the adventures of Hanno, and the expeditions of Eudoxious, recognized in Ptolemy's geography. But what we now know as modern Europe remained in ignorance of the ''Dark Continent.'' The Greeks and the Romans knew the Africans chiefly through those who infiltrated into the Mediterranean world to be immortalized occasionally in their painting and sculpture as mascots and curiosities in the homes of the aristocracy, or through expeditions sent to conquer other nations bordering upon Africa.

Such accounts as we have, however, are not without some value. From time immemorial there has persisted the story of the Atlantis as old as the imagination of Plato. This legend deals with an extensively talked of people pictured as inhabiting various parts of the world but located by a few writers on the West coast of Africa, or on a land now sub-merged in the Atlantic, with the exception of such remains as the Canaries and Azores. These writers have depicted the life of the Atlantis as idealistic with all features of superior cul-ture known to the ancient and medieval world. From the West of Africa it is believed by Leo Wiener that African influence and commerce became so universal that natives, looking for new fields to conquer, braved the high seas and established contact with America probably thousands of years before Europeans had sufficiently advanced to have any such dreams. Words in the language of the American aborigines, parallels in their religions, and Negroid skulls found in caves in the Western Hemisphere are cited as evi-dences of the African discovery of America.[2]

Exactly what the civilization of the Atlantis was the chroniclers who have brought us this story do not give any reliable data. Far from being imaginary, however, is the story that there were actual dwellers who left along the West African coast traces of their regime, the remains of which evidence a great civilization. The most striking of these have been referred to as the figures of Sherbro, the megaliths of Gambia, and the findings about Ife. In spite of speculation to prove foreign importation, these antiquities are evidently indigenous. Aggry beads found also in this region, and re-sembling others dug up in both Asia and Europe, have been more generally regarded by Europeans as imported; but there is just as much evidence of the migration of this aspect of African culture to foreign points as there is to the effect that Africans borrowed it. Of the antique works in bronze, in which is depicted the whole life of the Benin around the mouth of the Niger, foreigners spoke likewise of borrowed

---

[2] The evidence to this effect is treated in more detail in the first chapter of Leo Frobenius's *The Voice of Africa*, Volume I; Woodson's *The Negro in Our History*, Chapter I; *The African Background*, Chap-ter I; Justin Winsor's *Narrative and Critical History of America*, Chapter I; and Leo Wiener's *African Discovery of America*.

ideas in thinking that the Benin had been influenced by the Portuguese, but a later study of a more scientific character has led to the conclusion that this contribution is also indigenous.[3]

How these civilizations arose and perished in the distant past long before Europeans touched the interior of the "Dark Continent," farther back than runs the memory of some of the natives now occupying the site of their predecessors, is still a mystery. Yet it is known that other parts of the world have had similar experience. Excavations around Troy have revealed relics of a score of civilizations, one buried upon the other. Even in America the study of the background of the aborigines is revealing the same picture of the past. How many African civilizations there have been no one knows.

Some scientists have found in the Bushmen of South Africa what they believe to be primitive man. Others supposedly more "scientific" have penetrated the past sufficiently to "discover" another "imaginary" race designated by them as the Grimaldi. Yet some of these writers find that the Grimaldi were the ancestors of the Africans who have resulted from changes which have worked likewise in other parts of the world as in France and Spain. There remains, too, the question as to what is a Pygmy, or whether the Pygmy is the same as a Bushman. In the early accounts there is a confusion, but scientists of today make a clear distinction between the two.

On the West Coast it is now all but evident that the prehistoric nations which developed kingdoms and empires perished because of a change in climate which converted fertile and well watered land into an arid area now constituting the lower fringe of the Sahara. This desert in the most ancient times did not cover as much of West Africa and the

---

[3] See the discussion in Delafosse's *Negroes of Africa*, Chapters I and II, and *African Background Outlined*, pages 4-18.

Sudan as it does today. Historic points later noted by foreigners and well established by the traditions of the natives are not today what they were a thousand years ago.

The African "aborigines" of the interior are spoken of as Negrilles or little Negroes, not a black people, but one of a reddish-brown color with a head of the size öf the man of today but a disproportionately small body and short limbs. They were supposed to dwell in trees and to live mainly by hunting. The later development seems to have been a change to dwelling in caves on the walls of which they probably left interesting paintings. How these little Negroes came into Africa thousands of years ago and from what point we do not know, but they seem to have settled near the Equatorial regions.

Some years thereafter, it is said, the real Negro of the present day type came into Africa from some place which no one knows. Yet some have spoken of this unknown abode as the now submerged land in the Indian Ocean designated as "Lemuria." The Negroes from this land pressed upon the Negrilles in Central and Equatorial Africa and pushed them from their former position. Concerning how much of Africa they covered there is a difference of opinion, for some recent writers ignorantly contend that the real Negro has never been an inhabitant of North and Northeast Africa. Yet there is just as much prehistoric evidence of the Negroes' presence in those parts as in other sections of the continent. Negroes were in Egypt throughout its history and figured in its development. In most of Egypt and in Ethiopia and in practically all of North Africa Asiatics and Europeans, because of the proximity to their continents, came in such large numbers that the complexion of these parts decidedly changed toward white. The Sahara was a barrier to still greater changes, but this handicap was finally overcome by the Mohammedans whose religious zeal and slave-trading brought them into North Africa and then into West Africa and the Sudan. There the African blood was still further diluted with that of the Asiatics.

Before this took place, however, the Bantu, a Hamitic people from an unknown area, had come into Africa. They pressed down upon the Negroes, mixing with some and driving others into the equatorial forest, a work further accentuated by the Mohammedanized Arabs who came later. The aborigines, the Bushmen, not yet extinguished by other movements of population, were driven toward the South. It is believed by some that the mixture of the Bantu with the Bushmen produced another people called the Hottentots. This is *a priori* reasoning, however, because the color of the Hottentot is not black, and the size of his body is intermediate between that of the Bantu and the Bushman. The Hottentots resemble in their characteristics the Bushmen. The former, however, are better hunters in having sufficient knowledge of chemistry so to poison their arrows as to kill the beasts without spoiling the flesh of the animal.

Where the Bantu first developed and from what place they came no one knows. Scientists now believe that before their movement into the heart of Africa they were settled somewhere in Asia or in the horn of Africa. They then moved for some reason into the interior of Africa in a southwesterly direction, forcing the Bushmen and Hottentots, if there were any at that time, into the extreme southern end of Africa, leaving that part of Africa below the Equator dominated by the Bantu. The Bantu were both pastoral and agricultural. It may be that these habits were determined by environment. Some parts of Africa are not suitable for tillage, and in some cases pasturage is seasonal, making it necessary to move from one area and back to another in order to raise cattle.[4] The life of the Bantu was sufficiently stable, however, to

---

[4] S. M. Molema, *The Bantu;* C. G. Seligman, *The Races of Africa;* W. D. Hambly, *African Ethnology; The Cambridge History of the British Empire,* Volume VIII, Chapter II.

show tribal groups under kings restricted by elders of the tribe, the land of which the chief could not alienate although he was their supreme judge, leader in war, and sometimes the high priest.

The tendency is to consider pastoral habits as coming from the Arabs, but certain Bantu who have not recently had contact with such Asiatics raise cattle. In explanation a few writers offer the Hamitic origin of the Bantu. It is believed that they are a branch of the white race which in moving originally out of their first home in Asia resembled the Caucasians more than they do today. In the migrations they took on a Negroid aspect by mixing with Negroes. Be that as it may, the Bantu, while being mainly of a chocolate brown rather than black, have practically all other features of Negroes and are regarded by "scientists" as "blacks."

If there is doubt as to some of the contacts of the African with certain foreign shores there is no reason for discrediting the assertion that on the east coast of Africa the natives had much intercourse with people from various parts of Asia and visited their countries. Trading centers along the east coast were frequented by the Asiatics from time immemorial. Northeast Africa, characterized by high plateaus and infertile desert regions near the coast, was left more inaccessible to the world than was the East Coast of the continent.

It is now known that early adventurers from Asia touched these eastern shores. The Chinese had early contacts with the Africans, but apparently left no deep impressions, although records of Chinese take Africans into account as constituting a social and economic factor in that land. The Japanese reached the same distant shores, for Negroes passed into Japan, where they were assimilated. The Japanese record in their history the deeds of Sakanouye Tamuramaro, a Negro, who distinguished himself as a general leading them to victory over the Ainu.

People from India had some commercial intercourse with the East Coast of Africa, but likewise left little impression except at a few trading posts, which apparently had been established by those of the Hither Orient—Arabs and Persians. Yet in spite of much investigation there is little evidence of any of these people's influence on the general development

MAP OF AFRICA

of African culture. Such impressions at coastal trading posts on the continent might have been made but were effaced by the migrations and immigrations which followed.

The outstanding trading posts like Sofala, Melinde, Mombasa, Kilwa, Magadosho, and Zanzibar established by Asiatics along the East Coast probably had sufficient foreign support to prevent their annihilation by social and economic forces which had free play among the natives of the interior. These factories had varying experiences according to the changing fortunes of those by whom they were maintained. Trade was the dominant force in their development, and the commodities of commerce, the methods of trading, and the routes pursued all changed during ancient, medieval, and modern times. In Africa were sought gold, precious stones, ivory, slaves, and skins, but because of influences from without, the demand for these was not coterminous or contemporary. The greatest change in the course of commerce was the Mohammedanization of Africa which entered rather from the North and penetrated the Sudan in order to proselyte the African at home rather than depend on the effort of Eastern posts to transport them. Africans were desired to serve as laborers and as soldiers in the Mohammedan armies. The interest in the picture then shifts from those trading into Africa to the larger number of Mohammedans settling there for permanent homes and actually transforming the country by race admixture—the fusion of Asiatic and African culture.

Supporters of the theory as to foreign influence in Africa, unwilling to believe that the actual Negro has ever made any contribution to progress, ascribe to the ingenuity of Asiatics the building in Southern Rhodesia of the advanced civilization indicated by the ruins of Zimbabwe. These massive ruins of a tremendously large fortress of ten concentric circles of imposing walls, built doubtless to guard the palace standing as the center of the life of the people, awaken in the observer wide speculation or imagination of what these people achieved and how they ranked among their neighbors in East Africa.

The solutric rock painting left on the walls of the caves of South Africa by other natives, probably the ancestors of the present Hottentots or Bushmen, have been long spoken of

also as of foreign production, but for this position there is
no evidence. Recently some have said that this rock painting was done by prehistoric people called the Grimaldi.[5] Yet
other writers say that these aborigines were progenitors of
the Bushmen or Hottentots in South Africa.

Egypt first felt the force of foreign contacts from the
East. The country was originally settled by Negroid people
as excavations clearly show. These people developed from
clusters of villages in the Nile valley until the nation attained a position of stability under King Menes about 3400
B. C. Following him came other enterprising rulers among
whom stood out Cheops, the builder of the Sphinx and the
Pyramids at Gizeh, and besides reservoirs, canals, and tem-
ples which show the grandeur that land attained. Negroid
rulers like Nefertari sat on the throne of Egypt. But foreign kings, the Hyksos, checked this prosperity for two hundred years, and Egypt slumbered until she was led toward
prosperity again under Thothmes III, who, about 1450 B. C.
conquered Syria and Ethiopia. This contact with the interior of Africa to the South and with Asia to the East,
even as far as Babylon, made Egypt a force for uniting
the peoples and ideas of both continents as she flowered
forth under Rameses II with his new capital at Thebes. This
advanced nation, attracting the covetous from foreign shores,
became later the victim of conquest by the Persians under
Cambyses in 527 B. C., by Alexander in 332 B. C., by the
Romans in 30 B. C., and by the Mohammedan Arabs in 638
A. D. Coloured Egyptians had their skin further whitened
by immigrations resulting from these conquests, and their

---

[5] This Grimaldi theory may be found in almost any recent work of
Europeans and Americans dealing with the prehistory of Africa. In
recent years it has spread like a fever from one to another without any
factual basis. Read G. W. Stowe's *The Native Races of South Africa*,
G. M. Theal's *Ethnography and Conditions of South Africa before A.
D. 1505*, and Schapera's *Khosian Peoples*.

religion changed from pagan to Christian and from Christian to Mohammedan.[6]

In Abyssinia Asiatic immigration had been early in evidence, but natural barriers prevented the rapid influx which overwhelmed Egypt. Yet so many foreigners came that writers still insist that the people of that country are not Negroes but Hamites, a Negroid stock, or persons whose origin is both black and white. Sometimes they are thought of as aborigines and then as Asiatics who have immigrated into and have undergone some racial change in Africa. Abyssinia received a large influx from Yemen which at one time dominated parts of the continent across the Red Sea and in turn was dominated by Abyssinians. The most important infusion of new blood, however, came from the Hebrews, even if we discredit the legendary offspring of the Ethiopians from the union of Solomon and the Queen of Sheba. The Hebrews took possession of that part of the country toward the north and organized there the Axumite Kingdom. This Hebrew nation did not endure, but it left its impress upon the Abyssinians whose culture today is Amharic rather than Christian in spite of the introduction of the new faith there by Bishop Fromentius in 330 A. D., and the much-talked-of role of Prester John.

The isolated position of Abyssinia on high elevated plateaus, however, has tended to make the people African. They were satisfied to go their way. Nothing like contact with modern nations yielded much knowledge of the country until we come to the reign of King Theodore about 1855. He brought under his sway most of the chiefs to constitute a limited feudal monarchy of which they recognized him as Negus Negasti, king of kings. His somewhat modern

---

[6]For the Nordic theory as to the origin of the races in Egypt J. H. Breasted's *History of Egyptians* and other works in this field is the best authority. A few other writers like Seligman, however, give a little ground for the more reasonable contention that the Egyptians were of mixed breed. The general facts of this early history may be found in almost any history of the ancient world.

policy led to frequent contacts with European nations and their rivalry for supremacy in that sphere.[7] The African area along the Mediterranean, long since internationalized by the immigration of both Asiatics and Europeans into that part of the continent, gradually experienced the absorption of one race or stock by the other or the destruction of one by the other for political or religious reasons. From the very beginning race admixture was evident. Egypt had this experience and North Africa underwent the same change. Carthage, founded by the Phoenicians, the first conqueror of North Africa, became almost a parallel of Rome. North Africa proper rapidly became Roman while Egypt united the best in Asiatic and African civilization for the benefits of the ancient and modern world which it was to influence. After the Romans came the Vandals, hoping to overcome both Romans and Berbers in North Africa. The Greek Empire, ruled from Byzantium, extended its sway over North Africa under Justinian. Next came the Arabs, and following them the Turks who have been dispossessed by European nations, mainly the French.

Foreign conquest was facilitated by lack of union in that area. Enthusiastic Berber leaders did not agree among themselves. No one was recognized as a central authority for the land. Strife developed among them, raids of one on the other followed, insurrections occurred frequently, and incessant wars plagued the land for centuries. Three distinct centers, however, did emerge as the nuclei for the well known areas of Morocco, Algeria and Tunis, sometimes called the Barbary States because the aborigines inhabiting them were known as Berbers, a people of Caucasian and Negro blood.

North Africa and Spain had all but natural contact. In

---

[7] F. E. Work, *Abyssinia, or Ethiopia, a Pawn in European Diplomacy;* Henry de Montfried, *Vers les Terres Hostiles de l'Éthiopie;* Henriette Celarié, *Éthiopie XXe Siècle;* Richard C. Thurnwald's *Black and White in East Africa;* La Comtesse de Jumilhac, *Éthiopie Moderne.*

those days of difficult navigation the Strait of Gibraltar offered the shortest route for passing from the one continent to the other. Adventurers from Europe followed this route into Africa, and Africans likewise in reaching Europe. Men of the Far East even knew of it. The Arabs, after conquering Egypt in 638, pushed on through North Africa. Tripoli fell to them in 643, Morocco in 681, and most of the other important parts of North Africa by 703. Berbers with some black blood mixed with Arabs and produced a race that developed later in North Africa as a conquering nation. These were the people who crossed the Strait of Gibraltar, took over Spain in 711 and would have taken all France had they not met Carl Martel at Tours in 732. During the two centuries following, these Arab-Berbers under the Ommeyades dynasty civilized backward Spain. The court of the rulers at Cordova became the center of culture. Art, learning, refinement, and elegance marked the reign of these conquerors. Commerce flourished, mathematics, science and medicine found a way through darkness. Contact with the Far East brought to Spain a real renaissance when other parts of Europe were spending a thousand years passing through the dark age which the destruction of Rome by the barbarians had produced.

Weakening as early as 1000, the Ommeyades dynasty ended in 1031, but prior to this Al Mansur as Caliph had established a kingdom of consequence in Western Africa. Dissension set in, however, since he was considered a usurper. The Berbers arose against him. Claimants of the throne following Al Mansur, used African troops in their conflicts, and the reigning Caliph employed a black bodyguard from Negroland. The Caliphs' power declined, and in both Spain and Africa the empire broke up into provinces. Thus came the opportunity of the Christians in Spain to drive the "infidels" out.

Driven back into Africa, the Arabs had to expand to maintain their position, and this brought them into closer contact with Negroland. The Spanish Arabs naturally pressed down upon the Berber tribes—the Goddala, the Lemtunah, the Messonfah, the Outzila, the Tuareg, the Zegowah, and the Lamtah, all brothers of the Senajah dwelling between the Atlantic Ocean and Ghadames, the western half of North Africa. These Berbers in consequence of wars among them-selves and against incoming Arabs pressed down upon the West African Negro kingdoms and forced Mohammedanism upon some of them. To Tiloutan the Lemtunah king who brought this African desert kingdom to its eminence before he died in 837 twenty Negro chiefs paid tribute. His suc-cessors held out against their foes until 918, when they were overthrown by the Senajah.

These tribes were later united under Yaha about 1048, and from a pious pilgrimage to Mecca he brought back with him Ibn Yassin, a teacher and stern reformer whose work was to restore the orthodox Mohammedan faith from which the dwellers in the desert had strayed; but against this reform pressure the tribesmen rebelled. Ibn Yassin, there-fore, retired with his faithful followers to seclusion on an island in the Senegal from which his inspired disciples un-der the name of Morabites or "Al Moravides" came preach-ing a holy war. This new movement brought him into power in both Africa and Spain. Yaha died in 1056, when he was succeeded by his brother Abou Bekr who, with the sup-port of the Almoravides, advanced to further conquest than the Southwestern Morocco kingdom left by Yaha. They had the territory stretching across the Atlas mountains to the western coast.[8]

Because of dissension among the tribes in the south in 1061, however, Abou Bekr returned to his desert kingdom and assigned his cousin Yusuf (Joseph) Tachefin to take charge in the north. From his desert base Abou Bekr made

---

[8] C. A. Julien, *Histoire de l'Afrique du Nord;* Stéphane Gsell, *His-toire Ancienne de l'Afrique du Nord;* E. Mercier, *Histoire de l'Afrique Septentrionale.*

YUSUF

another attack on the kingdoms of Negroland, advancing probably no farther than Hausa since he had to return to calm things to the north. In 1062 Yusuf established the city of Morocco and asserted his independence of the other part of the kingdom. With this as a beginning he extended his conquests in North Africa. About this time he established such a center of culture that the place proved attractive to the Arabs then being driven out of Spain by Alfonso. These emigrés begged Yusuf to take up their cause against the rising Christians in that country.

Now Yusuf was not an Arab himself. He did not speak that language. He was an African in every sense of the word. He was a "wise, shrewd man, neither too prompt in his determinations, nor too slow in carrying them into effect." He finally yielded to the urgent appeal of the Arabs. Yusuf crossed into Spain with a formidable army, drove his opponents from their all but impregnable positions and won a great victory on the battlefield of Zalakah in 1086. It is said that no tribe of the western desert was not represented in his army, and it was the first time the people of Spain had seen camels used for the purpose of mounting cavalry. In this army were some thousands of blacks armed with Indian swords and short spears and shields covered with hippopotamus hide. This conquest, as a writer has said, then, must be regarded as an African conquest by an African dynasty. These Almoravides thereafter ruling Spain, it has been pointed out, were identically "the same race which, moving from the West, imposed Islam on the races of Negroland."[9]

Yusuf died in 1106, when he was succeeded by his son as ruler of both North Africa and Spain. He maintained alternately a court on both continents. The African kingdom, however, was overthrown in 1142 and that in Spain

---

[9] Lady Lugard Flora Shaw, *A Tropical Dependency;* Stéphane Gsell, *Histoire de l'Afrique du Nord;* Monod, *Histoire de l'Afrique du Nord,* pp. 42-51.

in 1145. The last Almoravide African ruler was defeated by an Almohade, who not only conquered but killed his victim in 1147. This temporarily brought to a close the long intercourse between Spain and Negroland which had been freely maintained.[10]

From North Africa and from settlements on the southern border of the Sahara the new stock of a Berber, Arab and Negro admixture continued to encroach upon the West African and Sudanese kingdoms of the blacks. At times the adventurers came upon the blacks and dispossessed them, but often their introduction into Negroland was merely an infiltration. On the other hand, the conquering African blacks sent their armies to subdue these neighbors to the north and incorporated them into their kingdoms. Other states of these dwellers in and near the Sahara were permitted to take their regular course subject to the will of the blacks to whom they had to pay tribute. The most important of the native African states were Kumbi (Ghana), Manding (Melle), Mossi, Songhay, Bornu, and Hausa. These centres had relations with certain smaller states of mixed breed—peoples like Bagirmi, Wadai, Darfur, Kordofan and Sennar, of which we are to hear later.

Africa as a whole, however, was still unknown to Europeans. Directing their attention to the importance of that continent was no sudden feat. The coast of Africa to them was long a mystery and the interior was a puzzle. The outer world remained content with what the Greeks and Romans knew of North Africa and with what percolated from the interior through Ethiopia into Egypt.[11] Commercially it was always considered the land of the abundance of ivory and the immense deposits of gold. The stores of these treasures had

---

[10] The Almoravides, the Almohades, and Yusuf are amply discussed in the first three chapters of Lady Lugard's *Tropical Dependency*, and in Stéphane Gsell's *Histoire de l'Afrique du Nord*, pages 374 to 417.

[11] Monod's *Histoire de l'Afrique Occidentale Française*, pp. 13-51; Delafosse's *Negroes of Africa*, Chapters II and III; *The Cambridge History of the British Empire*, Volume VII, Chapter III.

been touched by such few adventurers from Europe and Asia that the extent of such natural wealth remained also in the sphere of the fabulous or mythical until modern times.

Contacts of the African interior with the Mediterranean world were mainly indirect. A few Africans reached Europe through Asia with which the Eastern and Northeastern section of Africa had early, though difficult, contact. European warriors conquering in the East often found Negroes among the captives of Oriental armies which they defeated, and they sometimes secured Negro captives in the slave markets of the Arabs and Jews. A still larger number of black men went out of the Sudan and across the Sahara to trade with European ports, and not a few of them remained in such city states as Venice, Genoa, and Marseilles. In the fifteenth century there were as many as three thousand blacks in Venice. The people of the interior of Europe during those days of difficult communication, however, knew practically nothing about Africa.

The wanderings of the Normans which probably brought them down the West coast as far as Guinea before the end of the thirteenth century did not result in an adventure of much benefit. They accomplished little more than the Moors and Arabs who, penetrating the interior four or five hundred years earlier, had made some unsuccessful efforts to explore the same parts. The travels of Marco .Polo did not serve to open up much of Africa. A more serious effort to explore this unknown land developed from the commercial expansion of Portugal as represented by the exploits of its adventurous Prince Henry, beginning with the year 1418. How early Negro captives in wars reached Portugal to be enslaved is not known, but early in the fifteenth century traders had brought Africans there from the West coast in such large numbers that they constituted a considerable portion of the population. With respect to Spain, which succeeded Portugal in this African trade, we have more information. Negroes, as shown by the career of Juan Latino, Juan de Pareja, and Sebastian Gomez, had reached a larger proportion in Spain, especially in the provinces of Algrave and Estremadura where they had become a large element of the population.[12]

To make the picture clearer we should note these ex-

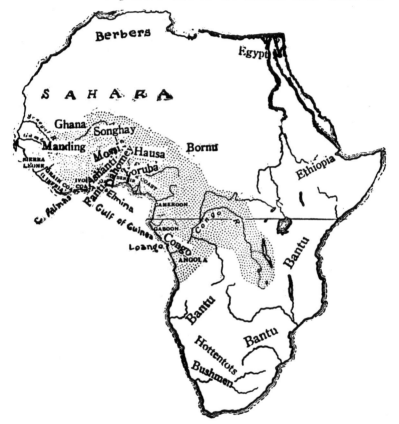

AFRICANS AS THE TRADERS FOUND THEM

plorers in the order of their appearance in the African sphere. In 1482 the Portuguese sailed as far south as the mouth of the Congo. Two years later Diogo Cam under the

[12] *The Journal of Negro History*, XX, pp. 190-243.

guidance of Martin Behaim, the cosmographer, had reached the mouth of the Kumesie, the southern boundary of Angola. In 1486 Bartholomew Diaz rounded the Cape of Good Hope. Pushing still farther, Vasco de Gama touched the shore at St. Helena, Mossel Bay, and Natal in 1497 and at the mouth of the Limpopo River in 1498. In 1502 he established forts at Beira and Sofala on the East Coast. In 1503 Antonio de Saldanha landed at Table Bay. In 1505 Pedro Anaya established a settlement at Sofala, and the following year the Portuguese discovered Madagascar. An epoch in the opposition of the natives was reached in 1510, when Francisco d'Almeida, the first of the Portuguese East Indian settlers, was killed with sixty-one men by the Hottentots at what is now known as Saldanha Bay. These adventurers hoped to intercept the much-talked-of lucrative trade between Asia and Africa, especially at the Port of Sofala and Mombasa. The natives, however, showed such determined resistance that the exploiters had to revise their plans.

For almost the next three generations there was comparative peace on the expanding commercial frontier with the exception of the stir made by Lourenço Marques in exploring Delagoa Bay in 1544. The Portuguese were endeavoring to strengthen their hold by visits and settlements at Sofala, Beira, Zanzibar, Kilwa and Lourenço Marques Bay. In 1571, however, Frances Barreto dared to navigate the Zambesi. In 1576 the Portuguese visited Natal, and in 1577 religious adventurers established the Dominican Mission at Mozambique. These explorations and that of Cabral and Albuquerque in Brazil made Portugal the world's greatest sea power. On land in Africa, however, no European nation was a great power.

Other elements were already in the picture to dispute the monopoly maintained in Africa by the Portuguese. On his way around the world Sir Francis Drake, a plunderer just as notorious as any of the Portuguese, rounded the Cape of Good Hope in 1581. Dutch ships on their way to India stopped at Mossel Bay in 1595. The British East Indian fleet visited the Cape in 1601. Isaac C. Maire touched Table Bay in 1614. The Portuguese, however, were to compete still further in the slave trade, colonize Congoland and Angola and even make war upon the Dutch in Brazil to which slaves were first carried in 1644. The Dutch became further acquainted in these parts in 1648 when one of their vessels was wrecked at Table Bay and the unfortunate sailors were entertained by the Hottentots for five months until they could be picked up by one of the home bound vessels from East India.[13]

European contact with Africa was facilitated by the collapse of the powers that had once ruled with great sway in North Africa. By the sixteenth century the Berber communities had become hopelessly disintegrated, and the anarchy which followed invited the intervention of the Portuguese, the Spanish, and the Turks. The Spanish conquered most of them, but these Iberians turned out to be so unsatisfactory that the Berbers invited the Turks. These newcomers developed into corsairs, who with Algeria as headquarters became all but independent of Constantinople, and for almost three centuries infested the Mediterranean as pirates. Europeans had constant trouble with them, and even the United States had to have a war with the Barbary States. These Turkish corsairs might have been more of a terror than they were had they not continually quarrelled and struggled among themselves. European nations, especially the French, began to deal later more effectively with the Barbary States. In 1830 the French drove the Turks from Algeria and then extended their possessions in that quarter in spite of warm protests to the contrary like that of Germany in 1909. The Portuguese and Spanish, however, have a foothold.

---

[13] These explorations are discussed in almost any work dealing with this aspect of European and African history. The following give useful summaries: Sir Charles Lucas's *The Partition of Africa; Historical Geography of the Colonies;* J. S. Keltie's *Partition of Africa;* H. H. Johnson's *History of the Colonization of Africa by Alien Races.*

Nominal possession, however, did not mean actual control. The Mohammedanized peoples in these parts did not have the same idea with respect to landownership which was found among the unadulterated natives below the Sahara. The latter thought of the soil as belonging to the tribe collectively and inalienable in the sense that no chief of the tribe could make a treaty transferring land. On the other hand, there were other racial, religious, and political questions which were just as troublesome. The Asiatics in North Africa were Caucasians mixed with Negroid stock, but they did not consider themselves as the same people as the Europeans then taking them over. In religion they differed widely from Europeans, and when other matters did not supply divergence of opinion sufficient to cause an uprising some Mohammedan prophet or functionary of that faith could proclaim a holy war which so gripped the adherents that it was difficult for the Europeans to deal with the situation.

The Mohammedans brought to Africa their conflict of religious beliefs. They found the Africans thinking of the world as the dwelling place of many good and evil spirits. In order to be happy the Africans thought that they had to avoid or please these spirits in some way. The Mohammedans believed, as the Africans did, in God, the creator of everything; but the Mohammedans taught that this Divine Being has been manifested even to the great prophets whom he has raised up to lead the people and that the chief duty of man is to recognize and worship Mohammed as the greatest of all these prophets. The sayings of this Prophet, collected in book form as the Koran, served his followers as the guide and inspiration of their lives just as the Bible has served the Christians who believe in the mission of Jesus Christ.

Most Africans until about one hundred and fifty years ago had never heard of any other religion except their own, but many years before that time the Mohammedans had begun to reach the interior of that continent. Yet the natives resisted any introduction of the new faith of the Moslems. Thousands of Africans died rather than change their religious customs; and thousands of Mohammedans, on the other hand, died in the effort to make the Africans accept their faith. These efforts multiplied "holy wars," conflicts drawn out mainly because of religious differences. The Mohammedans could always count on their home countries to aid in this effort, and they were delighted to have the opportunity to extend their religion. The natives long fought against this new faith, and the majority of them still believe in their world of spirits; but those Africans who did accept Islam becam more zealous in its propagation than the foreign Mohamme-dans themselves.

The Mohammedans, however, even while successful were failures. They, like the Christians, often separated into militant sects and organizations which gave their effort the aspect of a self-exterminating movement. In purely political matters, moreover, the Mohammedans had experienced gov-ernment so different from the more modernized form of the Europeans that it was difficult for things to work out har-moniously under direct rule. To reduce these populations to order it was necessary to resort to drastic measures tanta-mount to actual conquest of unsubdued people The work of Admiral Lyautey for France in North Africa is the best example of how the country was brought to order and started toward exploitation along modern lines.

In the course of these campaigns thousands of soldiers were brought into action, and numerous battles against re-calcitrant elements were necessary. The conqueror used the iron hand, however; these people were made to know that new lords were in the land, and that opposition of no kind would be countenanced. Yet in spite of these harsh measures it required generations to pacify the country sufficiently to justify the hope that European settlement, backed by European capital, would be a safe investment. The mere crushing of opposition was not sufficient. The defeated elements, dispossessed and exterminated in these contests, however, finally gave opportunity for the expropriation of lands which might be offered to the conqueror. The Moslems, moreover, have been inclined to offer less opposition recently for the reason that they have finally learned that Europeans do not mean to disturb them in the exercise of their religion. European nations have interfered in behalf of their coreligionists in Africa not to promote any particular faith, but only with this as an excuse for colonial expansion. The religious aspect of the Moslem question, then, has ceased to be a question of much import in preventing the furtherance of economic imperialism.[14]

---

[14] The role of the Mohammedans in North Africa and the Sudan may be studied in almost all histories of North Africa. European histories treating the middle age bear especially upon the onward sweep of the Mohammedans through North Africa into Spain and France. The African aspects, however, are better developed in the following: Stéphane Gsell's *Histoire Ancienne de l'Afrique du Nord;* Ch.-Andre Julien's *Histoire de l'Afrique du Nord;* Lugard's *Tropical Dependency;* E. Mercier's *Histoire de l'Afrique Septentrionale depuis les Temps les plus reculés jusqu'a la Conquête Française.*

CHAPTER II

IN WEST AFRICAN STATES

Below the Sahara and the upper Sudan developed typical African organization antedating the Mohammedan influx which culminated about the year 1000 A. D. The Western African and Sudanese kingdoms which the Mohammedans found on reaching the interior and the West Coast offer evidence to this effect. The first to be noticed was Kumbi, called Ghana by the Arabs.[1]

KUMBI

No one knows exactly how early Kumbi developed. The records show that the empire was in action at least fifteen hundred years ago. The Mohammedans who settled in this area say that they founded this kingdom, but what happened was that after they had made some settlements along the border they were conquered and brought into the Kumbi empire which in its glory covered most of West Africa. There is no record of any but black kings and emperors who ruled in this part of Africa. These black people were called the Sarakolle.

These people rose to heights under a great prince bearing the title *maga* or *maya* of Kumbi, or the *tunka of Ghana*, as

---

[1] Kumbi (Ghana) and all the West African and Sudanese kingdoms are briefly treated in Maurice Delafosse's *Negroes of Africa*, pages 42-129; J. L. Monod's *Histoire de l'Afrique Occidentale Française; The African Background Outlined*, pages 31-127. The best sources are the works of those who traveled in these parts—such as Ibn-Haukal, El-Bekri, Edrisi, Yakut, Ibn-Batuta, Ibn Khaldun, and Hassan-Ibn Mohammed, or Leo the African. Two histories have been left by native Africans themselves, namely, *The Tarikh Es-Sudan*, by Abderrahman Saadi, and the *Tarikh El-Fettach*, by Mahmud Kôti.

the Arabs called him. This prince was respected as far as Cairo and Bagdad. He and his successors extended his power over the Arabs immigrating into that area. They were not many in number and were absorbed by the blacks with whom they mixed without leaving any such trace of white blood as that seen among the people of North Africa or even in Ethiopia. Kumbi expanded too so as to extend south to the gold mines of the Faleme and the Bambuk. The production of the precious metal made Kumbi a prosperous country with a rich treasury sought by caravans from Tafilalit and Dara. Kumbi extended even as far as Manding, on the Upper Niger, and expanded towards the east as far as the region west of Timbuktu near the Great Lakes.

The empire was well organized from the point of view of its time. It showed as much evidence of political progress as was found in most of the kingdoms and empires then developed in Europe. At the head of the realm was the *maga* or *tunka*, and each of the provinces had its *maga* subject to that of the capital at Kumbi. In its golden age before the drying up of its principal streams these people had become sedentary and cultivated land while others devoted themselves to cattle and sheep-raising. Being thus attached to the soil, they developed that solidarity which enabled them to deal successfully with the scattered settlements of Semitic peoples who claimed that they once ruled that land and were determined to do so again, but the blacks had too much power of resistance to recognize any such false claims. The popularity of the place as a result of the exploitation of its gold mines and the profitable caravan trade over the Sahara stimulated industry in Kumbi. There were workers in gold, and in other metals. Spinning and weaving industries supplied cloth of various kinds for the rich and the aristocratic in Kumbi. Commerce in kola-nuts and cattle figured in the occupations of Kumbi.

Great prosperity was brought by trade, but the people were settled and depended upon the cultivation of the soil and the raising of animals for a living. The soil was fertile, and they raised two crops a year. In the groves were date and gum trees. Wheat had to be imported as a rule, but durra, another grain, was abundant. Honey was common in the land. Large pastures in which grazed sheep and cattle accounted for the abundance of meat. Ivory was a valuable commodity. Gold dust and gold worked into the form of wire served as a medium of exchange, and with the precious metal the people of Ghana purchased copper and dress goods from the visiting traders. Some of them, of course, traded slaves, kola-nuts, skins, and cotton, for these luxuries. Traders came especially from Angila in Tripoli, from Wargelan or Wargla in Algeria, and from Sidjilmessa in Morocco. Although it required some of these traders months to cross the Sahara with their caravans, the trip was always made worthwhile by the enormous profit made in disposing of these commodities in both Asia and Europe.

The king whom the invaders found ruling in Kumbi in such great sway was Tenkamenin. In 1062 he succeeded his maternal uncle, Beci. When Tenkamenin gave audience he appeared in great state under a pavilion round which were ranged ten horses caparisoned in gold. Behind him stood ten pages bearing shields and swords mounted in gold. On the right of the king stood the sons of the prince of the empire magnificently dressed according to Oriental style. The governor of the town and all ministers of the empire sat upon the ground in front of the ruler. The door of the pavilion was guarded by pure bred dogs whose collars were of gold and silver with bells made from the same metals. These dogs were supposed never to leave the spot occupied by the king. The royal town surrounded by beautiful gardens was guarded by priests. In that important place no one was allowed to enter except those invited by the king, for in it were kept the idols of the nation, the tombs of the kings, and the royal prisons.

The religion was animism, a belief that all things have good or evil spirits to be appeased in order that man may not be disturbed by the evil ones and may be blessed by the good. Under another ruler the people were introduced to Mohammedanism which was the religion of the traders and settlers reaching Kumbi during the ninth and tenth centuries. The royal and aristocratic later accepted Islam as a mark

TENKAMENIN

of distinction and scholarship because they taught the Arabic language and the Koran. Some of the rulers of the empire even had Mohammedan advisers, but the people as a majority remained animistic. Education from the African point of view had been made practical—teaching the child to do what was required of his parents in raising a family, defending the country and preserving the customs of the people. When the Mohammedans brought the written language and the study of books education reached a new stage in Africa.

Magic was believed and practiced in these parts; and the ordeal, which often became a practice of the magician, sometimes figured in the administration of justice. In the king himself, however, justice finally resided, for one of standing could always appeal to the sovereign. He presided over inquiries into the grievances of the people and his decisions were carried out by his ministers. The lieutenants in addition to serving as a cabinet had jurisdiction in the various parts of the empire organized along feudal lines, except that land could not be alienated by the chiefs and subchiefs inasmuch as it was considered the property of the collectivity rather than that of an individual.

The empire of Kumbi, however, was not weakened by this African conception of land. The sovereign had an income from his own domains administered under his personal control. The income of the state was increased too by certain royalties based upon custom. To the king went the first fruits of the harvest whether of skins of animals, of ivory, or of gold dust. The wealth of peoples conquered in war increased this revenue, especially that of rich centers like Howdaghost, which was conquered in 1054. The lucrative trade which sprang up between Kumbi and the outer world had to pay a tax, and it brought to the public treasury considerable income.

These financial resources enabled the sovereign to maintain a court of great luxury and an army of consequence to defend the empire. Kumbi had a military force of 200,-000 men, one-fifth of whom were equipped with bows and arrows. The rulers had wrought so well that Arabs who visited the country in the ninth and tenth centuries found it flourishing with an imposing capital. The capital city was situated between Gumbu and Walata in the region of the Hodh, in the sub-Saharan area. Since this region is arid today and does not show signs of much life it is believed

that the climate changed to the detriment of the country,
that the rivers dried up, the Wagadu especially, or became
small and underground streams; the soil ceased to produce;
the Sahara extended itself into that area, and Kumbi, or
Ghana, no longer continued a flourishing country. With only
thin pasturage, a few gum trees, and spiny bushes to encourage them, the farmers and shepherds moved to other parts.

Then too the decline of Kumbi was due to having other enemies. The Almoravides, enthusiastic Mohammedans of a
fanatical type, coming from a monastery where they had been
trained, invaded the country in 1076. The king of Soso,
Sumanguru Kannte, invaded the country in 1203, and the
king of the Mandingo, Sundiata Keita, in 1240. In its condition, weakened by nature which had ceased to yield her
increase, Kumbi fell. The Almoravides captured the capital and put to death all who would not accept their religion.
This religious sect which already had Morocco had conquered
Spain earlier under the leadership of Yusuf (Joseph) ben
Tachefin, the cousin of Abou Bekr, the leader. The latter
was killed not long thereafter by a revolt of his subjects
in Adrar, and with this as a start downward the Almoravides declined rapidly and lost their power, both in Africa
and Europe. Kumbi, however, could not recover when nature
was against her. There were among those Arabs and Moors
adherents who wanted to shake off their allegiance to Negro
emperors of Kumbi. Some of the African peoples accepted
Islam because of its prestige. Others moved from their habi-
tations as did the Serers and Fulani rather than yield to the
foreigners. Some natives remained all but neutral, as did
the Wolofs and the Mandingo. The Tukulors, the Songhay,
the Sarakolle and the Jula accepted Islam.

The new religion proved to be an apple of discord. Some
of the provinces of the empire became Mohammedanized
and others refused to go that way. No longer was there the
same loyalty as before this innovation. The important provinces under their respective *magas* who had once acknowl-

edged allegiance to the *maga* of Kumbi declared their independence and set up kingdoms of their own. Thus from the ruins of the empire of Kumbi came the kingdom of Diara and the kingdom of Soso. The latter became ambitious and tried to become an empire itself. At one time its ruler expanded his country by the conquest of Kumbi itself, and, turning to the south, he took the Manding. This was only temporary. His fortunes were reversed, and his kingdom and other provinces of Kumbi went to constitute once a part of Manding and again a part of the Songhay empire.

THE MANDING

About midway between what is now called Siguri and Bamako on the left bank of the Niger developed heroic leaders. Operating from Kangaba, sometimes called Kanga, the capital of Manding, they made for themselves a place in history among the greatest rulers of their day. Strange to say, too, that, with the exception of an interregnum of fifteen years, from 1285 to 1300, this city has been the center of the Malinké, or Mandingo people, either as an ordinary tribe of natives, a kingdom, or an empire for more than thirteen centuries. For several hundred years this city was the capital of one of the greatest empires ever developed in Africa and one of the most considerable that ever existed in the history of man. The first time the outside world ever had a glimpse of this empire was about 1050, when one of its rulers, converted to Islam, made a pious pilgrimage to Mecca to bow at the tomb of the Prophet. This ruler went in such gala array that the East was startled at the evidence of wealth and splendor indicated by his retinue and sought, therefore, to enter into trade relations with the Mandingo Negroes. By that time this sovereign had raised his country from vassalage to Kumbi into independence and recognition. The Mandingoes were then exploiting the gold mines of Bure which brought the trade at that center into competition with the gold trade of Kumbi, which it finally surpassed. The prestige of the Manding was further increased by Musa or Allakoy, who in 1213 made also a pious pilgrimage to Mecca, and subsequently three others during his reign. Eastern traders flocked to his country.

This prosperity was coveted by the neighbors of the Manding, and in 1224 the king of Soso, Sumanguru, conquered the country. His success was only temporary, for Sundiata Keita came to the throne of the Manding in time to unite the people and organize their resistance. In 1235 he defeated and killed the king of Soso. Sundiata Keita then took Kumbi, which Sumanguru also had conquered some years earlier. Sundiata devoted his time, however, chiefly to the arts of peace. He improved agriculture, introduced the weaving of cloth, stimulated the gold trade and made the kingdom peaceful and secure throughout.

This ruler lost his life by an accident at a festival in 1295. His successor, Mansa Ule, lived up to the traditions of his predecessor and expanded the Manding as far toward the west as to include the Bambuk, the Boundu and a part of the valley of Gambia. He was followed by a usurper named Sakura, but he proved to be the man the situation required. He extended the country by conquest toward the northeast into Massina and Jenne, toward the northwest into the region stretching toward the lower Senegal, into the Tekrur to measure swords with the kings of Diara and to make vassals of them. He established direct commercial relations with Tripolitania and Morocco and made a pious pilgrimage to Mecca, when returning from which he was assassinated by a Danakil near Jibouti.

These deserving rulers paved the way for the still greater work of the most distinguished ruler of the Manding, Gonga-Musa, Kankan-Musa, or Mansa Musa. He brought the Manding to its apogee during his reign from 1307 to 1332. Building upon the conquest of his predecessors, Gonga-Musa expanded the Manding empire in all directions so as to include practically all of the advanced parts of that section of the continent. His territory comprised nearly the whole of what is now called French West Africa and the colonies of other nations enclosed by it with the exception of the dense forests and the region near the bend of the Niger. Ibn-Khaldun learned that the power of the Mansa of Manding extended over the entire desert of Sahara, that the king of Wargla showed deference to him and all the Tuareg paid him tribute.

Gonga-Musa made a deep impression on the outer world when he went on a pious pilgrimage to Mecca. The Mohammedan religion had then become a political advantage among the royalty and the rich, and the pious pilgrimage of rulers from the Sudan and West Africa became popular. The journey was not so much the performance of religious duty as it was an effort to make a display. This pilgrimage of Gonga-Musa in 1324 was probably the greatest cortege ever to leave Africa on such a mission. He had a caravan of 60,000, a considerable portion of whom constituted a military escort. Servants to the number of 12,000, dressed in tunics of brocade or Persian silk, constituted his personal retinue. When on the way 500 of these servants marched before him, each carrying a staff of pure gold weighing sixty ounces. The remainder transported the baggage. Good cooks preparing for the king and those whom he entertained en route rendered the procession a great joy to those thus favored. To bear this and other expenses Gonga-Musa took with him gold worth more than a million stirling in eighty camel loads of 300 pounds each.

Gonga-Musa was generous in his gifts along the way, for he went first westward through his own dominions as far as the conquered Kumbi and then eastward that his subjects might be impressed with his cortege and profit by his generosity. He made gifts to towns to assist in their educational and religious aspirations. He was so generous that he had to borrow money in returning from Mecca. This he

GONGA-MUSA ON THE WAY

could easily do for the reason that the richness of his country was well known abroad. The pilgrimage helped both ways. He strengthened his trade relations with the East just as he had done in the case of the centers of North Africa. He made contacts with literary men of the East and profited by their knowledge. While returning, moreover, he learned that his general Sagamandia had taken Gao, the capital of the Songhay, and he went there also with his cortege to receive the homage of that king and his country.

Returning from this pilgrimage in 1324, Gonga-Musa met in the Holy Land an Arab of a Granada family called Ibrahim-es-Saheli, an architect, whom he induced to accompany him to the Sudan. El-Mamer, a descendant of the dynasty of the Almohades, also joined the sovereign and his companions and came as far as the Manding. Inasmuch as these orthodox Mohammedans did not like the unpretentious and mediocre straw huts as buildings used in West Africa for mosques, Gonga-Musa requested Es-Saheli to improve them throughout the empire, especially at Timbuktu, Jenne, and Kangaba. This added splendor to these cities and further impressed the world with the greatness of the Manding. For this fine work of reconstruction Gonga-Musa paid the architect 40,000 mitkals of gold, 180 kilograms. The buildings replacing the huts were brick edifices with crenulated flat roofs, pyramidal structures which varied from place to place to assume the aspect of modified castles.

Travelers who visited the empire, Ibn Batuta especially, who passed through the country less than a generation after the death of Gonga-Musa, when he had been succeeded by Suleiman (1336-1359), say that the Manding was in every respect a representative political organization measuring up to the standards of those of that day. The administration of the state was efficient. Ibn Batuta noted especially "its prosperity, the courtesy and discipline of its officials and provincial governors, the excellent condition of public finances, the luxury and the rigorous and complicated ceremonial of the royal receptions, the respect accorded to the decisions of justice, and to the authority of the sovereign.''

To reach this position Gonga-Musa had an efficient system. The finances were well organized. Taxation was imposed upon the royal domains, on minerals, and on foreign trade, especially upon imports. The provinces under rulers known as the ''koi,'' with subchiefs under them, were the units through which the administration operated. The administration of justice was an important concern of both the central and local authorities. In the judiciary were representative lawyers, judges, juriconsults, and the like, frequently mentioned by those commenting on the Manding. The people were in good circumstance because of their trade and industry. They exported gold, ivory, skins, and kolanuts; and they exchanged cattle, durra, and cotton for European woolens. Signs of wealth were in evidence, and the people seemed happy. Towns, which flourished as an outlet of what the people produced, introduced among them a desire for imported luxuries for which these commodities were exchanged.

The army was organized on the same basis of efficiency. It was composed of both infantry and cavalry armed with bows and arrows, swords, and long and short spears. The army was divided into units under captains or commandants. Smaller military units were grouped to form the larger. The army as a whole had two divisions, one of the north under one general and one of the south under another general. While the cavalry served as the eyes of the army the system was otherwise made efficient by the well organized ''telegraph'' system of public criers. By passing a message from mouth to mouth they could communicate an important matter over a large area in a short period, and the possibility of variation or misinterpretation in communicating it was reduced to a minimum.

THE SONGHAY

Great as was Manding, however, it had its day, declined and ceased to be a powerful empire. The ascendancy in West Africa and the Sudan next went to the Songhay. This empire, some have said, was probably founded in the seventh century of the Christian era. Others think that its beginning belongs to an earlier date. About the year 1000 A. D. these people had developed sufficiently to occupy a considerable area along the bend of the Niger and to have there a capital which they called Gao. From this point they ruled over other settlements which had a nucleus around Gungia, or Kukia, about one hundred and fifty kilometers down the Niger. Not many years thereafter, the power of the Songhay extended to Timbuktu, to the zone of lakes and to Walata; but the day of the Songhay had not yet arrived. The Manding under Gonga-Musa had become a power. He conquered the Songhay in 1325 and made it a vassalage, although Timbuktu and Walata remained subject to the Songhay; and so did the lake district, Massina, and Jenne. The Tuareg Chief Ali a century later drove the Manding administration from Timbuktu in 1433. On January 30, 1468, the Songhay took the city from the Tuareg. The Songhay conquered Jenne and Massina in 1473. This area with that of the lakes and the possession of Walata made the Songhay the formidable rival of the Manding.

This unusually rapid rise of the Songhay was due to the splendid leadership and remarkable foresight of one of the greatest rulers to appear in Africa. We first hear of him as one of the sons of the Dia Assibai, taken as hostage by Gonga-Musa when on his return from his pious pilgrimage he went to Gao to receive the homage of the Songhay after the capture of that city by the Manding general, Sagamandia, in 1325. These young men later distinguished themselves in the service of the *mansa*. One of these sons, however, watched every opportunity for escape after he reached his majority. He made friends there, and along the way toward his country he stored arms in order that when he escaped he would have some way to defend himself against his pursuers. And thus it worked out. He escaped, the alarm excited the guard, and an army rushed in the pursuit; but the project had been too well planned to be foiled. The young man reached Songhay, reorganized its defense, defeated the Manding army and made the Songhay independent.

This new ruler founded a dynasty called the *Sonni,* and he himself assumed the name of Sonni Ali. The Songhay under this renowned ruler began its ascendancy in West Africa and the Sudan. He was the first empire builder in those parts to appreciate the importance of getting control of the Niger. Establishing his power first on one bank and then on the other, he found it easier to repel attacks of enemies and to extend his territory at their expense.

In the working out of this plan to control the Niger Sonni Ali introduced something all but new in African military development—the use of a navy. Boats, of course, had been used before in African wars, but never before had a nation in these parts thought and planned the use of a navy for the conquest of the Niger and its defense. The plan as conceived by Sonni Ali showed the foresight of a great statesman and empire builder. The project worked out admirably in connection with his general plans which were so systematically carried out as to assure triumphant success. Striking to the right and then to the left bank of the stream, he compelled the neighbors of the Manding to yield. The Manding empire went mainly to build up the Songhay.

Sonni Ali, one of the most effective conquerors and organizers of Africa prior to the European conquest, however, has been unfavorably presented to history by the Mohammedanized elements under the fanatical influence of religion. Being possessed of a written language, these partisans left in written form the only data from which the history of the Songhay may be written. To do this properly the historian must keep ever before him the bias in these records. Sonni Ali incurred the displeasure of Mohammedans because as a conqueror and organizer he could not carry out his great task of centralization and at the same time respect the differences and ambitions of these centers of the new faith which agreed with nobody and did not agree among themselves. Having some new ideas as to progress not yet admitted gen-

SONNI ALI

erally among African Negroes, these teachers of the new faith considered themselves the advance guard of civilization, and the impression made by the adherents to Islam was usually favorable enough to secure special privileges from rulers to whom they first agreed to swear loyalty in return for the right to proselyte the African blacks. When they gained sufficient power they overthrew such rulers in order to have everything their way.

When Sonni Ali began to rule in the Songhay he soon

discovered that his plans could not be thoroughly successful if he recognized any group or center as above the law. The religious propagandists, calling themselves the educated, stirred up opposition to Sonni Ali; and to get rid of this as he would any other opposition he destroyed such antagonists, root and branch, regardless of their station and pretensions. Sonni Ali, although he had accepted the Mohammedan faith, was in heart an animist, and he had sufficient vision to understand that an empire with people divided on the question of religion could never become a strong force. The Africans had not become Mohammedans as a majority, and in most parts of Africa they have not become so even today. The wise ruler, as he understood the situation, would ignore religion as a state question and base his empire on loyalty to the government.

Reading what the Mohammedans have recorded, one would receive the impression that only centers of their teaching were especially attacked, but Sonni Ali stormed every hostile stronghold. Schools and mosques favorable to him were protected and supported. On this basis many of the centers devoted to Islam fell in the onward sweep of the Songhay to imperial status. These formerly all but independent settlements, expanded from those first established along the Southern fringe of the Sahara, were conquered and brought under the control of Negro rulers whose people the Moslems had long proselyted while mingling their blood with that of these aborigines. The time had passed for isolation and the recognition of special privileges for the socalled learned who dubbed as debauched, impious, and infidel all who did not conform to their religion. A new order of larger political import was necessary. The country could not be advanced without the change from segregation to aggregation. Sonni Ali was the man of the hour. He had the vision of a new type of government. Men of foresight agreed with him and cooperated in constructing the army necessary to make his dreams come true.

This achievement, however, was not an easy task, for the conquered in those days did not always remain conquered. The king of the Mossi of Yatenga, of whom we shall hear later, attacked Massina in 1477 and pillaged Walata in 1480 in his expansion of another empire in that direction. This brought Sonni Ali to realize the need for the improvement of the facilities of transportation between centers in the empire. He could relieve some of these outlying places more quickly if he connected Walata and Timbuktu with a canal starting from Ras-el-Ma, two hundred and fifty kilometers long. This constructive plan he undertook to carry out. It was not completed, however, for, hearing that the ambitious Mossi had again invaded his domain, he directed against them an army which drove them back; but, on the way, Sonni Ali was drowned November 6, 1492, while crossing a swelling current.

The direct descendants of Sonni Ali failed to hold the throne of the Songhay, and his able Sarakolle general, Mamadu, or Mohammed Ture, secured the throne with the title of Askia. He became such a successful ruler and organizer that he is generally referred to as Askia the Great. He was a man of so many desirable qualities that it would be difficult to praise him too highly, but to estimate his career properly it is necessary to eliminate from one's mind the insidious comparisons made of him and Sonni Ali by the Mussulman writers who denounced the latter while lauding the former merely because Askia Mohammed was a loyal Mussulman and Sonni Ali was not. Sonni Ali was a stern, austere, and fiery man of steel who with the assistance of men like Askia Mohammed made the Songhay empire possible. Askia Mohammed was just the type of man to succeed the conqueror of blood and iron and give the country the organization which it needed. Both were great men, one as a conqueror, the other as an organizer and reformer. Without Sonni Ali, Askia Mohammed would never have been known. Without Mohammed, Sonni Ali could not have built the Songhay empire.

During his long reign from 1493 to 1529, Askia Mohammed accomplished much to secure for him and his country a place in history. In the first place, he won the loyalty and cooperation of his ministers and provincial governors. His brother, Omar, whom he made his chief lieutenant, stood loyally by him. Askia Mohammed put the army on a professional basis by recruiting mainly among slaves and captives in war in order to leave the farmers and artisans free to develop the country through agriculture and industry. This army was organized under the leadership of native rulers, but with Songhay representatives supreme everywhere in the home provinces and four vice-royalties.

In contradistinction to Sonni Ali, Askia, an orthodox Mohammedan himself, conferred special favors upon the Mohammedan mosques and schools. Askia Mohammed even communicated with centers of Mohammedan learning outside of his dominions, hoping to be of some service to them and to derive therefrom some benefit. He made the acquaintance of such Mussulman scholars as Merhili, the Moroccan reformer. In 1497 Askia went on a pious pilgrimage to Mecca where he made the acquaintance of Soyuti and other Mussulman doctors. Askia was signally honored on this occasion in receiving from the Grand Cherif of Mecca the investiture of ''Khalife'' for the Tekrur or Sudan.

The chroniclers of that day point out especially how the pious pilgrimage of Askia Mohammed differed from the imposing cortege which displayed the power of Gonga-Musa of the Manding when he made the pilgrimage to Mecca two hundred years before. Askia Mohammed had a smaller number with him and less wealth to dispense as gifts, but he had sufficient funds to give 100,000 gold dinars to pious alms and to purchase land where he had a hostel built for Sudanese pilgrims. He had a military escort of only 500 cavalry and 1,000 infantry. He carried with him holy men,

ASKIA MOHAMMED

brilliant scholars, learned teachers, and the greatest notables. His court, however, was magnificent and well furnished.

The purpose of the pilgrimage, too, was different from the spectacular one of two centuries before. Askia Mohammed wanted to learn about government and administration, principles of taxation, verification and inspection of weights and measures, the regulation of trade, the reform of banks and markets, laws of inheritance, laws for the suppression of immorality, measures to be taken for the introduction of better manners among the people, and the limits of religious tolerance and persecution. He was concerned with the study of surgical science, anatomy, law, literature, and grammar. Returning to the Songhay, Askia Mohammed made some effort along all these lines. Although he was ahead of his time in thus looking forward to what was practically the modernization of his country he accomplished much to make the Songhay an empire long to be remembered.

While thus giving attention to his internal policy Askia could not neglect the defense and extension of the empire. By the end of the fifteenth century the outposts of Manding began to fall to the Songhay. In 1494, Omar, the brother of Askia Mohammed, had conquered all of Massina, which included at that time the Fulani kingdom of the Diallo. Askia himself captured Bagana in 1498. He conquered part of the kingdom of Diara in 1500, and in 1506 extended his sway as far as Galam, the Bakel on the Senegal. Askia Mohammed made some conquests in the Hausa country to the east but lost the ground gained when his ally, the king of Kebbi, turned traitor and compelled the Songhay to withdraw.

Unfortunately, near the end of his life Askia Mohammed became blind and was dethroned by his own son, Mussa, in 1529. Disorder then set in; murders, massacres, and insurrections became the order of the day, and the empire gradually declined. One of the sons of Mussa, David, who held the throne from 1549 to 1583, endeavored to restore the Songhay to its former greatness. He was generous and charitable and thus won friends. He reorganized agriculture, stimulated local industry, encouraged science and promoted education.

David won the friendship of Ahmed Ed-Dehebi, the Sultan of Morocco, but it was from this source that the fall of the Songhay came. When David died Ahmed Ed-Dehebi, in order to obtain information about the forces in the Songhay available for defense, sent there a delegation of spies. From David he had obtained in 1578 for 10,000 gold dinars the use of the salt mines at Tegazza which the Sultans of the Maghreb had long coveted. Now they saw that it was the time to take them by force, for great profit had been obtained even from the concession. He sent an army of 20,000 men to Tegazza, but they perished of hunger and thirst. Now he wanted both salt and gold. He then sent under one Juder, about 3,000 Spanish renegades, the scum of the earth. When they reached the Songhay they had become very much decimated, but, having modern arms, they easily defeated Ishak II, the ruler of the Songhay, who took flight among the inhabitants of Gurma and was killed.

Under Juder, Gao was taken, and soon followed Timbuktu, which served as a capital for the rulers calling themselves the Pashas of Timbuktu. At the end of seventy years, however, they had no authority outside of Timbuktu. The country had broken up into independent parts as it existed before the days of the Songhay empire. The Pashas for a time were designated by the Sultan of Morocco, but the subalterns soon became a law unto themselves and were brought to the position by their own coterie or soldiers. The Mandingo emperor, after the fall of the Songhay, all but took Jenne in 1599, but some of the Jenne stood with the Pashas. The Manding, however, made such an impression as to win respect. After 1660 the Pashas of Timbuktu exercised little more than nominal authority. From about this time they had to pay tribute to the Bambara king of Segu or to the

Tuareg Oulmidden to the north. The Pashas disappeared about 1780, and the source of authority there became first Bambara and then Tuareg. The French under Major Joffre took the country in 1894.

THE BAMBARA

The Bambara, referred to here as controlling Timbuktu from the south, had first been subjects of the Manding and next of the Songhay. While the latter was declining these people were developing two kingdoms, one with a capital at Segu and the other at Kaarta. These kingdoms finally united and formed a force strong enough under Biton Kulubali to compel the Manding in 1670, after failure to capture their stronghold, to agree not to trespass in those parts. This marked the end of the Manding empire. Biton next raised a professional army somewhat on the order of that of Mohammed Askia. He organized also a navy to operate especially on the Niger. With these he conquered all the territory between Niamina and Jenne. He subdued the Bagana, and took over also Massina and Timbuktu. His brilliant reign came to an end in 1710 when he died of tetanus fever resulting from an accident.

Biton's power went to his army, which deprived his children of the succession. A new dynasty was founded by Molo, the servant of the royal family, in 1750. He was noted especially for making war upon Kaarta and Timbuktu. From his successor, Da, Massina obtained its independence under Seku-Hamadu. This new conqueror captured Jenne, built a capital at Hamdallahi, and reorganized the administration. He converted the Fulani to Islam, forced Timbuktu to respect his authority, and captured it in 1826 or 1827. He was hated there, however, and his garrison could not remain. This king was followed by his son Hamadu-Seku, who added nothing to his father's record. Hamadu-Hamadu, the grandson of Seku-Hamadu, was vanquished by El-Hadj

Omar in 1862. The Bambara kingdom of Segu had gone down the same way before El-Hadj Omar in 1861. The Bambara kingdom of Kaarta founded about 1660 or 1670 did not hold out even so long as the one at Segu. King Sie did do as much as to capture Diara in 1754, and his successor conquered the greater part of the country north of the Upper Senegal and took Bambouk and Kuta from the Mandingoes.

CHAPTER III

AMONG THE MOSSI AND SMALLER STATES

A little later, or so far as we know, a little earlier, developed two Mossi states about the time that Kumbi, or Ghana, was well on its way to full growth, probably about the middle of the eleventh century, as Delafosse conjectures. These states often are taken to be one and the same because they were composed of the same people and had rulers known by the same title *morho-naba*.[1] They are, however, distinct, one with its capital at Wagadugu and the other a little over a hundred years younger with its capital at Yatenga. Toward the beginning of the fourteenth century they had the same extent of territory and the same organization as they have today. Each consists of several kingdoms whose rulers acknowledge allegiance to a central imperial authority and the kingdoms are divided into provinces under hereditary governors responsible to the king. These subalterns reside sometimes in their own provinces and sometimes in that of the emperor.

The empire centering around Wagadugu was made up of four vassal kingdoms besides the one which the *morho-naba* held in his own right. His empire was composed of five provinces whose hereditary rulers resided at his court and made up the imperial council. These were designated as functioning in such capacities as comptroller, chief of the eunuchs, chief of the infantry, chief of the cavalry, and guar-

---

[1] The sources cited in the footnote on page 25 will be helpful in studying further the history of Mossi and these other states. Consult also M. Delafosse's *Haut-Sénégal-Niger, Soudan Français;* Louis Tauxier's *Le Noir du Soudan;* his *Le Noir de Yatenga; Études Soudaniases; Les Nègres Gouro et Gagou; Le Noir du Bondoukou;* and *Nouvelles Notes sur les Mossi et Gourounsi.*

dian of the royal sepultures. With these served on the council eleven other ministers who as the dignitaries of the empire held such positions as the grand-master of the army, the commandant of the imperial guard, the grand priest of the local religion, the master of ceremonies, the chief of the servants, assistant to the chief of the servants, the chief of the musicians, the chief of the butchers, the chief of the royal stables, the collector of taxes and the trustee for the Mussulmans. The governors of the province ruled or administered their respective areas with courts of ministers modeled after that of the *morho-naba*.

The emperor was surrounded by a large number of pages, palefreniers, guards, and servants charged with rigidly defined tasks. Their life was ordered according to a minutely detailed rule. Everything done was indicated by airs from flutes or the beating of drums. Every morning the *morho-naba*, or emperor, received his ministers to learn the state of the country and to devise means for its welfare and prosperity. On approaching the emperor each minister would prostrate himself before the ruler, touching the ground with his forehead, striking the soil with his elbows, and covering his head with dust. Then these lieutenants took up with their sovereign the matters of state decided upon as the order of the day. Should certain affairs require an inquiry or the hearing of testimony the longer time necessary for their solution was allowed. It was customary for the emperor to hold such meetings in the evening to deal with matters of public order and criminal justice. The inquiries which he made and the procedure in hearing the matter brought to his attention showed all the beginnings of trial by jury. Doubtless here the Africans anticipated the Nordics in the development of our jury system, as contends Professor Nathaniel Cantor, of the University of Buffalo.

In this procedure, however, the emperor was governed by custom which had the force of law. If he made a procession through his capital in the daytime, he went on horseback accompanied by his entire court. Servants drove the horse, held the stirrups, and carried the sword and the large umbrella to protect the emperor from rays of the sun. Drums would beat and griots chant to signal throughout the city the time for a cessation of activities. At night the emperor would go out disguised, accompanied by one page only. He would proceed through the quarters of the capital incognito and enter homes in order to inform himself as to what was being said or done. At fixed periods or on specified dates he would repair to designated places on the borders of the capital to offer sacrifice that he might be preserved from all misfortune.

This organization resembles, in fact, almost parallels that given by the Arabs of the early African kingdoms which they visited—such as Ghana, Diara, Songhay, Manding, Ashanti, Abomey and several kingdoms of the Wolofs. Mossi, however, shows this type of state as more nearly perfected than elsewhere. This was probably the type of all states developed in Africa—those known and those of which we know nothing. It was a demonstration of the African idea of government, for these kingdoms did not expand widely by territorial conquest to include settlements of foreigners infiltrating into the Sudan and West Africa, and the Mossi owed practically nothing to foreign influence. The Mossi of Yatenga on several occasions left their territory as in taking Timbuktu in 1333 and making an incursion into Massina and Bagana as far as Walata in 1480, but they did not hold those as dependencies. They stayed at home and developed solidly in order to be able to resist the attacks of the Askias of the Songhay, the Pashas of Timbuctoo, the sovereigns of the Manding, the kings of Bambara, and the kings of Segu.

The Mossi resisted especially Islam. They admitted a few Mussulmans to their land for trade and had a special trustee to look after those of this faith, but the Mossi never permitted themselves to be converted to Islam. They stuck to their belief in animism. The rulers of the Mossi did not let their people act like a sponge which takes up any moisture with which it comes into contact. They insisted that they knew as much about the revelation of God as did the Mohammedans. In thus being arrayed against foreign influence the Mossi rendered a distinct service in showing the possibility of government among distinctly Negro people. When comparing their social and political order with those centers where foreigners settled in considerable numbers the slight variation which one finds shows how little West Africa was influenced from without by foreign cultures.

AFNO, OR HAUSA

The Afno city states to the east of the Songhay offer few examples of outstanding builders of kingdoms and empires. The principal reason seems to be that they were traditionally city states which, although in a sense tributary to each other, never united to form a large and enduring political organization. Yet they deserve notice. The kingdoms of Zinder, of the Zanfara, of the Kantagora, and the Bauchi were in this area. Especially noted was Gober, known far and wide for its cotton fabrics. There flourished also Kano, the walled industrial and commercial center dominated by scholars of Islam; Katsena, rich in agricultural resources and military prowess; and Zaria, which, thanks to an efficient and popular queen, became a commercial center with extensive power over the other Afno cities.

In the fifteenth century the kings of Kebbi, ruling from Sokoto as a capital over people supposedly a mixture of Hausa-Afno and Songhay folk, claimed jurisdiction over these cities and expanded westward. The Sultan of Bornu opposed this claim and attacked the Kebbi at Surami but had to retire and was killed in the retreat by Katsena people. His successor, the next king of Kebbi, made an alliance with Askia Mohammed to conquer the Afno states and with the aid of the Songhay forces in 1513 brought most of them under his sway. Against the forces of Askia Mohammed, however, he revolted or broke the alliance and kept the conquests. The King of Kebbi defeated an army sent against him by Askia Mohammed in 1517, and next he established his authority over the Afno. By 1600, however, the kings of Gober and Zanfara with the aid of the king of Air attacked the king of the Kebbi, destroyed his three principal towns, Gungu, Surami, and Liki, and made the Afno people independent. The country then remained largely in the city-state status which characterized it before these movements. The next stir came much later when Islam was extended from Kano, the only stronghold of the kind there for many centuries. This was the work of Ousman the Torodo, of whom we shall learn later.

BORNU

On both sides of Lake Chad and east of the Afno territory lived the Bornu people of decidedly mixed origin—some Negroes and others Negroid with an infusion of Semites, Arabs, and the like. In their origin they were distinctly Negroes, but the Berbers, Moroccans, and Mohammedanized Arabs immigrated into the country in sufficiently large numbers to change its aspect. Their first line of rulers were the Negro dynasty called Teda which was overthrown by the Kanembu, a Mussulman line, about the end of the twelfth century. But the Teda Negroes frequently arose against the usurpers, and they had difficulty in holding the country during two centuries of practical anarchy under Dunama I (1220-1259); under Ibrahim (1352-1376); and under Omar (1394-1398). The last mentioned was so hard pressed by the Bulala Negroes that he abandoned the Kanem to them and settled in Bornu, where one of his successors, Ali (1472-1504), had established the empire of Gassaro. His son and successor, Idris II, recovered the Kanem from the Bulala.

It was not until Idris III (1571-1603) reached the throne that Bornu assumed imperial proportions. He extended his authority over Kano, Zinder, and the Air, over the Kanem as far as the Fitri, over all the countries inhabited by the Teda, and to the South of the Chad over the Mandara, the Kotoko and the Mosgu. The empire was only for a brief period, for after the death of Idris III the Bulala regained the Kanem, although they soon had to yield it to the Tunjur proceeding from Wadai. The conquerors ruled it with a capital at Mao, but they paid tribute to the king of Bornu. Things continued very much on this order until 1808, when Bornu was attacked and defeated by Ousman-dan-Fodio, the Tukulor conqueror who drove king Ahmed from Gassaro. The Negro troops of Bornu under Mohammed-el-Amine, otherwise known as "the Kanemi" because he came from Kanem, rallied, however, forced the Tukulor army to retreat and brought Ahmed back to his throne. But this king and his successors became merely puppets in the hands of the Kanemi and his family. Sheik Omar, son of the Kanemi, ascended the throne and in 1846 proclaimed himself the Sultan of Bornu with his residence in Kuka. Hachen his successor was attacked in 1893 by Rabah who defeated and killed him and transferred the capital to Dikoa. Rabah was killed at Kusseri by the French under Major Lamy on April 22, 1900, and the country became a French protectorate.

BAGIRMI

Directly below the Kanem developed another such Sudanese kingdom known as Bagirmi. The founder of the kingdom was the hunter, Bernim-Besse, sometimes called Dokkengue, who built Messenya, the capital, in 1513. This pioneer built as he had learned from his ancestors. He did not depend upon foreign influence, for neither he nor any of his successors embraced Islam until we come to Malo (1548-1561). Yet it is said that his son Abdallah (1561-1602) brought that religion to Bagirmi. The next in line from this ruler, Borkumanda-Tadele (1734-1739) became a great warrior. He attacked Borku and Kawar and twice vanquished the king of the Wadai. Alawine (1739-1741), the son and successor of the great warrior, was subdued by the emperor of Bornu, to whom the Bagirmi became vassals. The next in line, Mohammed Alamine (1741-1784), seized the Fitri and Kuka and established the independence of Bornu. Abder-rahman-Gaurang I (1784-1806) renewed the struggle against the Wadai, but was defeated and killed by the king of that country, who reduced Bagirmi to vassalage. The son of the king of the Bagirmi placed in charge was dethroned by another son, Tchigama; but he was overpowered and imprisoned. He was later permitted to return and rule as Ousman Borkumanda, a vassal of Wadai, from 1807 to 1846. He led several expeditions against Bornu but was defeated by the Kanem in 1824 at Lederi near the Chad. The latter was aided by the British Major Denham, who sent two cannon to support his ally. Both Abdelkader (1846-1858) and Abu-Sekkine (1858-1884) tried to throw off the vassalage to Wadai. The former won a victory over the Wadai, and the latter succeeded in taking back his capital from which he was driven by the king of that country but only after the death of the latter in 1875. The cruelty of Borkumanda (1884-1885), the son of Abu-Sekkine, caused the Bagirmi to replace him with Abderrahman-Gaurang II, but he was so hard pressed by Rabah in 1896 that he came under the protection of France in 1897.

WADAI

Wadai, another of the Sudanese kingdoms in the much troubled area, was of pagan Tunjur origin, of the people who had their capital at Kadama. Other people of both Arab and Negro origin constituted the few mixed breeds among the Wadaians. This kingdom developed along the

customary African line with the people content as animists.
Finally about 1615 came Jameh, or Saleh, to convert the
people to Islam. He caused complications beyond their frontier leading to so many disputes and struggles with Bornu
on one hand and Bagirmi on the other that Wadai passed for
a number of generations as a sort of football kicked about
between the two neighbors.

Islam was forced upon the Wadaians by the son of Jameh,
who secured sufficient military support to proclaim himself
Sultan of the Wadai in 1635. He reigned for twenty years
but had to pay tribute to the Darfur; and his successors,
Kharut (1655-1678), Kharif (1678-1681), tried without success, while advancing Islam, to shake off this vassalage to the
Darfur. The next ruler, Yakub-Arous (1681-1707), succeeded in 1700 in defeating Omar-Lele and made the Wadai
independent of the Darfur. The next ruler had to fight the
Bagirmi, and then Joda (1745-1795) again attacked the former sovereign, the Darfur, and conquered a part of the
Kanem. Saleh-Derret, or Dered, his successor, was not strong
enough to prevent his warring son, Saboun, from seizing the
throne which he held by bloody and despotic rule (1803-
1813), during which he was victorious in his expeditions
against the Bagirmi. His son, who succeeded him, was still
more despotic. Abdelaziz, who was the grandson of Saboun,
usurped the power about 1829 but only to be disturbed by
numerous rebellions. When he died in 1835 the Darfur conquered the country and placed on the throne Mohammed
Cherif on the condition of vassalage to the Darfur.

This sovereign had a peaceful and prosperous reign and
attained such prestige and power as to attack and defeat the
Sultan of Bornu and force him to pay an indemnity of 8,000
thalers. He then moved the capital from Wara to Abecher.
He had troubles in revolts of tribes as a result of becoming
blind near the end of his career, and he died insane in 1858.
But Ali, his successor, rebuilt the waste places and estab-

lished a profitable trade with Mediterranean countries. He erected a fine royal palace and annexed the Rougna and the Kuti. These conquests, however, were not to remain long in the grasp of the Wadai. Under Yusuf (1874-1898) the Bagirmi became independent. Rabah invaded the country. The Rougna invaded the southern parts of the Wadai territory and made Senussi Sultan of the Rougna and the Kuti; but this new ruler, scared by Rabah when he reached Bornu, came to Wadai for protection and later appealed to France.

Their day was then almost done. The Europeans had their hold on the country and full possession was only a matter of time. Ibrahim (1898-1901) died of wounds inflicted by rebelling subjects. Abu-Ghazali (1901-1902) had to contend with a rebellion led by one of his officers, Acil, who drove him from the capital, and then, hard pressed himself, appealed to the French for "protection." Dudmurra ascended the throne, but in 1909 the French took the capital and reinstated Acil, his rival, as the ruler of the Wadai. Dudmurra defied the French, who, in order to obtain the country for themselves, had championed the cause of the weaker whom they could control. Taking refuge in the northern part of Wadai, Dudmurra gave battle to the Europeans and their allies. He defeated the invaders and made them realize the serious effort being made by the natives to defend what they held as dear as life. At the end of two years, however, his supplies and resources reached an end, and he had to surrender in 1911. Having thus disposed of the stronger party, France deposed their former ally, Acil, in 1912.

THE DARFUR

The Darfur apparently originated among the Tunjur to whom they were subject. Things continued thus peacefully under the domination of native rulers until this calm was disturbed by the Mussulmans coming into the country in sufficiently large numbers to convert a part of the Negroes to that faith and set up among them rival claims. By the fifteenth century the adherents to the new religion were dominant in this sphere, and a Mussulman, Soloun-Sliman, half Negro and half Arab, usurped the throne and established his capital at Bir-Nabak. Omar-Lele, fourth in line from him, however, moved the seat of government to Kabkabie. Under him, as noted above, the country lost prestige in being defeated by the king of Wadai in 1700. During the eighteenth century kings of various types ruled. Next came Abubekr, and then Abderrahman I. The following king, Teherab, distinguished himself by conquering the Kordofan and imposing Islam upon its people. Abderrahman II, the next in line, merely left the record of moving the capital to Tendelty, or El-Facher.

A step backward was noted under Mohammed-Fadel (1800-1840), when the Kordofan established its independence of the Darfur only to remain a short while as food to be plucked by the conqueror. Then Hossein ruled the Darfur and next his successor, Haroun, who permitted the Darfur to be annexed to the Egyptian Sudan by Zobeir-Pasha (1874). Haroun, still hopeful, would not remain under the yoke and rebelled, but his forces were no match for the modernized army sent against him; and he was defeated and killed at Kulkul by Slatin Pasha in 1879. This conqueror was made governor of the Darfur.

KORDOFAN

The Kordofan, frequently herein mentioned, lies east of the Darfur and west of Sennar, from which it is separated by the Nile. The inhabitants are Negroes. They were once governed by the Tunjur, the people about whom we know less than we do about their dependents, but who doubtless must have developed and maintained a powerful political and social organization during medieval and possibly ancient times. The name was probably applied to all the Non-Mussulman people of Negro origin dwelling east of the Chad. The Kordofan passed from under the control of the Tunjur when a Mussulman called Mussaba conquered it. Teherab of the Darfur, as noted above, conquered and Islamized it. He established a governor as a vassal at Bara. The next change was the conquest of the Kordofan under Mohammed-Fadel by Mohammed Bey who made El-Obeid the capital. From the Egyptian Sudan it went to the British Empire.

CHAPTER IV

MOHAMMEDANIZED HEROES

OUSMAN THE TORODO

Mohammedanized Africans count several important personages as heroes, although the Europeans, inconvenienced by their exploits, refer to these leaders as felons. The difference is in that of points of view. Among those working for the new faith was a great figure in the Hausa country or the Central Eastern Sudan about the beginning of the nineteenth century. This was a Tukulor marabout, a native of Futa-Toro, the sheik called Ousman the Torodo. He was the son of Mohammed, called Fode, or Fodio, which means "the savant." Sometimes Ousman the Torodo was called Ousman-dan-Fodio.[1] A marabout was one of the famous sect of the Almoravides (al-morabatine), those who had been thus designated because they had first shut themselves up in a monastery (ribot) for secret prayer and communion and then set out to preach Islamism and to wage war from the Sudan on Spain. Tukulor means (touscouleurs) all colors, people who had been produced by the admixture of several stocks but decidedly Negroid.

Ousman proved himself to be one of the greatest fighters to battle for the Mohammedan faith and for the glory of the Tukulor empire which he built up during the fifteen years of his activity. The empire lasted about a century.

---

[1] The sources already cited above account for the career of Ousman dan Fodio. It may be pointed out here, however, that Delafosse's works are especially helpful. Consult his *Negroes of Africa*, pages 2, 106, 107, 112, 280. See also the *African Background Outlined*. pages 81, 85, 120-121.

OUSMAN THE TORODO

The dissensions in Africa offered him the opportunity for his exploits. When in 1801 Ousman learned of difficulties between the Fulani shepherds of the Gober and their Hausa patrons he proclaimed a holy war against the inhabitants and their neighbors, taking the part of the Fulani, who spoke the same language as that of his people. He enlisted a large number of soldiers among the Futa Toro, the Massina, the Liptako and the Songhay and set out with an army with which he conquered most of Hausa. This country, with the exception of Kano, had not tolerated the faith of the Prophet. Ousman made Sokoto his capital and in its suburb of Wurno established a princely residence. He soon expanded his empire to include all the Hausa kingdoms, a part of ·the Adamwa, the Nupe, the Kebbi, and the Liptako in the bend of the Niger. This was the high tide of his success. Hoping to annex Bornu also, Ousman invaded that country but could not hold his ground against the Kanemi, who compelled him to retire beyond his border in 1810. Ousman died five years later after having made himself in. ten years the greatest conqueror and ruler in the Central and Eastern Sudan in his day.

The empire which Ousman had founded soon experienced serious difficulties although the Mohammedan faith secured a foothold in these parts as a result of the enthusiastic efforts of this zealous propagator. Ousman's brother Abdullahi took over the control of the western provinces, and the other possessions passed to his son, Mohammed Bello, who ruled from 1815 to 1839. Provinces rose against both the son and brother, however, and it was not long before all the Hausa countries rebelled. Then followed combinations with the Tuaregs as enemies of the empire. The Kanemi gave assistance to the rebellion, and likewise the Wadai and the Bagirmi in the attack on Mohammed Bello. Although one of the two armies sent by Mohammed Bello to combat the rebellion was defeated he saved the day with the other.

While Mohammed Bello did not measure up in military

prowess with his father, Ousman the Torodo, he did make an impression upon his time with his poems and prose works in Arabic, dealing with historical and religious problems of his day. He respected the learned and carefully watched administrative matters in order to see that justice be done to every citizen.

His brother, Atiku, served as a sort of austere ascetic who so restricted his subjects that during his reign from 1837 to 1843 he was in constant turmoil; and more trouble followed when Gober and Katsena revolted against the Tukulor princes who had been sent out to rule the vassal provinces. Ali, the son of Mohammed Bello, sat in uneasiness on the throne shaken by revolts against Islam from 1843 to 1855. Matters grew worse under the five successors starting from 1855 when the empire had so disintegrated that Sir Frederick Lugard did not have serious difficulty in occupying Sokoto as a British conquest in 1909. Be it said to the credit of Ousman the Torodo, however, that he did so well his work of building during the years from 1801 to 1815 that the Tukulor empire endured for a century.

EL-HADJ OMAR

Of the Mussulman Negroes who attained distinction as warriors and empire builders El-Hadj Omar stands second to none. His opportunity came in the effort to Islamize the Negroes of West Africa, many parts of which accepted the teachings of the Prophet, long before Mohammedanism made much headway in the Sudan and East Africa where Christianity had been early introduced as in Egypt and Abyssinia. The first opportunity for staging the Islamization of the Negroes of West Africa came in the revolution in Futa-Toro which took place in 1776. The Tukulor Negroes, who as a majority had been Mohammedans for six centuries, conquered in this conflict the Fulani, who had rigidly adhered to their own religious beliefs in things as being animated. Abdul-

kader, the *iman* or *almani,* led the Tukulor soldiers to victory
over Soule-Bubu, the last king of the Denianke dynasty established by Koli. The victor then set up in Futa-Toro a state
of the elective monarchy type, but supposedly directed by
divine authority. This state, under the guidance of the aggressive and statesmanlike Tukulor rulers, endured until it was annexed to the Senegal by the French in 1881.

In the building of this Tukulor empire, however, the usual
vicissitudes of nations were no exception to the struggles in
this momentous undertaking. The Bambara, to the contrary
notwithstanding, were making some progress at this time toward the establishing of an aggressive nation of their own
liking. In 1810 these people succeeded in extending their
power over the Khasso (around Kayes), where Diallo, a
mongrel of both Fulani and Mandingo blood, had established
a state. In 1846. moreover, Kandia, the king of the Bambara and of the Kaarta, established his capital at Nioro.
At this psychological moment El-Hadj Omar appeared upon
the scene in 1854 as the Tukulor leader, took Nioro, the
capital, and executed Kandia. These operations put an end
to the kingdom of the Masasi, and in eight years brought
three powerful states under the control of El-Hadj Omar.[2]

This conqueror was a Tukulor of the Torodo caste. He
was born about 1797 at Aloar, in the province of Podor. A
devotee to Islam, he made a pious pilgrimage to Mecca in
1820. He was admitted to the brotherhood of the Tijania,
and made the "Khalife" for the Sudan. In the pursuance
of his new mission in returning he sojourned with the
Kanemi, the ruler of Bornu, with Mohammed-Bello, the. emperor of the Sokoto, and with Seku-Hamadu, the Fulani king
of the Massina. El-Hadj Omar did not return to West Africa
until 1838. He first took up his abode in Futa-Jallon. In

---

[2] For more detailed treatment see Maurice Delafosse's *Negroes of
Africa,* pages 91 to 94; his *Haut-Sénégal-Niger,* Volume II, pages 380
to 418; *The African Background Outlined,* pages 106 to 107; J. L.
Monod's *Histoire de l'Afrique Occidentale Française,* pages 229 to 236.

1848, however, he transferred his operations to Dinguiray, where he organized an army in order to use the sword in the furtherance of religion. With this army he set out from Dinguiray about 1850 along the Bafing, captured Bure, subdued the Mandingo, took Bambuk, and brought under his control the territory as far as the Senegal. In order to convert the Bambara to Islam he attacked the Masasi and took Nioro, the capital, in 1854, as noted above. He placed in charge as governor of Nioro, a former slave, Mustafa. El-Hadj Omar then proceeded from the southwest toward Segu. He next conquered Merkoia, Damfia, Nyamina and Sansanding.

Endeavoring to extend his authority further by peaceful means, El-Hadj Omar proposed alliance to Hamadu-Hamadu, king of the Masasi, and to Turukoro-Mari, the Bambara king of Segu; but both rulers refused to make any such connections with this soldier advancing a new faith. El-Hadj Omar next directed his efforts toward the Khasso and in April, 1857, brought an army of twenty thousand to lay siege to Medine, its capital. The siege was sustained for three months with rare courage by Diuka-Sambala, king of Khasso, and by the brave mulatto, Paul Holle, in charge of the French fort in that area. The French Governor Faidherbe arrived on the 18th of July in time to force the conqueror to abandon the siege. El-Hadj Omar attacked in vain the French post of Matam in retreating from this area in 1859 when Paul Holle, reenforced with modern equipment, proved adequate to turn the tide against the invader, and he came back to Nioro in 1859.

The natives with the aid of the French might thwart El-Hadj Omar's efforts, but by themselves they had no hope to stop his progress. Facing the conqueror as a common danger, the king of Segu and the king of Massina united their Peuhl and Bambara forces and gave El-Hadj Omar battle on the right bank of the Niger. There they were disastrously

EL-HADJ OMAR

routed by the Tukulor army. Attacking him later with 40,000 soldiers, these allies were again ingloriously defeated. El-Hadj Omar then began a campaign against the Beledugu, and after a few battles between the Bambara and the Fulani captured Segu March 10, 1861.

El-Hadj Omar organized Segu. He executed hostages to assure the submission of the chiefs. He forced the Mussulmans to shave their heads, to pray five times a day, and to observe the rules of the Koran. They must not eat fish, dogs, horses, or dead animals or take fermented drinks. A mason, Samba N'Diaye, fortified the city as a royal residence.

Still restless for further conquests for the faith, El-Hadj Omar hurled his army upon Hamadu-Hamadu, subdued Hamdallahi and had the king of Massina executed in 1862. These further successes caused great consternation throughout the Sudan and in Europe. Not yet satisfied with what had been done to expand the Tukulor empire in behalf of Islam, El-Hadj Omar entered upon the conquest of Massina. Next he took Timbuctoo, but deemed it advisable to withdraw from the city state after levying heavily upon it. He then returned to the Massina, where an uprising had resulted from the stern and rigorous rule imposed. Going next to Hamdallahi, he was blocked in his efforts and retired during the night under the cover or camouflage of a fire. El-Hadj Omar died in 1864 in a grotto where he had been cornered by disgruntled Fulani.

El-Hadj Omar's empire had extended from Massina to the Faleme and from the Tinkisso to the Sabel. This had been accomplished between 1848 when it began and 1864 when it reached its greatest limits. The empire then comprised four practically independent states. The results which El-Hadj Omar had thus achieved as a soldier brought him a high rating. His fame spread rapidly abroad. With meager resources and no rallying cry but that of a religion which most of the natives of that area had refused to accept, he built up an empire of consequence which all but equalled those of

Gonga Musa and Askia Mohammed. Observers from afar inquired as to who was this new figure on the horizon and how he had contrived to perform these feats in such a short time. And in this shortness of time was the trouble. He had conquered more rapidly than he had organized. In each one of the kingdoms conquered he left a son or relative as governor. These became jealous of one another, and Ahmadu at Segu claimed supreme authority. With petty strife they weakened the empire, and peoples thus forced together availed themselves of the opportunities thereby offered for revolt. Both animists and Mohammedans united against the oppressive rulers. This offered the European imperialists their opportunity. At the psychological moment they further intervened as "friends of humanity coming as liberators." French troops under Lieutenant-Colonel Archinard entered Segu April 6, 1891; and, promoted to the rank of general for doing the task so well, he captured on April 29, 1893, the city of Bandiaga, the Tukulor capital of Massina.

SAMORI

Another of these Mohammedan leaders of more than religious objectives was Samori, a black man of slave ancestry. According to the best records available, he was born at Sanankoro about 1835. Lafia Ture, his father, and Massokono Kamara, his mother, were both Mandingoes, following the occupation of colporteurs. Samori began his career in the same business. He reached a turning point in his life, however, when, at the age of twenty, he returned home one day and learned that warriors from Konia had raided the community and carried off his mother as a captive to their chief, Sori-Ibrahima. Because of his unusual love for his mother, Samori went to this chief and earnestly pleaded for her release but suffered enslavement also by the captor himself.

Samori succeeded, however, in reaching his objective another way. In the service of Sori-Ibrahima Samori so distinguished himself as a soldier that this rising military hero became indispensable to that country. The conqueror desired to shower upon Samori various honors including that of commander in chief of his armies, but Samori availed himself of the opportunity to accept, as the best reward available, permission to return with his mother to Sanankoro. There they again resumed their occupation as colporteurs.

With such a long experience in the army and with a growing thirst for power to defend the oppressed, Samori could not long continue as a colporteur. He next entered the service of Bitiki-Suane, king of Torongo, whom he easily supplanted as king of the country by showing great military ability and capacity to organize. Samori then went forward to extend his kingdom by conquest. In carrying out this new program he first met in battle Famadu, the chief of Kanadugu, whom he defeated and beheaded. Frightened at this triumphal approach, Bisandugu and all Kanadugu humiliatingly submitted to the conqueror. Samori easily defeated next the army of his former chief, Sori-Ibrahima, and decapitated his two brothers who had been sent with these forces against the invader. With Konia added to his territory Samori could establish his capital at Sanankoro as the center of immense territory which with the exception of Keniera constituted all Wasulu. Sori-Ibrahima, hoping that all was not yet lost, decided to take the field against his former slave in order to save at least some part of his kingdom, but he, like his two brothers, went down in a disastrous defeat. He was taken prisoner, but Samori, sparing him the decapitation which his brothers had suffered, condemned his former chief to follow in the rear of the Wasulu army and pray for its success.[3]

---

[3] Samori's career may be further studied in almost any of the European histories of West Africa and the Sudan. These writers with the economic imperialists' point of view generally brand Samori as a felon. Consult, however, the following: Monod's *Histoire de l'Afrique Occidentale Française*, pages 244 to 250; A Mevil, *Samory;* Lt. Colonel Baratier, *A Travers l'Afrique.*

In eight years of conquest Samori had established an empire of 400,000 square kilometers. He then entered upon the career of religious reform. He had been an animist himself from birth and ruled over a million and a half of such believers, chiefly the Mandingoes and the Bambaras; but Samori knew the influence of Islam as a rallying point in the Sudan. He therefore assumed the title of *almany,* which means commander of the believers with authority from God. He undertook to make this title more than one of snobbishness as it had been used by so many of his predecessors in the advancement of the faith. He endeavored to have himself respected and increase his influence by teaching the principles of the Koran. Samori made the Mussulman faith the state religion. He had mosques built in each city. He could not at once bring all his subjects to a strict observance of the Mohammedan customs, but he constrained the majority of them to do so; and to root the faith deeply in the minds of coming generations he had the sons of the chiefs sent to school that these principles might be mastered and taught by them during coming years. He had fines imposed on those who would not conform to his orders.

Samori's financial policy required little of his people. He compelled each village to cultivate a field for his good; and he collected the tenth part of the yield of gold in Wasulu. Other revenues came as spoils from conquered territories. All this income went into the military budget which, because of the demands upon the army for constant service, was the most important of the state. Everything centered around the activities of the army, and the state had to be organized and conducted in keeping with this policy.

The army had ten corps or divisions. The generals were governors of the corresponding ten provinces. In time of war the army corps were assembled by threes as three divisions, each under the command of a brother of the sultan. The tenth corps was a reserve force directly under the control of Samori. The corps contained about 5,000 men each, sub-

SAMORI ON THE WARPATH

divided into divisions of 1,000, which were further divided
into companies of 100, formed of ten squads. All the chiefs
were mounted and the commanders of the corps had with
them at their expense two or three hundred choice troops, the
"Sofas" and some cavalrymen. The guard of Samori, the
Almamy, was composed of 500 young men chosen for their
intelligence and their physical make-up. They were arrayed
at the side of the Almamy, and stood ready to sacrifice their
lives in his behalf. The guard of honor only had rapidly
firing guns. The equipment, however, improved in the
course of time, but not sufficiently to compete with the more
modern equipment of European troops.

With this military machine thus built up Samori held his
own with the French, who saw that they had to overcome
him or be driven out of that part of Africa. When he finally
conquered so much of their surrounding territory the French
found themselves humiliated by seeing the natives trampled
upon after the French had guaranteed them "protection,"
and the immediate danger was that the French themselves
might be bottled up in the Bakoy. Samori was the most
dreadful enemy encountered by the French in Africa. He
showed himself to be a leader of the people, a strategist, and
a shrewd politician. As a soldier he showed unfaltering
courage, relentless energy, perseverance, foresight, and, above
all, an unwonted tenacity which knew no such thing as
discouragement.

To dislodge and conquer a soldier of this type required all
but supreme effort by the French troops in Africa. By 1881
when Samori's conquest had made him such a power, Borgnis-
Desbordes had just established the French post of Kita. He
established that at Badoumbe in 1882. Apprised of the approach of Samori, the French commander tried to enter into
negotiations with the formidable leader through a native
lieutenant, Alakamessa. The intermediary, however, obtained
nothing from Samori but an expression of contempt for a
native who would bargain to surrender his own native soil.

The French commander could do nothing then but engage in battle—the thing which he had so much dreaded. The French contingent directed its course southward and crossed the Niger near Siguri and dispersed the Wasulu troops below Keniera, who had just taken the town. Retreating to the post at Kita, however, the French troops were harassed by the Sofas under Fabou, the brother and lieutenant of Samori. Borgnis-Desbordes took a position at Bamako in February, 1883, but Fabou gave him battle in that quarter. After a number of attacks to the south of Bamako, Borgnis-Desbordes and Captain Pietri, with 400 well-armed men, drove back beyond the Ouyako the 3,000 inadequately armed soldiers of Fabou.

During the years from 1884 to 1886 Colonel Boylève, Commander Combe and Colonel Fry engaged in several battles in the Bakoy basin, fighting forces under Malinke-Mori, another brother and lieutenant of Samori. Boylève was chiefly occupied in protecting the line of communication with supplies. Combe cleared the approaches to Bamako, scoured the Manding, and established the ports of Kundu and Niagassola. In the meantime the French under Captain Louvet had been surrounded and besieged by Samori's troops in Nafodie and the French post at Niagassola had been attacked. Combe unblocked Captain Louvet, besieged in Nafadie; and Frey freed Niagassola where the post recently established had been attacked. Defeated at Fatiko-Djimgo, Malinke-Mori turned back toward the south. Samori then thought it best to make peace, which the French on two occasions had proposed in 1886 and 1887. This resulted in the treaty of Bissandugu, signed on March 25, 1887.

This agreement fixed the limits of Samori's empire. His possessions which extended from Tengrela in Futa Jallon must be limited on the Tinkisso and by the Niger as far as Bamako. A French post was established at Siguiri. The French claimed the right of protectorate, but Samori denied that the protection of their country was thereby accepted for the Wasulu empire and its dependencies. To prove that he really meant to carry out the terms of the treaty as he understood it Samori gave as a hostage his son Karamoko, whom the French government invited to visit Paris. In the meantime, Samori, who had learned much by observing the French at close range, sought to extend his empire in other parts toward the east. He conducted a campaign against Tieba, the king of Kenedugu. He then besieged Sikasso, which held out successfully for sixteen months and cost the invader so many men that when a revolt of his subjects of Wasulu and Sankaran took place he had to return to Bissandugu to restore order. For the failure to carry Sikasso Samori blamed the French. He insisted that Kenedugu was included in his empire according to the treaty of 1887 and that the French should have supported him in the effort to take possession of it. Samori, therefore, disregarded thereafter the treaty with the French. Another treaty signed in 1889 limiting his territory on the Niger to what was between its source and Siguri and allowing a French post at Kurusa was also ignored.

Samori's troops crossed to the left bank of the Niger and took away people, alarmed by the approach of the French as related. Here his method of warfare changed. He saw the French were his real enemies and that he must dislodge the French or be ruined himself. He saw that mere resistance against armies with modern equipment would not solve his problem, and he could not depend upon a united front of African chiefs against the French. The only two remedies left him were to devastate the country to make it impossible for the French or their allies to live on it and seek the alliance of some other European power against the French.

Samori proposed to bring the Wasulu empire under the protection of the British in Sierra Leone and sent envoys to London for the negotiation of the pact. Chambers of commerce there supported them, but the negotiations did not succeed. Samori, however, did contrive to get some advice from that quarter, and British merchants sold him some modern rifles and munitions. Better equipped and wise enough to know that an army is at greater advantage when free to move than when besieged in a fortified town, Samori kept going to pillage and to destroy all tribes under the protection of the French, and devastated all areas likely to fall into their hands. It was another case of Sherman's march from Atlanta to the sea during the Civil War, or Napoleon's enemies retreating before him in Russia.

There were natives who were too much attached to their homes to join in making such a sacrifice, and it was impossible to dislodge all the people in this way. His method, however, injected terror into the situation, and few in the beginning dared to oppose him. Samori's method differed too from that of other Africans with whom the French had dealt. He showed foresight in having his well-equipped soldiers retire before the French inch by inch while those with old equipment were functioning as two distinct groups, one to guard the conducting of the dislodged formation, while the third would conquer in the east native territory to which the exodus would be directed. This enabled Samori to do the exceptional thing in military history of accomplishing three objectives at once. His people changed countries every year, pressing toward the east into districts already subjugated by his advance guard without leaving the conquering French even an old man to impress into their service or a morsel of food with which to feed him.

The importance of this method of warfare, the French with their modernly equipped men did not realize when they started upon their campaign in 1891 and suddenly attacked Kankan. The French believed that this campaign would be a triumphant march from the Niger to Sanankoro, and they regretted that there were not sufficient obstacles to render the conquest one of a little glory. Setting out from Bamako to Siguiri, they found their triumphal march turned out to be a hard and painful campaign, a raid of thirty days only.

Kankan was taken by Archinard, and Bissandugu was captured, but the French had to evacuate it the same day and
fall back to Kankan, the occupation of which was necessary
to save their face and maintain their position on the right
bank of the Niger. There the French had to remain until
the close of the rainy season near the end of the year.
Samori, however, had been warned of the imminent danger.
He spent the next six months preparing and organizing his
army, buying rifles and providing his forces with supplies.
While Samori would not stand prolonged battle with the
better equipped French, his method of retreating into the
barren or devastated country where the food supply of the
French became a difficult problem was as effective as gun-
fire. When Colonel Humbert marched again upon Bissandugu he had to contend with a resolute foe in fifteen combats
in a mountainous and woody area afflicted with yellow fever
and cattle plague. Bissandugu was retaken and then Keruane
and Sanankoro, the second capital of the Wasulu empire,
but the French force, diminished by fire and privation, could
not go any further. In the meantime Samori hurled his
faithful allies of Kabadugu upon Bagoe and gave full license
to one of his best generals, Sekuba, who conquered all the
country at the extreme limits of the Bambara regions occupying the upper Sassandra Valley. In this campaign Sekuba
defeated and killed Captain Menard in a battle at Seguela.

Samori ordered in April, 1892, that the French posts be
attacked and their line of communication be cut. Samori
himself in charge took the province of Nafana, executed its
hostile king, Liala-Koro, and made himself master as far as
Bandama. This victory assured the liaison of the troops of
Sekuba in the South and those of Kabadugu in the North.
Thus while slowly retreating and leaving for the French a
few states in the West Samori had doubled his possessions in
the East. An appearance of defeat resembled very much
success. This at least showed strategy.

·On the approach of the dry season in 1892 the French ex-

pedition forced Samori in the direction of Sanankoro, where
he came face to face with a former opponent, Colonel Combe.
In the wake of this warrior the sharpshooters and Algerian
horsemen accomplished a clever feat. They advanced as far
as the limits of Nefana, took possession of Guelaba, but had
to stop there before winter. Samori, unmoved, continued his
tactics of withdrawing before the enemy when it seemed unwise to risk battle but destroying everything as he retired in
order to starve out the pursuer. He reached the Bandama
frontier and approached the French colony of the Ivory
Coast. The campaign of 1892-1893 cut Samori off from
Sierra Leone as a result of fourteen battles in thirty-four
days. There he had hoped to obtain further provisions.
Samori had to leave the Milo valley and fall back beyond
Odienne. Combe established forts at Farana and Kissidugu.
The French now held all Wassulu.

Samori, however, reestablished communication with the
Gold Coast after his connections with Sierra Leone had been
broken. In 1894 Samori reduced Kong, the Djimini, the
Diammala, and established a capital at Dabakala. He so
menaced the Ivory Coast that the French considered the campaign of 1894 and 1895 necessary. Colonel Monteil conducted
the French force but, having first to pacify the Ivory Coast,
lost time and men in that area. When he attacked Samori's
army with three hundred soldiers he did not find the reenforcements promised from the government, and had to
retreat exhausted and humiliated. Colonel Monteil himself,
severely wounded, returned to the Ivory Coast. His losses
in killed and wounded had decimated his ranks to two-thirds.
The Sofas next undertook to take the offensive in the east,
but the French Buguni and Beyla kept them in awe. A son
of Samori, Sarankieni Mori, extended his incursions toward the
French zones of influence and protectorates into Bobo Diulaso, Lobi, and Gurunsi. Near Gao he exterminated an
English detachment under Lieutenant Henderson. He con-
sented to cede Buna to the French, they contend, and author-

ized Captain Braulot to march upon the town to take possession, but when the Captain reached the place he found it occupied by Sofas who exterminated him and his detachment. This much talked of treachery of one of Samori's lieutenants determined the French to subdue him at all hazards. Samori, now near the Ivory Coast, however, was about at the end of his resources. He could no longer outwit the French by disputing the ground foot by foot while devastating the country to starve out the invaders, and conquering new lands ahead with his advance guard. Samori was now facing impenetrable forests settled with natives untouched by outside culture and unable to sympathize and cooperate with the defender of the native soil. The people had become tired of the exhaustive warfare and longed for some less expensive adjustment of affairs. His warriors, moreover, had less ardor than formerly. He vainly tried during a respite of 1896-1897 to restore the morale by rejuvenating his staff and replacing generals who had been often defeated. Caudrelier set out from Dobo Diulaso in 1897 and drove the forces of Samori from Kong. He forced Samori's army from the west to the east and fortified the ground gained by establishing permanent posts. French soldiers from these posts then surrounded Samori's army on all sides except the west. Next Pineau forced Samori to abandon the territory between the Camoe and the Bandama. Thus pursued and abandoned, Samori thought of connecting with Liberia. He concentrated his forces at Seguela and plunged into the forest. Detachments from the north under Colonel Bertin, and of Commander Lartigue, closed in on Samori. A reconnoitring conducted by Captains Gouraud and Gaden surprised Samori on September 29, 1898, and he was taken prisoner at Guélémou on the upper Cavaly by Lieutenant Jacquin and Sergeant Bratières. By way of Beyla, Nafadie, Niagassola, Kita, and Kayes, Samori was directed to Saint Louis, where he tried to commit suicide rather than be made a prisoner. He was deported to Gabon with his son Sarankieni Mori. He died at Niolé on the Ogooué in 1900 at the age of sixty-five. His career had been very much like that of Napoleon. His death was very much like that of the Corsican at St. Helena.

RABAH

One of the bravest of these religious leaders of whom Mohammedanized Africans still sing the praises was Rabah. The economic imperialists think of him, however, as a cruel religious fanatic who drenched the Eastern Sudan with blood. Rabah was made possible by troubles developing in the Eastern Sudan about 1875. Zobeir-Pasha, around whom the beginning of this story centers, was a Jaaline Arab who had been a slave-trading merchant and who, with an army of native soldiers, had assisted Egypt in conquering the Upper Nile. For this service Zobeir-Pasha had been made Governor of Bahr-el-Ghazal. Called to Egypt to confer with his superiors, he left his son Suleiman in charge of his office. Enemies of the Jaaline Arab caused Suleiman to believe that he was in disfavor with the rulers of Khartum. Suleiman therefore took up the fight of Haroun, the dethroned sultan of the Darfur and Babel, against Egypt. Gessi Pasha, sent against Suleiman, disastrously defeated him; but Rabah, his principal lieutenant, son of a Negro woman, the wet-nurse of Zobeir-Pasha, and consequently his foster brother, escaped from the bloody encounter with the remnants of Suleiman's army and began conquests which made him the dominant figure in the central Sudan for twenty-two years.

Starting out from Bahr-el-Ghazal in 1878, Rabah entered the territory of the Banda the following year. He took Kuti in 1883, organized it with Rougna as a kingdom and installed his lieutenant Senussi as sultan there in 1890. The explorer Crampel lost his life in a conflict with Rabah's forces in 1891. In 1892 Rabah invaded Bornu and attacked that same year the Sultan Hashem, whom he put to death. Rabah next destroyed Kuka and transferred the capital of

Bornu to Dikoa. Thus at the end of fifteen years of uninterrupted success he appeared to be the invincible conqueror in control of practically all the territory between the Nile and the Tchad. He levied duties upon the caravans and subjected his subjects to heavy taxes.

Coming into countries which the French natives claimed as under their protection, Rabah found obstacles which he could not so easily surmount, but his successes continued.

RABAH

He marched upon Gober, in pursuing Abubekr, Hachem's nephew and successor, but Rabah was stopped at Sokoto by the army of Emperor Meyassu. Later Rabah turned to smaller states to the south of Chad and took Gulfei, Busso, and Kusseri from the Mandara and Sogone from the Kotoko. Next he invaded again Bagirmi, which at that time had come under the protection of the French. By agreement with the sultan of Gurang the French had placed one Gentil at the capital as their representative. Rabah launched an attack on Massenya which he burned while taking 8,000 Bagirmi as captives. Then with an army of 8,000 men he pursued the Mbang under the protection of the French. On the 18th of July, 1899, Rabah encountered a detachment of the advance guard of Gentil, commanded by Bretonnet, and annihilated them in a desperate fight lasting for eight hours. On April 22, 1900, however, Rabah's career came to a close when he was met in battle at Kusseri by the French commander Major Lamy, and both Rabah and his conqueror were killed.[4]

MOHAMMED-AHMED, THE MAHDI

Mohammed-Ahmed, the Mahdi, was a militant Negroid devoutly attached to Islam. He was a native of Dongola and belonged to a Nuba family, a non-Arabic race of the Sudan, not to be confused with the Nubians. He proclaimed himself Mahdi in 1881. By this he meant to say that he was the inspired representative of Mohammed and a prophet himself. His position among those of his faith was that of an inspired leader with authority to proclaim holy wars upon those whose policies did not harmonize with the teachings of the Mohammedans or who stood in the way of the carrying out of Islamic designs. Accepted as such by his followers and dominant over areas brought under his subjection, the Mahdi became the controlling force in his day in the Eastern Sudan, which bowed to his will for sixteen years.

The rise of the Mahdi was all but phenomenal. He began his career with the defeat of Rachid-Bey, the governor of

[4] Rabah's record is set forth in numerous works such as Delafosse's *Negroes of Africa*, pages 113-114 and 122-123; Monod's *Histoire de l'Afrique Occidentale Française*, pages 304-306; *The African Background*, pp. 125-126 and 184-185; E. Gentil, *La Chute de l'Empire de Rabah*.

Fashoda, in the Southern Kordofan. There the Mahdi's family had come and set up its residence. His career gained further momentum in 1882, when he defeated an Egyptian army and seized all the Kordofan. El-Obeid, the capital, fell into the Mahdi's hands in 1883. On November 4, the same year, he drove into ambush Hicks-Pasha's army of 10,000 men and annihilated them at Chekan. Frightened at those sweeping victories and shaken by the consternation which they caused, Slatin Pasha, governor of the Darfur and Lupton-Bey, governor of Bahr-el-Ghazal, surrendered without much effort in 1884. Only Emin-Pasha in Equatoria, and Mustafa-Bey, at Dongola, then persisted in combating the Mahdi, but Berber and the Sennar had fallen into the hands of the "Dervishes," those thus designated as the partisans of the Mahdi. On January 15, 1885, the Mahdi seized Omdurman, a suburb of Khartum, and eleven days later rode triumphantly into the citadel there and put Gordon-Pasha to death. These conquests in five years had made the Mahdi the master of four-fifths of what had been the Egyptian Sudan. The long train of successes was ended when shortly thereafter the Mahdi died of typhoid fever at Omdurman.

The Mahdi's work, however, was not yet undone. He was succeeded by Abdullah, or "khalife," the term by which was designated the heir to the kingdom by the dying Mahdi. Abdullah belonged to the Baggara (cow-herders) of the Darfur, who were a cross between Arabs and Negroes. He had been the friends and chief advisor of the Mahdi. Abdullah ignored the relatives and fellow countrymen of the Mahdi and reorganized his empire with natives from his own people of the Darfur, thousands of whom he brought to Omdurman. Abdullah built up a powerful army, launched an attack on Abyssinia, and took the city of Gondar in the battle in which the Negus John was killed in 1888. By 1892 these victorious troops established their power in Equatoria, which had held out against the Mahdi, but had been abandoned by Emin Pasha in 1889.

THE MAHDI IN ACTION

At this point, however, the tide began to turn. In 1896 the Dervishes lost Dongola to the Anglo-Egyptian troops and Berber in 1897. On July 10, 1898, Captain Marchand seized Fashoda in carrying out the French design. Kitchener took Omdurman on the second–of the following September in the furtherance of similar aims of the British. By diplomacy he forced Marchand to leave Fashoda in conceding it was the British sphere of influence. Both the French and British imperialists now were lying across the Mahdi's path. The French were trying to conquer that section of Africa to connect its possessions in East and West Africa, and the British were invading the same territory to make it the connection between their possessions expanding north from the Cape and south from Egypt. With the English in all but complete ascendancy the Mahdi had to abandon his empire. Forced to take refuge, the Mahdi was defeated and killed in the Kordofan in 1899 by Colonel Wingate.[5]

---

[5] The rise and fall of the Mahdi may be traced in many works, among which the following will be of service: R. C. Slatin-Pacha, *Fire and Sword in the Sudan;* G. Breul, *L'Afrique Equatoriale Française; The African Background Outlined,* pages 126-127.

CHAPTER V

IN ASHANTI AND DAHOMEY

Although the public is still misled by ignorant and biased writers who point out as an outstanding weakness of the Negro his so-called inability to govern, the evidence runs decidedly to the contrary. In that part of Africa where the real Negro of unadulterated blood is found, the European conquerors met their greatest opposition because of the governments which the Negroes had established without European or Asiatic experience in state building. With the exception of Abyssinia in East Africa, where there has been so much admixture with Asiatics that writers refer to those people as white Africans, the African kingdoms and empires of great import developed in the truly Negro Africa above the equator on the West Coast. The most outstanding of these were Dahomey, Ashanti, Yoruba and Benin. Of these we have learned much to admire in their culture, their social organization, their industry and their art. The Benin excelled especially in their aesthetic expression, as evidenced by specimens of their art found in the best museums in this country and Europe. These people developed a government of force and influence, but did not manifest as much power of resistance as did Dahomey and Ashanti. What their government meant is best expressed by the difficulties encountered by the conqueror.[1]

Ashanti owed its stamina mainly to a line of unusual kings. The first king of worth, well known to Europe, was Osai Tutu, the fourth of the line. He is known, however, as the

---

[1] More details with respect to the Ashanti may be obtained from R. S. Rattray's *Ashanti*, his "Arts and Crafts of the Ashanti," in the *Journal of the Royal African Society*, Volume XXIII, 265; and his *Ashanti Law and Constitution*.

founder of the empire. During his reign from 1700-1730 a
man of mystery, called Anotchi, claimed that he had received
from heaven the mission to make the Ashanti a great nation,
the symbol, or palladium, of which was a wooden throne
partly covered with gold. In this throne was the soul of the
Ashanti nation. As long as they safeguarded this they would
be a great people, but if they lost it the nation would come
to an end. It should never touch the ground and no person
should sit upon it.

With these insignia for right of ascendancy the king was
easily the supreme authority over the chiefs of the provinces.
These in a somewhat feudal arrangement ruled over subchiefs and the last mentioned over the families in the villages,
exercising legislative, judicial and administrative powers.
The king, however, was not absolute, for he was to some extent controlled by a council in foreign affairs. The government was more of an aristocracy except that in all cases the
king had the right to impose the death penalty. The king
was supported by an army of companies officered by a commander from the respective provinces. The army was maintained by levies made according to those areas and supplied
somewhat after the order of European feudal armies.

This well developed part of Africa, like other parts of the
West Coast, had long been desired for Europeans, first for
trading posts to secure palm oil and slaves and later for the
expropriation of the whole area for colonial expansion. The
Portuguese, first upon the scene, built Elmira Castle in
1482, preceding the British, who did not become active in
this area until 1533. The Dutch, French and others cast also
their wishful eye in this direction. The Swedes concentrated
at Cape Coast, the Danes at Christiansbourg. In the course
of time these trading posts expanded and gradually fell into
the hands of the British through the operation of the Royal
African Company. Facing bankruptcy, as a result of the
abolition of the slave trade in 1807, however, the Royal
African Company surrendered its charter in 1821 and turned

over its forts to the Imperial Government. These forts, Cape Castle, Accra, Sekondi, Winneba, Dixcove, Anomabu, and Commanda, were placed under the Governor in Chief of the British West Africa Settlement, and thus constituted an imperial stronghold or colony on the coast.

The people along the coast were Fantis, Gas, and Krebos, while in the interior dwelt various tribes of the Akan stock under the control of the Kumasi. Wise in their generation, the British with these forts on the coast as a foothold gradually worked their way into the interior by stirring up strife among the natives and then intervening to settle these quarrels. The British exacted the land as the fee for their restoration of order, or for extending *Pax Britannica.*

Sir Charles McCarthy, who was functioning as Governor of the coastal possessions in 1824, could not wait altogether upon diplomacy. Following the usual method of stirring up war between natives whose lands were desired, he incited the Fantis to attack the Ashantis and revoked the treaty made by the English consul with the Ashanti King Osai-Tutu Kwamina, by which he had the right to use the route to the sea by way of Cape Coast. Believing that he could now attack and vanquish the Ashanti with his British troops and Fanti allies and settle the question by taking the country, McCarthy rushed into the disputed area. He had made the fatal mistake of underrating the opposing force. The British represented the proudest nation on earth, but the Ashanti on the other hand represented a fearless fighting nation ready to die for their country. In spite of the able assistance given by the Fanti allies of the British the force was battered to pieces under the onslaught of the Ashanti. The survivors who could so contrive as to extricate themselves from this catastrophe retired the best they could, but they left Sir Charles McCarthy dead upon his own chosen battling ground at Assamako on January 21, 1824.

The results of this defeat were disastrous to British influence along the coast. The Ashanti were convinced that Euro-

OSAI-TUTU KWAMINA

pean soldiery is not invincible, and the natives allied with the British were inclined to think that the "protection" of the empire was a myth. Driven out of the Ashanti country, the British had difficulty in retaining their forts along the coast. For two years the Ashanti made attacks on these trading centers, but in the battle of Dodowa in 1826 a reenforced British army drove the Ashanti back. This victory was so expensive to the British, nevertheless, that the Imperial Government decided to abandon these forts.

British merchants, looking far ahead, decided in 1830, however, to maintain the trading posts along the coast at their expense until such time as the Imperial Government would change its policy. Captain George McClean, who was made the new administrator, abandoned the policy of dealing with the Ashanti by force since it had been so disastrous to Sir Charles McCarthy. McClean endeavored to reach the same end by diplomacy. The olive branch was thrown out to the Ashanti, and they made peace in 1831.

The outstanding provisions of the agreement were that the Fantis would remain the allies of the British and that the Ashanti would permit merchants to trade in their territory. McClean interpreted the so-called alliance of the Fanti a sort of surrender of their sovereignty, and he actually set up a government at Cape Coast Castle which exercised over certain natives legislative, judicial, and administrative powers. The Committee of Merchants to whom he was responsible was not thus interested in such an advanced step in colonial administration, for it might alienate the natives and cause a loss of trade. The Imperial Government, however, appeared upon the scene again, took back these forts, and placed in charge Commander Hill. He succeeded in 1844 in signing with the Fanti chiefs an important treaty called the Bond of 1844.

This treaty gave the British judicial authority over the Fanti, and thus legalized what had been questioned under McClean. The words of this treaty, the first of its kind in

the development of the African colonial policy, were unusually significant in that it was specified that the Fanti
were not a conquered people but friends and allies of Great
Britain. Resolutions of a Select Committee of Parliament in
1842 had said that their relationship "should be, not the
allegiance of subjects, to which we have no right to pretend,
and which it would entail an inconvenient responsibility to
possess, but the deference of a weaker power to a stronger
and more enlightened neighbor, whose protection and counsel
they seek, and to whom they are bound by certain definite
obligations."

In thus entrenching themselves among the Fanti by actual
exercise of power and diplomatic claims couched in evasive
terms herein set forth, the British without war got control of
the Fanti territory. This precedent served as the first step
in the conquest of the Ashanti area which was the hinterland
of Fanti. The Ashanti were not seriously disturbed for
thirty years, but trouble broke out again in 1872 when the
British in another effort toward expansion bought out the
Dutch African forts. Among these was Elmina, which the
King of the Ashanti claimed on the grounds that it belonged
to him inasmuch as he had only rented it to the Dutch, and
they could not sell what they never owned. The Ashanti had
no desire thus to part with their only outlet to the sea. On
the other hand, the British decided to support their claim
by force. The two opposite forces met in battle in 1873.
Again the Ashanti proved that they were more than a match
for the British and their allies. The Ashanti defeated the
aggressor and put Elmina in a state of siege. Realizing that
something drastic had to be done to save the prestige of the
British in Africa, the home government sent reenforcements
under Sir Garnet Wolseley, but these newcomers availed
little against the fearless and undaunted Ashanti.

To stem the tide more British troops had to be brought
into action. With superior arms on hand in 1872 the British
cut off the supplies of the Ashanti with a naval blockade,

invaded their country, and burned to the ground their capital, Kumasi. The victors demanded as an indemnity 50,000 ounces of gold, and the right to trade in Ashanti territory. Knowing, however, that the spirit of the people had not been broken, the British guaranteed the Ashanti political autonomy. The British did not actually occupy the country at this time. They deemed it wise to concentrate on strengthening their hold on the people and resources near the coast. The program of economic imperialism, growing out of agreements consummated in the Congress of Berlin in 1885, had not yet started the rush to the interior.

When the British about this time decided to annex the country they met stubborn resistance on the part of the young warrior and king Primpeh. To the ultimate request of the Governor of the Gold Coast in 1894 that he should surrender his country he emphatically replied that he would never thus bow to the aggressor. Instead of preparing to resist, however, the Ashanti made the mistake of sending a mission to England to adjust matters. While they were awaiting a negative reply from Joseph Chamberlain, who next to Rhodes was the greatest of all imperialists, the Gold Coast Government was concentrating its forces to take the country. The aggressors unexpectedly stormed Kumasi in 1896, seized Primpeh, the Queen Mother, the royal family, and administrators of the state and imprisoned them at Elmina. Primpeh was exiled to the Seychelles Islands, but in 1924 after the fires had been smothered he was allowed to return as a private citizen. It was not difficult then for the British to compete with the French and Germans in expanding toward the Upper Volta, but the French had made good their claim to Ivory Coast and the Germans to Togoland. The Ashanti, the most formidable force encountered by the British on the West Coast, had been removed, although the spirit of the people was not yet crushed.

Trouble developed in 1900 under Sir Frederick Hodgson, then in charge of that territory. He attempted to impose a tax on the Ashanti and to collect the indemnity exacted from them after the victory of the British in 1896. Knowing that this money to be thus raised was to finance campaigns against them and other Africans, the Ashanti refused to comply with these orders. Hostilities broke out. The old battles had to be fought over again. Since 1896, however, the Ashanti had not been able to organize any resistance, and their rising was suppressed. The whole country then together with the Northern territories was declared a protectorate. To show at least an inclination to concede something to the Ashanti and calm troubled waters the British returned the ''Golden Stool'' of which the natives had been dispossessed during the war; and Primpeh in the capacity of a marionette was elevated to the position of paramount chief of Kumasi. In 1935 Osai Agyeman, nephew of Primpeh I, was made the nominal King of Ashanti in the system of indirect rule. The aim is to keep the Ashanti separate and distinct from the Fanti, with whom the latter have recently developed too many ties to leave the British comfortable.

DAHOMEY

In no part of West Africa did the European conquerors encounter more formidable resistance than in Dahomey. This is admitted even by A. Le Hérissée and Henri LeFaivre, both of whom try to make a good case for the right of the French to take over the country. This resistance of Dahomey was due to the solidarity which the kingdom developed under its well connected dynasties. Their kings in ancient times united surrounding areas, defended their frontiers, maintained peace and stimulated the people toward becoming most prosperous farmers and artisans. These kings knew ''how to organiez their state and their army and administer their kingdom in a fashion which did them honor.''[2]

---

[2] Melville J. Herskovits' *Dahomey*, two volumes; G. L. Brunet, *Dahomey;* Edouard Foa, *Dahomey;* Henri Labouret, *Le Royaume d'Arda et son Evangelisation;* A. Le Hérissée, *L'Ancien Royaume du Dahomey;* A. L. d'Albega, *La France au Dahomey en 1890.*

That the Dahomans had reached such a stage in their development as to terrify the conquerors who coveted the land is everywhere evident from ruins excavated in those parts. Leo the African, who traveled in the Sudan about 1507, learned of this kingdom although he did not know its exact location. On the map of Joannes Janssonius, published in Amsterdam in 1627 under the title of Guinea, the city and country of Dauma, intended for Dahomey, are shown as located North of Arder (Ardra) and to the East of the Volta. Uninformed historians, however, have thought of the reign of Wagbaja between 1650 and 1680 as the foundation of the Dahoman kingdom and still others are conservative enough to fix the date as 1625.

At the beginning of the seventeenth century, however, Europeans did find in this area three states—the kingdom of Judas extending from the port of Widah on the Gulf of Guinea to its capital Suavi, the kingdom of Arda (Ardres) and the kingdom of the Foys, or Foins (Fons). Of these Ardra, or Ardres, was the most ancient and may have ruled over the others. The first known king was Kopon, the founder of the long-ruling Dahoman dynasty. When he died Hunugungung succeeded in forcing into exile his two brothers who disputed his accession. The next oldest of these brothers was received by Da, the king of the Foys, at Abomey, where with a little territory in the beginning he finally expanded and built up his possessions until he had power to overcome Da and erect a new palace over his remains. This he called Dahomey.

Not much of interest to the outside world was noted under the successor known as Adanzan I, and Akaba, who ruled from 1650 to 1680 and from 1680 to 1708 respectively, except that the country still grew. Then came Agadja-Troudo, who distinguished himself by important conquests among which was noted the taking of Allada, in the battle for which the successor to the throne of Kopon of Ardra was killed in avenging the exile of his grandfather Tacudunu. He next attacked and conquered the kingdom of Judas and united the three kingdoms under one ruler and made it the most formidable opponent to the Europeans trading along the West Coast of Africa.

About 1732 the power of the Dahomans became strikingly in evidence when Bessa-Abadee ascended the throne. During the forty years of his reign he solidified the conquest of his predecessor, got rid of the malcontents, dispatched his opponents, fought the Popos, the neighboring tribes, the Mahis, and the Egbas. He attacked the Portuguese at Widah and annihilated the entire garrison.

The three kings who ruled from 1774 to 1818, Adanzu II, Winuhiu, and Agonglo, accomplished nothing more than to hold the frontiers against neighboring tribes whom for first one reason and then another they had to fight. There was the short reign of Adanzan (or Adandozan) who before his father died had shown himself so cruel that Agonglo, contrary to the local custom, tried to have his younger son succeed him. Adanzan, in spite of these efforts, reached the throne and with the opposition to him as an additional reason for cruelty plunged into a vindictive despatching of almost everyone that displeased him. His enemies, therefore, invited trouble from without in joining with two Portuguese slave-traders, Francisco Felix Da Souza and Domingo Martins, of Brazilian mixed breed, who dethroned Adanzan and made Ghezo king. Under the influence of Da Souza especially, Ghezo did much for the economic development of Dahomey with respect to the culture and trade in manioc and palm oil, but just as much more was done to stimulate the slave trade by numerous wars which were stirred up to secure captives to supply the slavers which cast anchor at several ports along the coast. The Europeans and Americans profiting by this traffic had paid high tribute to this king who thus favored them, and they have pointed out as evidence of his greatness the splendor which Dahomey attained in art and commerce during his reign.

Trouble awaited Dahomey, moreover, in the establishment of Porto Novo by the son of Kopon of Adra, who had been driven out by Hunugungung, his successor. This exiled son crossed the Ouémé into the kingdom of Djaquin and started this Porto Novo in the establishment of the nucleus of the city of Ajachi. During the taking of Djaquin by Agadja-Troudo in 1724 Ate-Agbanlin, the descendant of the son of Kopon, had fled to Porto Novo, where he reigned without being troubled and maintained a flourishing trade in slaves. Sodji, who was ruling in Porto Novo in 1851, was disturbed by the aggression of the British, who about this time had established themselves at Lagos at the mouth of the Ougon after having driven the native king from that region. The British were now advancing with their vessel even upon Porto Novo and with a manufactured pretext bombarded the city. Hoping to play one European nation against the other, Sodji, not desiring to experience what the African king had at Lagos, signed with France a treaty of commerce and amity, February 23, 1863; and with the English as a scare ever hanging over the head of Sodji, the French induced him to transform this agreement later into a treaty to come under the "protection" of France, the second of the following April.

All was not finished for the French, however, for the successors of Sodji did not always respect their agreements. Meppon favored the English, who were still hoping to obtain that territory. Messy was followed by Bassy who was placed upon the throne with the support of Gle-Gle, the King of Dahomey, and the French merchants of Porto Novo, as Tofa II. He was a royal prince of Dahomey. He once put down a rising by calling the troops of Dahomey but attacked them in their retreat because of so-called misconduct. This alienated the Dahoman king. When the Dahoman king undertook to chastise Tofa for this and repeated insults the British under Admiral Brown appeared upon the scene to prevent the attack. Gle-Gle undertook several campaigns in which he failed, but he was successful in maintaining the frontiers of the kingdom. Yet this was done, his opponents report, not without much horrible massacre and imposing sacrifice of human beings, of which the French who had given him a modern education in the Lycee de Marseille expressed their horror.

The French, however, had the right to trade in the Dahoman country by virtue of a treaty of amity and commerce signed by Ghezo in 1851. Greater concessions were necessary from their point of view not only to force more out of the natives but to prevent the British from taking that country and Porto Novo in commercial rivalry. The trade rights and the possession of certain ports for traffic within the territory were always in jeopardy because of the construction placed at will upon treaties by the kings. Gle-Gle wrote the President of France protesting against their taking his country, and he offered Portugal the protection over it, which was refused.

In other words, the French had grown tired of the bilateral interpretation of their concession to trade and of the treaty of amity and commerce. Just as they had induced the kings elsewhere to sign agreements when in their ignorance of the European diplomacy they knew not what they were doing, so the French expected the Dahoman kings to comply. The Dahoman kings had no objection to the friendship and commercial intercourse with the French so long as that meant prosperity to their country and the getting rid of the British whose operations in the adjacent territory did not show that they would be desirable neighbors. When, however, the interpretation of the French claims meant interference with the Dahoman wars proclaimed to strengthen their hold on subject areas the Dahomans objected. For a generation the French had claimed to have a protectorate over Porto Novo, but the Dahomans pointed out that the kingdom had long been recognized as a vassalage of Dahomey.

To force another interpretation the king of Dahomey had to be brought to terms. The effort resorted to was the usual bribery with gifts and new professions of friendship. The Bayol mission sent to the capital in 1890 was thus charged to iron out the differences between the disputants. After undergoing difficulties in reaching the capital they were not able to accomplish anything satisfactory to the foreigners. Gle-Gle, the king at that time seventy-five years of age, was in such a state of health that he gave little encouragement to the leader of this mission. Behanzin, the son and heir to the throne, was not favorably impressed.

These rulers understood clearly what was desired, but they had no inclination to yield any more ground. They reiterated, however, that the French had long been friends of the Dahomans and had enjoyed profitable trade with them; and they could not now see the necessity of taking territory which long had been included in their domain or belonged to chiefs who were vassals of Dahomey. The Dahoman kings, too, in spite of knowing of the aggression of the French, the garrisoning of other forts, and the appearance of fresh troops which had penetrated the interior, cautioned peace, but with a firmness that, if their territory should be invaded, they would dispute every inch of the ground covered by an invading force. The Dahomans then had no recourse but to war. They could expect nothing from the British in Nigeria who seemed worse than the French.

The French, however, worked out a military campaign which would result in the dispossession of the Dahomans. Behanzin met their force first at Poguessa. The battle was costly to both sides. The French realized that it was not so easy as that of Sherman's march through Georgia, and the Dahomans realized the difficult task ahead to maintain their frontier. The defenders then fell back to Akpa, where they again gave battle. The French reinforced and with an army well organized under the mulatto General Dodds suffered losses again but compelled the defenders to fall back again to

BEHANZIN

Kotopa. Their lines were reorganized for another resistance at Djokoue, but here again under the fire of an
army trained in modern methods of warfare the native forces
were defeated.

The last obstruction to their access to the capital had
thereby been removed, but Behanzin, still with an invincible
spirit, took flight from the city with such supporters as he
could muster and sought a base of resistance elsewhere.
The French had the capital and soon the country, but the
ruler of the country whom they hoped to force to an abdica-
tion or vassalage was not at hand. Not wishing to lose all,
Behanzin sought from afar to treat for terms, but the French
believed that it was absolutely necessary to eliminate him
in some way. He was still the idol of the Dahomans and
their embodiment of authority. Without disposing of Behanzin they could never peacefully rule Dahomey. He finally
surrendered at Acachacpa.

What to do with Behanzin after he surrendered was a
problem. There was so much wavering about the matter that
when the conquerors began to move him from place to place
Behanzin thought that they intended to kill him. "If such
is your intention," implored the captive, "do not prolong the
agony, kill me at once." But it would never do thus to dis-
pose of a man who had been to his followers the symbol
of greatness. It was decided then to send him into exile
to Martinique with a few of his coterie known to be close
to him through his mature years. Upon urgent request the
French later permitted Behanzin to be transferred to Bilda
in Algeria in 1905. In 1906 his health became so poor
that he was permitted to move to the city of Algeria. The
change made little difference, however, for, humiliated and
broken-hearted, he died soon thereafter in that city on December 10, 1906.

Many persons came to do honor to this African prince
who surrendered only with his weapons in his hand. His
last request was that his ashes should repose on the native

soil of Dahomey, but for fear that the carrying out of such
an order at that time might rekindle flames which had hardly
been extinguished his wishes were not complied with until
1927, when the French thought it could be done without dis-
turbing the *Pax Gallica* in Africa. Thus passed into history
the king of a country not inferior in culture and achievement to many European and Asiatic countries in his day.
He was sacrificed and his country expropriated by French
imperialists who had no excuse but that they coveted it in
the carrying out of their designs.

In the European histories of Dahomey, with the exception
of a few like those of Le Herissé and Delafosse, is painted
a dark picture of the slave trade and the sacrifice of human
beings. In this they cannot be sincere, for the slave trade
in Dahomey received its main stimulus from the demand
in America which Europeans supplied by stirring up cruel
wars. Human sacrifice in Dahomey must be studied from
the point of the Dahomans themselves, from a study of their
whole culture. All kings of Dahomey did not carry this to
the extreme. Some refrained from it. The so-called human
sacrifice was mainly the execution of captives in war and
public criminals on festive occasion such as the death of a
ruler, a royal marriage or the coronation of a king. It
probably went beyond the cruelty of public hangings and
beheadings in America and Europe. But the so-called human sacrifice was no more justification for the French conquest of Dahomey than there would have been for Canada
to conquer the United States because of its lynchings. Here
newspapers carry the notice of these horrors beforehand and
encourage men, women and children to bring refreshments
to enjoy a scene as one does a picnic.

IN NIGERIA

Nigeria, the richest colony of England save probably India,
embraces several former African states and kingdoms along

the west coast and extending into the interior—Lagos on the coast, Yorubaland, Hausa, and Bornu, earlier mentioned in this work. The entire area now known as Nigeria embraces territory of 372,674 square miles, with a population of 20,-000,000 people, but this aggregation is a recent political organization since the conquest by the British. The states which existed in smaller form were taken over as separate units after more or less resistance to the British.[3]

The British in establishing trade connections along the west coast are said to have had their contact first with Benin in this area when in 1533 they made connections with the king of that country. Swedes were also early there at Cape Coast, and Danes built Christiansbourg near Accra as a port. Dutch, Portuguese, and French traders were in this area at the same time, trying to secure their share of this African trade started by Sir John Hawkins. Palm oil and slaves were the chief commodities. Native chiefs were encouraged to produce these—palm oil by natural methods and slaves by taking captives in war and driving them in coffles to the coast to be sold to European traders.

The Europeans of these years had little thought of the interior. Even after Mungo Park and the Lander Brothers explored the Niger about the end of the eighteenth century the interior was a deadly area for Europeans. Those who tried to live there died in large numbers. For centuries, then, the Europeans had only a few forts along the coast, and trading vessels, sent out by merchants to establish these centers, connected them with the outer world. Of the Royal Adventurers Trading into Africa and its more formidable successor, the Royal African Company, historians have taken note as the most advanced agents of the slave trade, espe-

[3] Some additional information and points of view may be found in the following: A. C. Burns' *History of Nigeria;* Brigadier Crozier, *Five Years Hard;* A. B. Ellis' *Yoruba Speaking Peoples of the Slave Coast;* Leo Frobenius' *The Voice of Africa;* Casely Hayford's *Gold Coast Native Institutions;* Mary Kingsley's *The Story of West Africa;* E. D. Morel's *Nigeria: Its Problems and Its People.*

cially after the concession to England in the Asiento in the
Peace of Utrecht in 1713.

Nearer to our day were other corporations of importance
even though after the abolition of the slave trade in 1807
the commerce with Africa had to be reorganized on a different basis. They had to connect with the interior and in
some way tap its resources. Mcgregor Laird, subsidized
by the British Government, interested in trading to Africa,
built the first iron ships to enter upon this trade and established the first British inland trading post on the Niger in
1857. Laird soon died in the effort, and his coworker, Dr.
Baikie, followed him likewise to the grave three years later in
1861. Great Britain did not push this enterprise as far
as it might have, had it not been for troublesome European
and colonial problems to which it had to give attention, and
the African economic imperial policy of the European nations had not at that time developed. It was not until 1879
that Goldie Taubman succeeded in amalgamating the trading
posts and individual traders interested in the Niger in order
to organize the United African Company. This enterprise
gave way to the National African Company, later designated
as the Royal Niger Company.

This corporation developed the trade in that area until
in 1898 it incurred the displeasure of the Fulani chiefs and
of the French, who were also expanding from the Senegal
toward the Niger. Only by rushing through an agreement
with the kings of Borgu and Nikki in 1894 had the British
the basis for a claim against the French with whom they
almost went to war on this account. For further security
of their claims the British had to work against even the
Germans. Although late in becoming a power in Africa the
Germans were making rapid strides as a colonizing power,
especially in the Cameroons which they hoped to expand into
this area. Sir Frederick Lugard was then ordered to take
over in the name of the British Empire the territory then
controlled by the Royal Niger Company. His forces de-

feated the Emir of Nube in 1898 and set up a capital at
Jebba. The Company withdrew its charter, and Lugard
was made High Commissioner for the Protectorate. Lugard
knew that his task had just begun, and he organized a new
force to conquer the adjacent territory.

The deed had already been done in Lagos in annexing
that country by armed force under the pretext of suppress-
ing the slave trade which the British themselves along with
other Europeans were carrying on with King Kosoko of
Lagos. A naval squadron ordered by Palmerston to drive
the king out, opened fire on the place December 25, 1851.
The British suffered severe losses but continued to drive
him from his throne. They set up their own puppet Akitoye
as king of Lagos, and in order to dispossess the natives altogether proposed to this marionette and to Dosumu, his son,
to sign a treaty ceding the territory to the British. Having
little self-respect, they at first refused, but had to yield.

Yoruba, then the hinterland of Lagos, fell an easy prey.
This country had reached a high level of culture as farmers
and artisans with such walled cities of large population as
Ibadan, Llorin, Abeokuta, Ogbomosho, Ede, Ogo, and Iwo.
They were united under a paramount chief or king ruling
over semi-feudal war lords at the head of smaller political
units. This area went also to the British. The deed was
done by chicanery. First the British sent to the king of the
Egbas at his capital, Abeokuta, a consul who would serve as
a spy. The king, knowing that such was the trap set, had
the courage to refuse to receive the consul. He remembered that the British worked their way into Lagos the same
way. The British then resorted to the usual policy of setting one native against the other by first proposing that the
Alafin bring their products through the province of the Ibadans without paying toll. Since this was refused Captain
Glover, of the Royal Navy, sent troops to take over the roads
of Abeokuta and incited the Ibadans to attack the Alafin.

The British could then intervene in 1895 in order to restore peace by taking the country. In 1897 the British boldly dethroned Overami, the king of Benin, and deported him. This gave them all of what is now Southern Nigeria. Hausa and Bornu, spoken of today as Northern Nigeria, next fell a prey to the British conquerors. The other European powers had declared in the Berlin Treaty of 1885 that they would raise no objections to the effort. France could at the same time advance north of Lake Chad and Germany could hold the Cameroons. The emirates of Sokoto, Kano, Katsena and Zaria, disunited, could offer no actual resistance and fell one by one under the fire of Lord Lugard, after Sokoto, the most important of them, had yielded in 1903. Property was destroyed, native girls were outraged and those shot down were looted for their jewelry Soldiers hacked the ornaments right and left from their arms and limbs for whatever gold they wore. This area with Lagos was organized in 1914 with Southern Nigeria as the Colony and Protectorate of Nigeria.

Chapter VI

IN STATES TO THE SOUTHWEST

Elsewhere the natives on or near the West Coast had not developed such political organizations as those which have already been noticed. Much has been circulated about the native Congo empire which the Portuguese finally christened as San Salvador under religious influence in the southwest, but even there trade and diplomacy under the pretext of modern enlightenment won the day for the imperialists. While there was imposed the yoke which the other natives wore it was carried out less hurriedly and more sympathetically than when the early European traders effected their occupation of the western littoral. Natives were made to believe that they were of the same human family as the Portuguese, selected youths were educated in Portugal under Christian influence, and a native prince thus prepared was elevated to the throne of San Salvador as a founder of a new dynasty which runs back with close connection and significant achievement in Christianization for about four centuries.[1]

In the carrying out of this early program, however, the Portuguese with all their profession of Christianity were considered by the Africans as enemies. The Portuguese encountered especially the opposition of the Ngola, from which comes the designation of that territory as Angola. A colony was established there in the name of the king who had no

---

[1] The rôle of the Portuguese in Africa is concisely given in the fourth chapter of the eighth volume of the *Cambridge History of the British Empire.* See also G. M. Theal's *Records of S. E. Africa;* his *The Portuguese in South Africa;* and H. H. Johnston, *A History of the Colonization of Africa by Alien Races.*

vassals since the chief had made grants only to the donatory. Troubles of administration arose out of trade in cattle, slaves and ivory. The Portuguese province of Benguela was set up especially for this traffic, and in order to extend the jurisdiction of it for the purpose of trade they encroached upon natives who protested. Luis Mendes de Vasconcellos, who became governor in 1616, undertook to dethrone the opposing Ngola chief and set on his throne another who would rule in the name of "Christianity" and for the extension of the slave trade. Although the chief's kraal was destroyed, his subchiefs forced into submission, and a tribute imposed upon them, the Portuguese governor was so hard pressed that he found it necessary to make peace with the chief and his fearless sister, Ginga.

Ginga came as the ambassadress to treat with the Portuguese, and as a stroke of diplomacy accepted Christian baptism. Dissatisfied with the way things had been going under her brother, she had him dethroned in the midst of a rising in which he lost his life in 1623. She next began to stir up against the Portuguese the chiefs who had submitted to the foreigners. A force sent against her seized her camp on Ndangi Island, in the Cuanza, but she escaped to continue as a thorn in the side of the invaders. The Portuguese with alacrity pursued her as far as Quissima, where they captured her two sisters, but Ginga escaped from them again, taking refuge far away in Congo, from which she continued to harass the conquerors. While others yielded this brave woman chose exile and hardships rather than abandon her rightful claims.

Portugal obtained in somewhat more imperialistic fashion a few other possessions, the most important of which is Portuguese East Africa. The policy in dealing there with the natives had been more direct and despotic, but Portugal had to go more slowly probably than it would have gone had it not faced the land-grabbing British and Boers, ever anxious to take advantage of their Latin neighbor on that

GINGA MEETS THE ENEMY

distant shore. The once extensive Portuguese African empire was lost mainly to the Dutch and British. Natives organized at various times to oppose measures for more thorough subordination and exploitation, but they could wage no formidable wars of which the natives in other parts showed themselves capable. That there was less manifestation of hostility was due to the more human attitude of the Latin imperialists than that of those of Teutonic origin.

The penetration of the interior on any great scale, however, did not follow for centuries after the early effort made by the Portuguese when European aggression became systematized by international agreement. Great Britain, like most of the European powers, had early established trading posts along the African coast; but, torn between the "Little Englanders," led by Gladstone against expensive colonization, and that faction led by Lord Salisbury in favor of a world empire, Britannia had not penetrated the interior, except when compelled by some great emergency so to act in its own honor as in taking over Egypt and annexing the Transvaal in South Africa. The early explorations in Africa of Mungo Park, Dorchard, Meslay, Molien, Clapperton, Denham, Lander, Laing, Duranton, Caillé, Rafanel, Planet, and Barth, stirred other countries more than they did England. Even Livingstone's explorations, followed by those of Stanley, moved Belgium toward taking over the Congo country, while Great Britain and other powers remained in doubt as to the wisdom of penetrating the African hinterland. Portugal had long been in possession of extensive territory stretching from various points on the coast into the interior, but had not been able to build on the dark continent an empire to disturb the calm of Europe. Portugal, internally weakened by political strife, by economic reverses, and by the loss of Brazil, had declined. Spain, with merely a strip on the Moroccan coast, the Canaries and scattering islands, was not much more striking in the field of economic imperialism.

Exciting action developed in France after 1870, however, when that country had been defeated by Germany and saddled with heavy taxation to pay the war indemnity of five billion francs exacted by the conquerors. The dark prospect for the French capitalists compelled them to look to distant quarters for an outlet. The French saw in African expansion the opportunity to acquire territory which might compensate in part for the loss of Alsace-Lorraine and extend the trade of an economically depressed victim of the sword of the Teuton. The desire for colonial expansion had been manifested by Wilhelm II, the new German Emperor, but Bismarck, the iron Chancellor, did not see the wisdom of it at that time. The permanent control of Alsace-Lorraine was considered by him sufficient to keep safe from European interference. The French upon the basis of explorations by De Brazza, who outwitted Stanley, took over and organized the French Congo, the beginning of what is now French Equatorial Africa. At the expense of the Belgian Congo, France expanded her claims in West Africa, and strengthened her hold on North Africa.[2]

If Africa was to be taken over without regard to the rights of the natives, however, some sanction had to be sought from without. The necessity for such understanding resulted from various causes. About 1882 the British imperialists desired to intervene to save the investments of their countrymen in Egypt, and they wanted to do it without the proposed joint intervention with the French. Leopold of Belgium, seeking to have sanctioned his rape of the Congo which the United States by recognition elevated to the dignity of international law through its minister to that country, H. S. Sanford,

---

[2] The partition of Africa is discussed in numerous works. Both entertaining and informing, however, are the following: Lamar Middleton, *The Rape of Africa;* J. E. S. Green, *Rhodes Goes North;* Sir Charles Lucas, *The Partition of Africa;* Jean Darcy, *Cent Années de Rivalté Coloniale;* J. S. Keltie, *The Partition of Africa;* E. L. Guernier, *L'Afrique Champ d'Expansion de l'Europe;* J. J. A. Pellenc, *Les Italiens en Afrique;* E. Bassi, *La Zona d'Influenza;* C. G. Woodson, *African Background Outlined,* pages 137 to 148.

thought likewise, with respect to the looted territory. Later
the people of the United States became terribly excited over
the atrocities in the Belgian Congo and loudly denounced the
exploiters as brutes; but few of the Americans of that time
knew of or referred to the fact that it was the recognition of
the Belgians' rights in the Congo by the United States Government which first gave their position in that area international
standing. In America where the undeveloped domain attracted most of its capital not much of our wealth could be
devoted to the exploitation of Africa, but there were always
those Americans who had dreams of making millions on the
"Dark Continent," and certain members of our diplomatic
corps sanctioned these deals in the hope that they would thereby profit personally.

In view of the complications resulting from claims and
counter claims and the desire of the non-colonizing powers
to take a part in the enterprise it was deemed necessary to
hold an international Congress to draw up rules for the
partition of Africa. This finally resulted in the Berlin Congress, which met in 1884, and continued into 1885. This
Congress, however, in keeping with the usual sham and hypocrisy of the time was not nominally called for political purposes but to civilize the Africans and suppress the slave
trade, as set forth in a preceding Congress of these powers
in Brussels in 1876.

In the Congress in Berlin in 1885 Bismarck followed the
policy of playing the small powers like Portugal against the
large powers like Great Britain. The members had the
vision, however, to see the necessity for considering freedom
of trade in the Congo, the application thereto of the principles adopted at Vienna in 1814, and the formalities to be
observed in occupying African territory. With the smaller
nations losing to the larger, however, the Congress provided
for the freedom of trade in the Congo and the Niger regions,
for some territorial revisions, and above all for the important
principle that to be effective the European claim of terri-

tory must be followed by actual occupation. In other words, a mere treaty secured from a native by a drink of gin and the mark on the dotted line was no longer sufficient. Money and rifles had to follow rum.

The scramble for Africa then began in earnest. The European had occupied only ten per cent of the African area by 1876, and by 1885, the date of the Berlin Congress, only twenty-five per cent of this area had been claimed. During the next five years, the British, although expelled from the Sudan, annexed Bechuanaland and north Somaliland; the Italians invaded and set up a protectorate over east Somaliland and pretended to have a zone of influence in Ethiopia; Germany established a claim in East Central Africa; France expanded her conquests in the Upper Niger; Belgium effectively occupied the Upper Congo; Portugal undertook an expansion into East Central Africa; and Spain made good her claim to Rio de Oro. In five years, between 1886 and 1891, most of the continent had been taken. The very fever of expansion of the British is explained by the cost which they paid in the annihilation of Hicks Pasha's force by those of the Mahdi who later destroyed also a more formidable force stationed in the Sudan under Gordon, and killed Gordon himself.

Italy and Germany, as it has been seen, came into the colonizing sphere rather late, and the former was permitted to acquire territory of doubtful value—mainly a desert region in North and East Africa. Italy obtained Lybia as a result of a war with Turkey in 1912, but it took her many long years to pacify it. Italy acquired parts of Somaliland and Eritrea, and was secretly promised by the French and English in the Treaty of 1916 a share in any possible partition of Ethiopia. Disappointed in this at the close of the First World War, as mentioned elsewhere, Italy finally conquered Abyssinia, which she was unable to pacify, so great was the resistance organized there before the forced departure of Hailie Selassie.

Germany obtained its own colonial charter in the Treaty of Berlin in 1885. By shrewd diplomacy Bismarck brought other European nations to consent to its participation in the partition of the continent on principles to which they agreed. The African chiefs were to be forced to sign on the dotted line an agreement to come under the protection of some imperialistic nation and thereby give that nation the right to declare to the world that this particular part of African soil was expropriated and other nations must not interfere. Thus agreed the partitioning of the remaining part of the continent was merely a matter of so much shot and shell.

The first objective of Germany was Angra Pequena in Southwest Africa, in order to protect the trade rights of its citizens who, under Luderitz, a merchant, in 1882 had established there a settlement for trading. Merchants of Hamburg and Bremen had induced Bismarck to support their expansion of trade into Africa. The German Government after outwitting the British imperialists by diplomacy declared the territory a protectorate in 1884. The rest of the program was simple; the natives were told to give the country to the Germans. This, of course, they refused to do. Rather than thus yield they said that they would die for their native soil. The roads to the interior did not permit easy access, and in their way of fighting the natives in the beginning inflicted heavy losses during the four years of conflict known as the Herero War.

Following the gaining of a foothold by Luderitz for commercial purposes, the Germans established there their first government under Theodor Leutwein, who served for eleven years. He was mainly the commander maintaining order at military posts supplied with mobile troops. Before this occupation could advance very far, however, the natives rebelled against the intruders. At first the tribes were temporarily overcome by playing the one against the other and by shooting down those chiefs who would not yield after apparent defeat. Both the Hereros and Namaquas found themselves cramped by being deprived of their lands which they felt that no chief had the right to alienate since land, as they understood it, belonged to the collectivity; and in face of the Germans as a common enemy the Namaquas and the Hereros tended temporarily to forget the old feud which had long caused many wars between them.

Trouble was ahead. Near the end of 1900 a quarrel between the Namaquas and a German official ended in the death of the German and a Namaqua captain. The Namaquas therefore concentrated their forces at Zandfontein on the Orange River, where they were reenforced by others from the Karas Mountains. It required all the German forces in South Africa to quell the disturbance and disperse the natives. Several engagements in which victory shifted from one side to the other brought the Germans to the point of concluding peace on as favorable terms as possible.

The rising of the Namaquas, however, gave the Hereros an opportunity to avenge themselves, and get back their lands as they thought. Their leader, Samuel Maherero, ordered the attack, giving instruction that only the Dutch and English missionaries should be spared. In the first attack, however, while the natives killed 123 German males, they spared their wives and children. The rebellion spread among other chiefs. Frontier forts of the Germans had to be abandoned and men, women and children rushed to the more densely populated coastal settlements for protection. The Germans received some encouragement from the Berg and Demararas whom they had once befriended in their struggles against the encroachments of the Hereros and the Namaquas; but reenforcements were long reaching them, and their situation became critical under the attacks of these fearless Hereros and Namaquas until 1904.

Reenforcements finally came from Germany, and the conquerors took the offensive. Numerous attacks followed, and heavy losses were sustained on both sides. The natives assembled at Great and Small Waterberg, where they seemed so formidable that at the command of the Kaiser operations were suspended until additional troops could be obtained from Germany. General Von Trotha was sent to assume the command. The new commander attacked the Hereros at Hamakari. The natives fought bravely and brought many of the invaders to the dust but deemed it advisable to abandon that hotly contested field. Samuel Maharero withdrew with some of his troops into British territory. His people followed in the easterly direction into the desert. The Germans could not overtake them, but the desert did the rest in working out their extermination. Natives died of thirst and their cattle perished. Only a few reached the British in Bechuanaland.

Raiding bands in guerrilla fashion, however, remained to torment the Germans. General von Trotha then entered upon the destruction of all tribes. His successor, Herr von Lindequist, modified this to the extent of sparing their lives that they might be apportioned as serfs among the farmers settling on the lands recently occupied by the conquerors. By 1907 the Herero resistance had been broken. At first they were not permitted to own cattle because this would require grazing lands, and they were to have no lands. This, however, was later slightly modified.

While the Hereros were being crushed and exterminated the Namaquas also took the warpath, although because of the pretended friendship of the Germans they had not been active during the attack on the Hereros, and had actually aided the enemy at Waterberg. Under one of the native leaders, Morenga, a German band had been routed at Dawignab, and Wasserfall had fallen. Von Burgsdorff, approaching Hendrik Witbooi, the Namaqua leader, to treat for peace, was killed. Under the inspiration of Stuurman, a prophet from Cape Colony, Hendrik Witbooi declared war on the Germans on October 4, 1904. The Germans were unable to cope with the situation, and were afraid to take the offensive. For two months the Germans had to con-

tent themselves with defending their own well occupied
ground. At the end of that period the Germans went forward to battle; but the Namaquas, wiser in their generation
than the Hereros, did not concentrate at one point where
they might be defeated and captured. The Namaquas resorted to guerrilla warfare. This strategical method proved
to be decidedly exhausting to the German forces, but they
derived a little consolation from the fact that they won
partial victories at Naris and at Gochas.

The turning point came in 1905 when General von Trotha
had finished his extermination of the Hereros in the north
and could march toward the Namaquas. Hendrik Witbooi,
however, had retired to the Kalahari Desert, into which the
Germans could not easily follow him. He returned, however,
to Vaalgras to give battle and was defeated and mortally
wounded. His son Isaac was inclined to make peace, but
Simon Koper, leading other warriors, continued the struggle
from his base in the desert. Morenga, the leader who had
carried by storm Dawignab and Wasserfall, was finally defeated and imprisoned at Prieska. He contrived to escape
again and make war on the German strongholds. Finally he
was disposed of when he fell mortally wounded on September 20, 1906, in battle with British troops. The last of these
warring tribes yielded in December of that year. Simon
Koper was pursued into the desert by forces under Frederick
von Erckert, who surrounded the native leader at Seatsub.
The native forces were practically annihilated, but the victorious forces left their German leader slain on that battlefield.

Thus ended the Germans' 88 engagements against the
Hereros and 295 against the Namaquas. In these battles the
invaders had lost 179 officers and 2,169 soldiers. The number
of natives killed by the aggressors has been estimated con-
servatively at 120,000, but there are investigators who have
insisted that this number reached at least 200,000. While
this is a terrible indictment of the inhumanity of man to

man it is at the same time an evidence of the bravery of the
Basters, Orambo, and the Hereros that so many of them chose
to die rather than to yield.[3]

And well might they take this position, for when the country was occupied by the invaders those natives who had not
been exterminated were rounded up without any thought as
to their tribal and social order and let out in lots as serfs
and slaves to toil on plantations opened on the lands par-
celled out to the German colonists. This territory was conquered by the British during the World War and afterwards
reorganized as a British Mandate. The masters remained
practically the same, and there is a strong agitation to turn
this territory over to the Boer element in South Africa, who
are the bane of the natives.

In 1884 the Germans further advanced their imperialistic
program by coming into possession of the Camerouns. Their
claim was based upon the exploration and treaties made with
the natives by Gustav Nachtigal and the need for extending
protection to trading posts established there by Woermann.
The Germans merely sent their warships into the port of
Duala and declared the interior to which this port was an
outlet a protectorate of Germany. The French, who had
especially disputed this claim by virtue of Pierre de Brazza's
explorations, had to agree thereto to secure German sanction
of their hold in North Africa. The British had sent their
ships on the same mission, but they reached the point too
late. The Germans forced an entrance into that territory
after promising the natives that they would be protected in
their right to the land. The natives here also resisted as they
had elsewhere. The Germans, however, were equal to their
task. They hanged the chief of Duala and Rudolph Bell
and all other opponents on the ground that they favored the

---

[3] The history of German colonization in Africa is summarized in the
eighth volume of *History of the British Empire*, on pages 694 to 709,
from the British point of view. The German point of view is given in
Sander's *Geschichte der Deutschen Kolonialgesellschaft für Sudwest-
afrika.*

cause of the British. The natives fought like men who had
some presentiments of what awaited them, but the resistance
could not withstand the attack of a modern military force
and had to yield except so far as a guerilla warfare could
fan the flames of the failing spirits of a dispossessed people.

True to their policy, the Germans ruthlessly killed and
cornered the natives and destroyed their property until subordination to the conquerors was assured. German settlers
rushed in, took the lands, forced the women into concubinage,
and compelled the men to supply the demand for labor on
land which they had always regarded as theirs by divine
right. The native had no redress. The only way to communicate with the home government was through their oppressors, and this was closed. Raw materials went to Germany
from this and other areas, and goods manufactured therefrom brought the desired profit. Humanitarian questions
had no place in the movement. German economic imperialism
was considered a success.

Togoland passed into the possession of Germany about
the same time. The Germans appeared upon the scene in
1884 and forced an entrance at Lome, the port of that country. Nor could any other European nation object, for
they were doing the same thing in probably a little more
humane fashion. France had thus taken Dahomey to the
East of Togoland and the British the Gold Coast on the west.
Climate in Togoland, however, helped the natives a little. It
proved so disastrous to the Germans trying to settle there
that they decided, as far as was necessary, to leave the natives
in charge of the plantations and exploit them indirectly.
Then followed the whipping of men, the outraging of the
women and forced labor.

In a more diplomatic fashion the Germans had to work
their way into East Africa. The British were not anxious to
have competitors in that quarter. In the development of
their economic imperialism requiring according to Rhodes'

dream the connection of Cairo with the Cape the Germans might be in the way. They might want to connect their possessions in the east with those in the west and thus conflict with the British scheme. According to the rules laid down for thus establishing trading posts, the Germans succeeded in bringing the English to agree to their claims in that area by virtue of treaties made by Karl Peters and his two disguised companions on a "scientific mission" in that quarter. Some of the claims, however, had to be abandoned.

From the time of their annexation in 1889 the natives boldly resisted. Risings multiplied through Tanganyika, especially against the hut tax, and stimulated an actual war known as the Maji-Maji Rebellion in 1905. The natives killed many of the invaders, but German superior forces turned the tide and finally shot down 120,000. Once on safe ground, the Germans expropriated the lands and reduced natives to serfdom. That the natives fought bravely, however, is evidenced by the fact that the Germans had to exterminate so many of them before they would yield. These excessively cruel methods served as one of the main excuses for depriving Germany altogether of her African colonies which were reorganized as mandated territory at the close of the First World War.

CHAPTER VII

THE CONFLICT IN SOUTH AFRICA

The most heroic stand of the natives was probably in South Africa. The Dutch under Jan van Riebeck undertook permanent settlement there with pioneers landed at the Cape in 1652. Hoping not to have to penetrate the interior where hostile Hottentots disputed their way, the Dutch established merely a trading post, and for what labor they needed they imported Malay convicts from their possessions in the East Indies; in 1654 the Dutch brought Negro slaves from the Guinea coast. To keep the peace the invaders had been forbidden by Holland to enslave the Hottentots, but when the Dutch tried to take everything for themselves and give nothing in return a feeling of hostility soon developed into a struggle in 1659 known as the first Hottentot War. The Hottentots raided the settlement, killed the herdsmen, carried off the cattle and reduced the outpost all but to starvation.[1]

Relief to the Europeans finally came, but not a permanent one. When the Hottentots saw the more formidable Company's soldiers stationed at the Cape and realized that it meant the expropriation of their lands they attacked again with such great bravery that they took away practically all the oxen of the colony and temporarily broke up agriculture which the Company had always urged upon the colonists. The idea of the Hottentots in taking away cattle was to obviate the necessity for the Europeans to occupy more land.

---

[1] For the European point of view with respect to South Africa read the eighth volume of *The History of the British Empire*. Useful also are two other recent works, J. E. S. Green's *Rhodes Goes North* and A. C. Raphael's *The Cape to Cairo Dream*. For the natives' point of view see S. M. Molema's *The Bantu*, and George Padmore's *How Britain Rules Africa*.

The more cattle the settlers had the more land they wanted and the more they crowded the natives.

The Dutch by the middle of the seventeenth century, however, had become a world power and could deal more successfully with the Hottentots. Although the French flag was raised temporarily in 1670, the Company was strengthened and a port was built in 1685. Peace was made with the tribes for a stipulated amount of goods which the Dutch never delivered; and the black captain, Gonnemma, contending that he, the real ruler, had been left out of the deal, went to war in 1672. He kept the Dutch and their native allies alarmed until 1679, when he finally agreed to make peace. So bravely had the Hottentots defended their soil, however, that the Dutch deemed it advisable not to penetrate the in-terior, and there was only one diversion from this rule from that time until 1795, when the Cape was temporarily taken over by the British. This exception was a visit of one of the Dutch governors to Namaqualand in 1685 when copper was discovered there.

When the French flag was hoisted at the Cape temporarily in 1670 the defense against the natives was accordingly weakened by the transition. The Hottentots, however, were losing ground. With bullets, brandy, and smallpox the Dutch gradually exterminated the Hottentots. In similar fashion the Dutch disposed later of annoying Bushmen. They raided the Dutch settlement persistently, killing both the colonists and their cattle; but the Bushmen, being incapable of organized resistance, could not succeed. Adrian Van Jaarsveld carried out the order to run them down and shoot them by the hundreds.

The European population at the Cape did not rapidly expand to open up the interior, for in 1680 the colony had only 600 inhabitants. While Africa farther north had become somewhat known as a result of the exploration of the Blue Nile and Abyssinia by James Bruce in 1768-1771 and of West Africa and the Niger by Mungo Park in 1796-1805, the South

African back country was still a mystery. A new factor to stimulate the penetration of the interior came with the religious impulse brought by certain Huguenots in quest of asylum from European persecution. These pilgrims as a result of the Revocation of the Edict of Nantes came to the Cape in 1688. Their work had little to do with the evangelization of the natives, for the Dutch did not look favorably upon such a mission and dissuaded Moravian missionaries therefrom as late as 1732 and deported the leader George Schmidt to Java.

Troubles within and without were facing the Europeans on the coast. In 1690 the Portuguese abandoned Delagoa Bay. In 1698 the Arabs repulsed the Portuguese north of the Mozambique. The Ama-Xosa complicated matters by threatening the Europeans from the rear when they crossed the Kei River. Weakened by disputes among themselves, the Dutch prohibited the use of the French language at the Cape. To add to these troubles came smallpox in 1713 and a cattle plague in 1714.

The Dutch, however, were not yet down. They succeeded in taking over much which declining Portugal had to abandon in South Africa. The Dutch settled Delagoa Bay in 1720. Some of their number dared to enter Pondoland in 1736 and were killed by the natives. Yet the Dutch had sufficiently expanded to make the Gamtoos River the eastern boundary of the Cape in 1745, and with 5,510 Europeans and 6,729 slaves in 1752 celebrated the one hundredth anniversary of the settlement at the Cape. The rage of smallpox in 1755 and 1767 did not destroy the colony or weaken it too much to make headway in the development of the Cape. In 1778 Governor Van Plettenburg met certain Xosa rulers and secured their agreement to the Fish River as the boundary of the expanding colony. This, however, was only clearing of the stage for a number of conflicts between the Europeans and the natives known as the Xosa Wars. The cause was the usual one between the conqueror and the conquered—

duplicity, treachery, forced signature of treaties by irresponsible persons and a unilateral interpretation of such agreements.

The tribes made conspicuous by these wars were called the Ama-Xosa or Xosas. The tribe was founded by Zwide, whose brilliant achievements were eclipsed by his illustrious son Xosa after whom the people called themselves. Zwide, however, had three sons, namely Mtembu, Xosa, Mpondo. These divided their father's kingdom and called their people respectively Ama-Tembu, Ama-Xosa, and Ama-Mpondo; a branch from this tribe became independent and took the name Ama-Pondomisi. The Xosas probably originated around the Great Lakes in the fourteenth century, but from the founder down to the ruler known as Togu there is a silence in their traditions covering a period of about one or two hundred years.

During the childhood of one of these intervening rulers, Tshawe, his provident mother, we are told, saved the throne to this house by escaping with the son from the clutches of those conspiring to murder him. When he had reached his majority he returned with power to dispossess his brothers who had usurped the throne. Under this King Togu the Xosas probably advanced from their position around the Great Lakes as far south as the Kei River by about 1687. Gconde, who succeeded Togu, his father; expanded the frontier to Umtata and made an alliance with the Hottentots by taking one of their women as his wife. This alliance with the Hottentots strengthened greatly the Xosas. The next ruler was Tshiwo, the son of Gconde. During this reign another tribe, the Amangqunukwebe, was founded by those escaping from a death sentence for witchcraft and taking refuge among friendly Hottentots.

Then came Tshiwo's son, Palo, a minor, all but dispossessed by his unscrupulous half-brother, Gwali, who, as regent, attempted to assassinate the boy king. Upon being detected he escaped from the country with a following and joined another tribe among the Hottentots called the Amatinde. Palo grew to manhood, ascended the throne, ruled successfully and left three sons, Gcalaka, Rarabe, and Langa, from whom came tribal division of the people known as the Ama-Gcalaka, Ama-Rarabe. Tiso, the brother of Palo, was already ruling a section of the father's tribe known as Amambula. In close connection with these were the Ama-Fengu, or Fingoes (meaning wanderers), who escaped from the horrors of tribal wars and were united by the common lot of seeking refuge which they found in the high mountain ranges.

This in brief gives an account of the people together with the Zulus mentioned elsewhere, who, after the extermination of the Hottentots and the Bushmen by the Dutch in their area, next disputed the authority of the Europeans in South Africa. While there was not a general policy of expansion of the Dutch into the interior there was a natural extension of their coastal settlement toward the Xosas who were coming in a southwesterly direction from the home of their origin. Certain of the Xosas at the same time began to cross the Fish River in 1778. That stream had been declared the eastern Dutch boundary in 1775 by a decree extending the European claims beyond the Gamtoos, which, until 1770, had been the Dutch frontier.

In this confusion and conflict of claims the Dutch Governor Van Plettenberg visited certain petty chiefs of clans and induced them to recognize the Fish River as the boundary line; but these subchiefs had no authority to make such a treaty, and the Xosa continued to cross the stream into the Zuurveld claimed by the Dutch. The Xosas attacked Hottentots there subject to the rule of the Dutch, ravaged farms and took away cattle, thus forcing the isolated Dutch pioneers in the Zuurveld to leave for safer posts. The Xosas, insisting that the land was theirs, refused to move, and the Dutch under Adrian Van Jaarsveld, the exterminator of Hottentots and Bushmen, employed force. In the engagements which followed between 1779 and 1782 the Xosas proved to the

Dutch that they were facing more formidable opponents than the "primitives" first encountered in South Africa. Victory shifted from one side to the other. With better military equipment, however, the Dutch defeated the Xosa in one bloody battle and forced them to retrace their steps across the Fish River.

The Xosas considered this advantage of the Dutch as only temporary. After recuperating, so to speak, the Xosas crossed the Fish River again in 1789 and roamed over that area as before. The Dutch forces sent against them in the Second Xosa War were completely disillusioned as to the Xosas' prowess in arms. The Dutch made practically no headway in trying to dislodge these defenders of their native soil. The Dutch raided the cattle of the Xosas and the Xosa returned the compliment, each one hoping to weaken the other by depriving the opponent of supplies, but the campaign ended with victory for the Xosas. The natives continued their course free and undisturbed on both sides of the Fish River.

At this juncture, however, the Xosa made a mistake in underestimating the resources of their enemies. Instead of remaining content with what they had won, they decided to penetrate further the Dutch colony and crossed the Gamtoos. Fortunately for the Xosas, however, the Dutch at this time had to deal with a revolt of some of their officials against the British who had taken the colony in 1795, though not permanently. Believing that the Xosas were supreme in the situation, many Hottentot servants of the Dutch and others of the Hottentot Cape Corps under the leadership of disaffected leaders like Klaas Stuurman deserted with arms and munitions of war to the ranks of the natives. Thus strengthened and equipped, the Xosa invaded Cape Colony in 1799 and struck terror to the heart of the European population. The Xosas and Hottentot forces pillaged farms, burned houses, carried off cattle, crushed opposing forces, and laid waste the country for many square miles. Unable to cope with the situation, General Dundaas made peace as early as possible with the Xosa and Hottentot invaders. This ended the Xosas wars with the Dutch government in charge, for the colony was finally taken over by the British in 1806. A new European nation had to deal with the Xosa people.

The British inherited the troubles of the Dutch, and a new conflict, the fifth Euro-Xosa War, broke out in 1811. The cause was the old question as to whether the interlopers or the natives should occupy the Zuurveld. The British commander sought to negotiate for an amicable agreement, but one of the Xosa chiefs, voicing without doubt the sentiment of all his coleaders, replied to such inquiries, "The country is mine; I won it in war, and mean to retain it."

By exterminating Stockenstrom and his thirteen companions, sent on a peaceful mission, after they had held a conference and exchanged tobacco in trying to work out amicably a solution of the differences, the Xosa precipitated hostilities. In retaliation the Cape military forces entered upon a vigorous campaign and punished the Xosa by driving them beyond the Fish River. The British then built military posts along this boundary to prevent further invasion by the natives.

In the midst of this defeat the misfortune of division in the ranks now overtook the Xosa just as it had formerly in the case of the Dutch. The Ama-Rarabe section of the Xosas had divided in 1796 into two branches—those following Chief Ngqika, or Gaika, and those following Ndlambe. A complication ensued when the British, represented by Lord Somerset, undertaking to decide between these tribal chiefs the matter of chieftainship, recognized Ngqika and formed an alliance with him, much to the consternation and disappointment of the Xosas. This was following the well established rule of the imperialists—to aid the weaker in the contest to defeat the stronger and then destroy the weaker. War followed between these tribes, and in 1817 the British came to the assistance of their ally Ngqika when defeated by the

followers of Ndlambe. The combined forces of the natives as
allies of the British defeated Ndlambe and reinstated Ngqika
as chief of the Xosas.

Makana, or Makhanda, the Great Prophet, then appeared
upon the scene, collected the scattered fragments of Ndlambe's army and preached a new crusade against the British,
with the destruction of Grahamstown, the British military
headquarters of the east province, as the chief purpose of
the rising. Makana, uniting religion with magic, attained
ascendancy among the Xosa. Practically all the Xosas except
the followers of Ngqika cooperated, and an army of about
10,000 assembled on the hills overlooking Grahamstown from
which Makana sent the British office an ultimatum saying,
"We shall breakfast with you tomorrow morning."

Makana, before leading the attack, thanked his men for
their loyalty and addressed them eloquently on their invul-
nerability from British bullets, the immortality of the soul,
and the resurrection of their dead chiefs. He then launched
the attack with undaunted bravery, but the British met it
with a destructive fire which left 1,500 Xosas dead or
wounded on the spot while the others withdrew in confusion.
Having failed, Makana gave himself up the following day as
he had declared that he would, if defeated. He was taken
prisoner; but he and his fellows overawed the prison guards
and escaped in a boat only to drown. In 1819 peace was
made between the warring tribes and between the British
and the Xosas.

By this agreement the country between Fish River and the
Keiskama was declared neutral ground. This meant trouble,
for the Xosa occupied it on one side and the European colonists on the other. Parts of the area were annexed to the
Cape by fiat in 1825 and 1831. The Europeans were
gradually pushing the Xosa back, and they resented the outcome. The old troubles on both sides recurred, and war
broke out in 1834. This was the Sixth Xosa War. Gaika, the
chief of the Xosas, had settled in this neutral area. He died,

and his son had been declared his successor. The new chief and his people were expelled from this neutral territory by the Europeans on the march to conquer all the territory, and his land in the Tyumie Valley was annexed to the Cape. In supporting him against his former rival the British had merely used him as the means to an end.

In retaliation for thus illegally annexing neutral territory the Xosas devastated the lands and, reenforced by the Hottentots, attacked the European aggressors, destroying much life and property. The Fingoes, other Africans repeating the history of Negroes in dealing with Caucasians, espoused the cause of the European intruders in assisting them to drive the Xosas beyond the limits of the neutral territory. Hintsa, the chief of the Gcaleka Xosas, was defeated and had to ask for peace. Instead of being treated as an enemy in war, however, he was taken as hostage. In trying to escape, he was pursued and shot down by one Southey. Peace, so-called peace, was then made with Hintsa's son, Sarili, or Kreli, his successor. All the territory between the Fish River and Kei River was then proclaimed a British sovereignty by Sir Benjamin Durban. The European pioneers lauded him for having made a master stroke in colonial expansion while the Xosas dubbed his action a downright robbery.

And it was so evident to the home office that an act of injustice had been inflicted upon innocent and unoffending people that in a dispatch of December 26, 1835, Lord Glenelg, the Secretary of State, ordered that these lands be returned to the Xosas. In this decision Lord Glenelg was influenced by Dr. John Philip, a Scotchman, who in 1819 had been sent by the London Missionary Society to work among the Bantu. He insisted that the natives had been barbarously treated and were justified in taking up arms to hold their lands. He said that they had been "urged to revenge and desperation by the systematic injustice of which they had been victims."

The European settlers in their turn branded this a grave error and said that it destroyed all hope of the enforcement of order, and placed life and whatever property was left in the eastern district at the mercy of the Kaffirs. Dr. Philip, therefore, was coolly received by the large circle in Cape Town. So incensed were some of the Boers by this affair that they joined the Great Trek. The abolition of slavery in the British Empire in 1833 had already upset the Boers. The British, moreover, had further frightened the Boers by adding to the concession of land rights the right of natives to live·among Europeans as equals. Rather than tolerate Negroes clamoring for social equality the Boers trekked toward the frontier and finally across the Vaal.

Further disturbance was noted in 1840, but the Governor, Sir George Napier, settled the matter peaceably at a conference with the Xosa chiefs before it became serious. In 1846, however, actual war broke out because of the arrest of a Xosa for stealing an axe. This Seventh Xosa War, then, is known sometimes as the Axe War.

The incident makes an interesting story. The Xosa who had been arrested for taking the axe was being taken to the nearest magistracy, at Grahamstown, manacled to a Hottentot culprit, both in custody of Hottentot constables. Overtaken by a detachment of Xosas, these officers were ordered to release their fellow-countryman. This request being refused, the Xosas proceeded to use force; and in the fracas the prisoner was released but not without killing one Hottentot and one Xosa. The Government demanded the release of the prisoner and the punishment of those who had taken him from the custody of the constables. The chief, expressing the opinion that the matter had had a just natural settlement in that one man was killed on each side, refused to comply with this order. Two years of warfare, therefore, followed.

During the first half of the struggle the Xosas held their ground and withstood the onslaughts of the aggressors. In the second year of the war, however, history again repeated itself in the Caucasians' success in dividing the unorganized

natives themselves. The Fingoes had again come to the rescue
of the Europeans and fought the Xosas more bitterly than
the colonists themselves. The Xosas lost in all the engagements on the Keiskama and the Kei. In the final blow Sir
Harry Smith, of Indian fame, routed the Xosa from the
neutral territory and proclaimed the land between the Kei
and the Keiskama a British Crown Colony under the designation of Kaffraria. He made a treaty of peace on these
terms with Sandili, chief of the Ama-Rarabe Xosas.

This was a complete reversal of the Government's policy
of non-interference with the affairs of the Bantu as shown
in Lord Glenelg's reversal of the annexation of this territory
by Sir Benjamin Durban. No longer the chiefs were to do
to suit themselves and conduct their affairs as they pleased so
long as they did not invade the colony. The administration
was to be headed by a Briton, and the Bantu must thereafter
recognize British suzerainty. This was the beginning of a
new day in British expansion in Africa, a token of a new
economic imperialism.

In 1850 followed the Eighth Xosa War, but the natives'
day was almost done in spite of heroic fighting in one of the
most serious conflicts on the African continent. Disquiet
had continued to reign on the new border; and, joined by
Hottentots, the Xosa attacked the military posts and captured
one of them. Next the Xosa invaded the large districts
known as Somerset, Albany, and Alexandria and assumed
fortified positions in the Amatola Mountains. From these
positions they descended from time to time to devastate the
European settlements. The Fingoes, however, true to their
tradition, were again allied with the British, who ultimately
defeated Sarili (Kreli), the chief of the Gcaleka Xosas, and
took one thousand head of his cattle. This advantage the
British retained in spite of losing the *Birkenhead*, which with
400 soldiers and munitions of war foundered at Danger Point,
although they were defeated about the same time by the
Basuto under Moshesh, mentioned elsewhere.

It was of some moment, however, that after sustaining such an unjust expropriation of the land belonging to the natives, the British appointed as Governor Sir George Grey, who proclaimed that his policy was to pacify rather than antagonize the natives, to uplift them rather than exterminate them, to educate them rather than brutalize them by whiskey, theft, murder, and war. Unfortunately, however, the Xosas entered upon a suicidal career. They came under the influence of a maniac, a misguided leader, who declared that the spirit of their ancestors bade the nation to slaughter their cattle and destroy their grain and in headlong fashion throw themselves upon the British and dispossess them of their abundance of grain and cattle. The Xosas were to build upon the ruins of this attack a great empire. The Xosas obeyed foolishly this order; and, unable to take possession of the British as prophesied, about 70,000 died of starvation. This was the chief factor in breaking their power in South Africa.

In their weakened condition, however, the spirit of resistance was not yet dead, and they plunged into the Ninth Xosa War in 1877 under Kreli, the leader of the Gcaleka Xosas. The Zulus arose against the British about the same time, but there was no concerted action shown in this coincidence. In fact, the Bantu were divided. The Fingoes fought with the British against the Xosas and 82,000 other native troops fought with the British against the Zulus. The British had the advantage of another efficient Governor, Sir Bartle Frere. The Xosas were defeated, and so were the Zulus, although there have been few demonstrations of greater or as great fighting qualities as those displayed by these Bantu. Their trouble was want of mutual confidence which has made cooperation among them always a serious problem.

CHAPTER VIII

CHAKA

Out of the fighting Bantu developed some exceptional military leadership. Of this class Chaka, the great chief of the Zulus, was outstanding. He made himself the dominant figure among the tribes in Natal, Zululand, and parts of Pondoland. Chaka sprang from a people constituting one of the three somewhat distinct ethnic groups, although there is a striking resemblance in all three, and they are all spoken of as the Bantu. The three divisions consist of the Bechuanas on the high plains together with the Basuto in the interior, of the Ama-Xosa, Ama-Zulu, and Ama-Swazi dwelling near the coast, and of the Damararas and the Ovambo inhabiting the West Coast highlands. Chaka belonged to the second group generally referred to as Zulus. This term, however, is roughly used to mean practically all people in South Africa when this designation should be given a more restricted definition of Zulu-Xosa natives. These three ethnic groups, to one, or rather to two, of which Chaka and his feats belong in history, are divided into numerous tribes and sub-tribal groups too numerous for us to set forth here in this brief account. Here we are concerned mainly with those who built political and military organizations of importance prior to the conquest of the Europeans and defended their native soil.[1]

Chaka appeared upon the horizon long after empire building by the natives had ceased in those parts of South Africa.

---

[1] Chaka's career is still a matter of mystery, but that he was a great figure no historian of Africa doubts. European authorities refer to him in the usual disparaging fashion. Mofolo, a native African himself, however, has immortalized Chaka in a most dramatic story.

CHAKA

The tribes were numerous and unusually small. At this time there was no state building looking toward such an imposing center of culture as the Mashona, who without knowledge of geometry, had made Zimbabwe, "that El Dorado of the early Portuguese and Dutch settlers in Southern Africa, the supposed Ophir of King Solomon, the palace of the Queen of Sheba." About the only remnant of this former culture of a great people, destroyed by migrations and raids, was that the natives discovered by the explorers in this area retained their skill in working in gold and other metals.

For the military leadership which such a state of retrogression offered, Chaka had the right sort of experience. Born of a humble mother unjustly treated by an ungrateful husband, Senzangakona, Chaka became an outcast when he was his father's rightful heir in his sub-chieftainship. Senzangakona, tormented with the spectre of dying without leaving a male heir, since none of his former wives had borne him a son, sought Nandi as wife, and in due time she delivered Chaka, the much desired heir to the throne. Finding more pleasure with other wives who thereafter bore sons also, Senzangakona cast off Nandi and her son, Chaka, because of the threat that the foes of Nanda would have him dethroned by proving to the satisfaction of the tribe that the union with Nandi was contrary to the rules of the people.

Some extremists insisted that Chaka should be killed because he was born of sin. When Chaka went herding calves with other boys,[2] they beat him because of the ill will en-

---

[2] Mofolo, going into the details of Chaka's life, tells us:

"Distressed at these afflictions Chaka had to suffer among the boys herding calves, his grandmother took him to live with her and set him to scaring birds away from the corn. The other boys employed to scare birds mocked him but did not beat him. Chaka could not understand what crime he had committed to cause himself to become the object of so much abuse. Never had a child suffered greater hardships. The herdboys were not through with him either, for they sought him out in the corn field one day when he had nothing to defend himself and was so surrounded that he could not escape. They beat him to death, as they thought, and threw him into a deep hole in the long grass. A woman who saw this malicious performance from afar, approached and

gendered against him. Defending himself against these cruel attacks one day, Chaka knocked out a boy's eye; and the aggrieved boy's father gave Chaka a terrible beating. This fighting, however, was a training for Chaka. He learned thereby to use weapons, to parry blows, to strike while keeping his head protected, to move swiftly and to run fast—in short, "to give ground and then leap up and strike home at the same time."

Thus attacked by his enemies even when a boy, Chaka had

found that he was merely unconscious. She placed him in the shade of a tree, poured water over him and he regained consciousness. He was too weak to walk; and the good woman sent for his relatives, who came and bore him away on a cow hide used for a stretcher. Nandi then appealed to Senzangakona to intervene and stop this cruelty to their son, but the messenger was intercepted. The chief was persuaded, moreover, even to stop sending cattle and goats as food for Chaka. To preserve the boy from untimely death his relative kept him at home scaring birds or herding calves, and he became an object of ridicule for the other boys who teased him as good-for-nothing.

"Then Chaka's mother, like so many others in such a plight, sought the advice of the wise men as to how she should order his life in order to overcome his enemies. Their advice was sound. They outlined the proper course for him to follow. When the boys attacked him thereafter he so bled them with deep wounds that they scattered. He never tired of fighting his enemies. He rather regretted that the combat ended. His weapons struck home with such force that none could withstand him. These same boys, then, seeing that Chaka was their superior, made him their leader. His cattle had the choice pasturage and drank first at the pools.

"One early morning when still a mere boy, Chaka drove his cattle to the fields only to find them dispersing precipitously at the sight of a lion. Men nearby, having heard the roar of the lion the night before, realized what the trouble was and began to disperse in all directions. The lion had seized a calf the evening before, and after eating what it wanted lay down in the tall grass. Some of the men, however, planned to pursue the lion, and Chaka, a boy, was brave enough to go with them. They formed a cordon around the animal so that when he attacked or tried to escape he would always face someone of the party, all of whom unanimously agreed to fight to death to deliver the one who might be attacked. And thus they proceeded to surround the animal, but when they heard the death-like roar of the beast everyone except Chaka ran in excited fashion, the one trying to outdistance the other. The only man left beside Chaka was the man caught by the lion when it sprang. Chaka realized the danger the man was in of being killed, and therefore yelled as he rushed toward the lion to draw his attention away from his victim. It was too late, however, for the lion struck the man's neck with his paw in the first spring upon him and broke it. When the beast turned upon Chaka, as he courageously approached,

to go to live with his mother in refuge, but even there his foes pursued him. His mother, dearly loving her son, believed that he would live to be useful and prominent, and staid by him through all his trials. Under the direction of the wise men of the tribe, she directed him in the right way. Chaka learned still better how to fight back—to defend himself against his attackers. Tradition would have it that he not only learned to overcome men but even the fiercest animals. Even before he became a man, he had delivered a girl

Chaka, true to his earlier training, stepped quickly to the side from where the beast sprang through the air to seize him and from the side stabbed the lion with his spear. Thus mortally wounded, the beast quickly died amid gruesome groans. Chaka then called to the men to come and see the dead lion, but they were hidden away in the huts of the village even to the exposure of their wives and children. The women, braver than these men, had the courage to watch from afar and see what Chaka had done. The men were reluctant to go to the place, too, for, if it were really true that Chaka, a boy, had killed the lion, they had been put to shame. The women led the way with expressions of great acclaim, singing the song of deliverance to honor Chaka. Other songs in honor of Chaka were composed and sung in Nandi's village to spread his fame abroad. This made her heart glad.

"The lion was carried to Senzangakona at Nobamba; and he, according to the custom of the country, sent it to Dingiswayo, the chief, the successor of Jobe. Senzangakona said that the animal had been killed by his son, Chaka, unaided when others at first accompanying had fled for their lives. The chief said in reply, 'Dingiswayo greets thee and says that it is now long since thou didst send things to Jobe, his father, that there was a man-child in thy house. When wilt thou send the child to him that he may see and know him? He gives thee thanks for the lion thou didst send him, and bids thee send Chaka that he may return to thee with the calf which my master will give thee as an offering of thanks.'

"Senzangakona was between two fires, however, for while the people were praising Chaka, the young man and the warriors whom he had exposed as cowards were plotting against him. The later wives of the chief who had borne him sons after the birth of Chaka had already poisoned his mind against his first son and had forbidden him to succor him and his mother. The father did not comply with the wishes of Dingiswayo, but instead began to plan for Chaka's destruction.

"Chaka, the man of courage, however, would still have opportunity to show that he was not of common clay. In the village, where Chaka was still looked upon with contempt, he was compelled to sleep near the door of the hut in which he lived so that if anyone were attacked it would be Chaka. Two or three times when hyenas were seen about the village Chaka's hands were tied that he might not resist. The chronicler informs us, however, that fate still stood with him, for the animal

from a hyena which he killed in combat and likewise delivered a man by felling the lion attacking him. Still trying to kill Chaka because of his prowess which attracted all eyes to him, his enemies finally received temporary satisfaction from seeing him resort to the bush. In that sequestered abode he finally developed into a man of great might and attractive qualities.

During Chaka's wanderings in the bush one great figure among his fellow Africans never forgot him and sent persons would not attack human beings at all or would pass by Chaka after smelling him and snatch someone in the middle of the hut.

"Once a hyena came into a hut at Quebe where slept the girl of Mfokazana and seized her while all, including the man who pretended that he loved her, skulked away to the nearest place of safety while hearing the distressing cries of the unfortunate girl. Chaka, sleeping in a distant hut, heard the shrilling appeal of this girl for deliverance, aroused all around him, saying: 'Rise up, young men; the hyena has taken a girl.' Listening for a moment to learn the direction in which the hyena had gone, Chaka rushed to the rescue, overtook the hyena, struck the animal under the shoulder blade with his hand and ran his spear through its body. The girl, rescued, sprang to her feet and, looking about her, saw an exceedingly tall man standing between her and the hyena. Not knowing that she had been delivered from the animal, she yelled again while the people in the village remained trembling, crouched in their huts, believing that she was lost forever, and hoping that fate might save them. But Chaka, taking her by the hand, reassured her that she still lived. He said, 'Thou hast escaped, be silent, rejoice, there is the hyena, it is dead. Rise up and see it. It is I, Chaka.'

"To the girl still unable to understand Chaka repeated these words, and she finally recognized his voice. She then looked him straight in the eyes and assured herself that it was Chaka. She next regarded the hyena and assured herself that it was dead. Appreciating as never before the value of life, she clung to Chaka and clasped him and kissed him again and again, saying, 'I knew that there was none but thee, Chaka, who could rescue the dead who have no hope. Mfokazana abandoned me when we were side by side alone in the hut.'

"She then rushed to the village shouting for joy and calling on the people to come and see the great feat which Chaka had performed. They came singing songs in praise of Chaka and in condemnation of Mfokazana, the disgraced runaway. And there was great rejoicing to see that the one counted lost had been restored to her friends and relatives.

"The covetous and begrudging enemies of Chaka, ashamed to see how far he had gone beyond such cowards as they were and at the same time anxious to stop his career, if possible, wondered what could be done to get rid of this mere boy who could perform feats which well-seasoned men dared not attempt. Mfokazana saw that the best way out

in quest of the young man. This was Dingiswayo, the chief under whom Chaka's father Senzangakona was only a sub-chief. Chaka finally came out of his hiding where he had communed with the witch doctors under whose influence he became a changed man. Prior to this time he had become a man of intrepidity, of great endurance, and manual prowess. To these he was to add the qualities of an indomitable will and an aggressive spirit which made him push forward to the ends he sought regardless of the cost in life or property of others. In this state he finally came to the home of Dingiswayo. As he approached the capital he heard the witch doctors telling how he had disappeared in death and would never be seen again. Seeking to approach Dingiswayo, he

of his embarrassment was to murder Chaka. When the people went out to see Chaka seated on the animal which he had killed, Mfokazana, on arriving, struck Chaka on the head and brought him face-forward to the ground. Chaka arose, seized his spear, rushed through the crowd, and then turned around to meet his assailant who was following him and gave battle. Thick indeed was the fight between Chaka's jealous enemies trying to destroy a man who had learned to fight against odds. Chaka by strategy, although outnumbered by his foes, emerged victor, leaving his assailant dead on the battle ground.

"When Senzangakona, the chief, arrived with his wives and saw their son lying dead on the ground they demanded of Mfokazana the death of Chaka. Orders were given to the men of Quede to dispatch Chaka, and the battle was on. A few of these men of Quede stood with Chaka, however, but these were soon overcome by the numerous foes and Chaka in fighting broke both his stick and his spear. He fled from them so swiftly that none could overtake him. He went from the scenes of his childhood, from the country where he was born into the veld, into the bush, where his enemies could not reach him. When Dingiswayo heard of this cowardly effort of the sub-chief Senzangakona he fined him some cattle, saying that he was teaching his warriors to be cowards. Dingiswayo ordered that Chaka be found and sent to him.

"While Chaka was in the bush he met Isanusi, the witch doctor, or sorcerer, who brought from Chaka's ancestors a new message that he was to be the hero of even greater achievements than he had known, provided he will hear the voice of the wise and sacrifice everything which he had held dear. Here Chaka breaks with the fearsome past—from such as the first plots of the herdboys against him, of the men who had tried to murder him, of the order given by his father to kill him when he was unoffending. Chaka was now convinced that among the selfish only might makes right. Under the spell of the witch doctor he binds himself to do whatever is necessary to obtain power, to put away all mercy and compassion in order to reach the goal.''

had to tell the guards who he was, not that he was Chaka, but a hare that has escaped from a brother to the owl, a vagabond fleeing from the spear, but a manchild whose hands knew how to grasp weapons of war and fight the battles of the Chief. Of Dingiswayo he asked protection. When he had told his story the whole court stood around and gave Chaka a great welcome. Nandi was called and, observing that her son still lived, fainted because of her inexpressible joy.

Chaka entered the service of Dingiswayo. His assistance was immediately needed. A mad man at the gates again ready to destroy Dingiswayo's cattle had to be dealt with more severely than formerly, for all sent against him hitherto had failed. The people thought the mad man had the advantage of possessing an evil spirit. Chaka agreed to join the defense against the raid of the assailant. The crowd went in pursuit. The assailant gave fight. The defenders fled. Chaka, biding his time, however, struck the man dead as he was trying to kill him with a spear. The people honored Chaka for his feat. They saw that the reports of Chaka's killing the lion and the hyena were true.

This delivery of the cattle from the raider convinced Dingiswayo that Chaka was the natural leader to be sent against Zwide, the neighboring hostile chief, who often raided Dingiswayo's cattle. Chaka went in the vanguard. Zwide's men advanced with furious fighting, and Chaka's companions fled. But Chaka dealt blows right and left with his short spear, cutting down those who approached him and parrying the blows of those attacking from afar. He brought low so many of Zwide's men that the remnant fled in all directions. Chaka had won the day fighting at times against enemies outnumbering his forces ten to one.

Next Chaka, coming more and more under the influence of sorcerers, was visited by Ndlebe and Malunga, who were to serve him as scout and protector respectively. These were the companions of Isanusi, whose influence over Chaka had already been noted. Dingiswayo did not like Malunga, and he stayed away from Chaka most of the time while Ndlebe, the idiot, was ever present. Malunga, however, appeared in time of great need.

These men the annalist makes of great importance to Chaka in the second war with Zwide. The enemy had tried to retreat as a ruse and draw Dingiswayo's forces into the bush where they would be overwhelmed by his hidden warriors. Ndlebe set fire to the parched grass of the dry season and drove the reenforcements out of the bush in disorder. This discomfited the army of Zwide, and Chaka did the rest. Zwide was taken alive, for Dingiswayo did not permit a chief to be killed. The army was received on return with great acclaim, and Chaka again became the subject of a song of victory. Dingiswayo was convinced beyond doubt that Chaka was the one whom he had long needed and made him the commander-in-chief of his forces whether Dingiswayo went with the army or not. But jealousy was not yet dead. Dingiswayo's uncle, and two others had raised a plot against Chaka because he had been promoted over them.

In the midst of this renown Chaka's father, Senzangakona, died in 1810, and another son, Mfokazana, undertook to deprive Chaka of the succession. Chaka had two younger brothers, Dingaan (Dingana) and Mhlangana. Dingiswayo heard of the death indirectly. The tribe sent no messenger to the chief, as was wont, for if a heifer had also been sent Dingiswayo would have sent a messenger in return to bear his condolences. Everything was hurried, however, for the burial and period of mourning were shortened to rush the acknowledgment of Mfokazana as sub-chief and to inform the chief after the thing was a *fait accompli*. It was believed advisable to rush matters thus and prepare for war since Chaka would doubtless claim the throne and would be recognized by Dingiswayo. The relations between the chief and his subvassal, Senzangakona, had been so strained that in recent years the former had not invited the latter to go to war with him. Dingiswayo, however, although ready thus to honor Chaka, bade him refrain from forcing his claims for six months during which his father's bones should not be dishonored by war.

In the meantime he suggested to Chaka that he should marry, but Chaka was reluctant to believe that any woman of worth would thus honor him. Thus was brought to him a problem that he could not solve. Successful in war but a failure in romance. Chaka had long looked with a wishful eye toward Noliwe, the daughter of Dingiswayo, but he had never thought that any woman of royal blood would accept a man of his station. Chaka had no idea that Dingiswayo was suggesting his marriage advisedly with the dream that Chaka, married to Noliwe, would unite the two chieftainships. It was finally revealed to Chaka that Noliwe loved him as dearly as he loved her. Yet he faced another problem in mustering up sufficient courage to approach Dingiswayo with a proposal which Chaka believed that he would never accept. The courage came indirectly. The chief was informed of their designs, and the consent was given.

At the grave of his father six months thereafter Chaka took courage to go forward with the work the fates had outlined for him. When the messengers finally came to announce the accession of Mfokazana, Dingiswayo informed them that they had proceeded wrong in the matter, that Senzangakona had notified him years before of his intention to have Chaka succeed him and that Chaka would. Chaka proceeded to the tribe and was met by Mfokazana, who was defeated and killed in battle. Chaka spared his other two brothers, who had not taken part in the war. He wrought terrible destruction among his former enemies and would have done more, but he was afraid of losing the good will of Dingiswayo.

Chaka became the sub-chief and as such was loyal to Dingiswayo. He braved the ill-will of the chief, however, in taking Malunga back with him regardless of Dingiswayo's desire not to have him around. Chaka had his usual seances with the witch doctors, Isanusi, Ndlebe and Malunga, and was installed as chief. In this situation he fell completely under their influence. They convinced Chaka that greater things awaited him than the succession to his father's and Dingiswayo's chieftainship, if he would agree to sacrifice everything to reach this ideal. Chaka had been inclined to seek the good and beautiful; but now he became completely sold out, soul and body, for temporal power.

Zwide recovered sufficient strength to battle Dingiswayo. Having unwisely permitted his forces to scatter after being tired with the fight against Matiwane, Dingiswayo was killed. This left the field clear for Chaka after the brother Mundiso had been defeated in trying to avenge Dingiswayo's death. Chaka engaged Zwide in battle and deprived him of all he had won. This made Chaka not only a sub-chief but a chief of chiefs. Again the loud acclaim and song of war in honor of Chaka.

Chaka gave his people a new name, the Zulus or Amazulus and he built him a capital, Umgungundhlovu ("The Elephant Abode"). Chaka then reorganized the people for political solidarity to support military conquest. Roads were built to facilitate contact with the capital. In the midst of the city was a large courtyard for drilling his regiments. On this spot assembled the troops returning from war as victors bringing the cattle and other property to present as spoils to the chief. Feasts and state functions took place there. Near this central courtyard lived the advisers as lieutenants of the chief. The best cattle were kraaled there, and near the enclosure stood the court of the chief. It had two entrances guarded by warriors. Everyone entering shouted his greeting, leaving his spear and blanket at the door with the guards. He must prostrate himself, crawl forward on his stomach and say "Bayate," and he remained in this position until his greeting was received. At the second entrance of the court was a high rock on which the watchman sat day

and night. No one was allowed to enter the city by night,
From the court was a palisade leading to the chief's hut,
Ndhlunkulu (the great house) to which one came 'under
penalty of death unless called by a messenger of the chief.
Out from this were the huts of the girls to whom he went
frequently and plucked their maidenhood. In another part
lived the city guards.

Everything was to be carried out in conformity with military needs. Chaka put an end to circumcision in that part
because the time required for this rite could be spent in
preparation for war. Warriors who had learned to fight
were distinguished from those in training. As soon as boys
had sufficiently developed to bear arms they were compelled to join the army. Parents saw them no more, and
they had no association with women. Afterward everything
with them meant war or the preparation for war. Removed
from the softening influence of women and the home and
made to think only of arms and how to use them, these
youths developed into military machines. They were not to
marry, for when in the heat of battle with men dying around
they might think of their wives and children. Those troops
who surpassed the others in war would be permitted to
marry. If no such troops excelled they were released from
celibacy in turn at the will of the Chief. A warrior for unusual bravery or some outstanding feat could likewise marry
as a reward.

In warfare itself several innovations were introduced.
The longhandled spear and the battle-ax, or knobkerrie,
which were thrown at the enemy, were abolished by Chaka,
and instead the short-handled spear requiring fighting at
close range was introduced. Chaka's men were to approach
the enemy without fear and dash them to pieces. A sort
of drilling like the modern method was introduced. System
and order became the distinguishing mark of these regiments. Every soldier had to obey his superiors. All had to
idolize Chaka. A soldier returning like a coward without

CHAKA IN WAR

his shield was promptly killed. A general failing to conquer
the foe suffered the same fate.

Forced either to conquer or die, the soldiers of Chaka
constituted the greatest fighting force ever developed in
Africa. Cowards were slaughtered by the thousands, and
sometimes innocent persons who had been forced to slaughter
cowards. Before this military machine thrones and seats
of governments tumbled. Chiefs and their vassals trembled
when they heard of the approach of Chaka's army. All
neighboring tribes came under his sway or underwent deso-
lation and extermination at the hands of Chaka's soldiers.
Moshesh, then trying to build up the Basuto nation, kept
Chaka out of his country only by sending the warrior word
that he recognized no other chief but Chaka. Moselikatze,
seeing that the shedding of blood had gone far enough, escaped with some soldiers across the Drakensberg mountains
and established a new nation in Matabeleland.

Everything must be sacrificed to the end of waging war.
Neither sentiment, nor love, nor religion must interfere with
his reaching the goal of dominating all the people within
reach. Chaka must, therefore, burn the bridges behind him.
It is said that he even put to death Noliwe, the woman
whom he loved, and his mother, who had nurtured him
when his father sought his destruction. After uniting by
conquest the thrones of the Ama-Zulu and the Aba-Tetwa
he overwhelmed the Undwandwe and incorporated their survivors into the Zulu nation. He next dashed to the north,
driving the Bangoni and the Ama-Gaza before him. Adjacent tribes at the same time were annexed to the Zulu
nation. He then took Pondoland.

Chaka sent to the English a proposal to cooperate with
them in further conquest, but his day was done. Chaka's
raids and slaughters tended to react on him and bring him
to a remorseful or weakened state of mind and to inaction.
Dingaan (Dingana) and Mhlangana, his brothers, hoping
to do the will of many in getting rid of the reign of terror,

stabbed him to death in 1828. He had enough self-posses-
sion to say warningly, however: "It is your hope that by
killing me you will become chief when I am dead. But ye
are deluded, it will not be so, for the white man will come,
and it is he who will rule, and ye will be his bondmen."

Chaka dropped out of the picture just about the time that
African affairs had become more complicated than ever
by the Great Trek. His war machine, however, remained
to play its conspicuous part for years to come. While the
Cape Government and the Home Government were trying
to decide whether they would stop the Trek of the Boers or
extend their jurisdiction over them in their frontier positions the trekkers rushed on into the territory of the High
Veld which the wars of Chaka had apparently left vacant.
The migrating Boers, however, had to deal first with the
Matabele who destroyed entirely one group while Hendrik
Potgieter could scarcely deliver another which lost to the
natives all their draught oxen at Vechtkop. The trekkers
recovered these animals by raiding the natives' stronghold
at Mosega early in 1837, and the Matabele, defeated again,
withdrew into what is now Southern Rhodesia.

Going down into Dingaan's Zululand, however, the Boers
alarmed the chief, although at first he had shown an inclination to cede the trekkers some land in Natal. Dingaan en-
ticed with promises certain Boers under Retief and slaughtered them. Next he sent his impis to attack others in Natal
and overwhelmed them while at the same time disastrously
defeating the English rushing with help from the coast.
Meeting forces led by Potgieter and Uys descending from
the mountains, the Zulus trapped and killed Uys and compelled Potgieter to withdraw. The way thus having been
cleared, the Zulus marched in triumph to the coast and
occupied Port Natal in April, 1838. The Boers who had
gone in quest of Natal thus found themselves suffering from
a loss of one-tenth of their men, while the remainder were
"cooped up in a laager."

Governor Durban, who had tried to stop the trek, could then say, "I told you so." It was unwise to stray so far from settlements thick enough to offer one another protection. Sir George Napier, who succeeded him, tried also to check the trek, but finally persuaded Lord Glenelg, the Secretary for the Colonies, that the establishment of a British administration at Natal was the only solution of the problem. Before the British could place their regulars in action there, however, the Boers had taken the offensive with Pretorius from Graaff-Reinet as leader. This attack was planned with more system than could be said of those efforts resisting surprise attacks of the natives when on the offensive. Time was taken, and the attack was made in laager form. The Boers fought behind wagons, by which they had practically surrounded the Zulus, and with a cavalry to pursue the natives should they undertake to retreat. The natives had numbers but no modern weapons. The assegais, their main weapons, could be effective only half as far as the crudest of the Boers' weapons, the smooth-bore flintlocks. At close range the natives were decisively defeated at Blood River on December 16, 1839. Only a few Boers fell, but three thousand Zulus perished. This victory is still cele- brated in those parts as Dingaan's Day.

This victory did not bring peace with the Zulus, but it was the turning point in the struggle of the Europeans for ascendancy. With the British officer as mediator, peace was negotiated between the natives and the Boers to whom the British at Port Natal had ceded their rights. Dingaan promised to deliver up the guns, horses and cattle which he had taken, and to cede St. Lucia Bay and the Southern half of Zululand. Pretorius thereafter played off the faction of Zulus under Panda against those adhering to his brother Dingaan and thus drove the king to his death in Swaziland in February, 1840. Panda, his successor, became a puppet for the conquerors.

The new policy of segregation came into force then in

DINGAAN

ruling the natives. Subject chiefs were allowed to rule their people on reserves only. Detribalized natives were to be subject to a pass law; they had to enter some one's service by contract and could not easily leave that employ. The natives were not to carry guns, ride horses, or take drinks. Natives were to be allocated to the farms in the proportion of five to each, and unwanted natives had to leave the areas opened for European settlement. At the same time was put in operation a system of apprenticeship which was virtual slavery.

The harshness of the Boer trekkers in practically exterminating the natives gave the British an excuse for annexation of Natal by force in 1845. It was insisted that the Boers thereby complicated matters by keeping the natives sufficiently disturbed to be a constant source of danger from war and devastation falling likewise upon the British in South Africa. On this point, however, the British administration at the Cape and the Home Government never adhered to a uniform policy.

CHAPTER IX

CHAKA'S SUCCESSORS

CETEWAYO

Against the new civilization, or the destruction of the native civilization, the Zulus made a final stand. Their military organization based upon a regimental system of celibate soldiery much like that of the Spartans was still intact. Brave Zulus still stood ready to wash their spears in the blood of the Europeans. Panda, who had suffered the warring ardor of the nation to dampen, died in 1872, when he was succeeded by the aggressive and undaunted Cetewayo, his son. After his trumph over his rival brother, Mbulazi, in a fiercely contested battle in 1856, Cetewayo had been the dominant force among the Zulus. The new chief had all the qualities of a popular leader. He was not only a successful warrior, but a handsome and intelligent man whom men delighted to follow. With these unusual advantages Cetewayo quickly restored the military discipline of Chaka's day.

On the death of his father in 1872, Cetewayo, hoping to forestall his brothers as rival claimants for the throne, sought the support of the Natal Government and that of the Transvaal to offset any recognition which Great Britain might give his rivals. By this time the British native policy had changed. They had annexed the new states founded by the trekking Boers and hoped to unite them and the Cape as one federation. In thus taking over this territory the British had annexed the very natives whose "protection" they had formerly championed to weaken the Boers. Now the British had to deal just as harshly with the warlike natives as had the Boers. The British eventually abandoned the philanthropic policy first advanced by Maynier and Shepstone. Instead of being able to play one European off against the other the Zulus had now no choice but to confront one strong power backed by their protected Swazi to effect their extermination. Not yet appreciating the gravity of the situation, however, they still fought for the continuation of the old civilization.

CETEWAYO

In his diplomatic move Cetewayo asked both Natal and the Transvaal to recognize him as king of the Zulus. Shepstone was designated by Natal to effect Cetewayo's installation as such a ruler but on certain conditions highly favorable to the Europeans and decidedly disastrous to the Zulu regime. Cetewayo was informed, moreover, that the long desired territory of Blood River between Rorke's Drift and the Pongola River would have to be abandoned since there had been a formal cession of those lands by Panda in 1861. The British had thus reversed themselves and veered around to the Transvaal point of view. Bishop Colenso, long the supposed friend of the natives, deserted the Zulus in this claim. Cetewayo, however, was determined to carry out his purposes. He established himself in the disputed territory and forced the Boers there to flee for their lives. He next proceeded to occupy a position north of Pongola, which compelled the exit of some German settlers from Lunenburg. Governor Frere, of the Cape, sent troops under Colonel Wood to the rescue, and a naval squadron to the Zulu coast appeared. No aggressive policy could be undertaken at that time, however, for the forces at the disposal of the Europeans were inadequate to cope with the rising Zulus. To the parsimonious Home Office went the appeal for reenforcements at the time that additional forces were needed to meet the situation in Afghanistan and Eastern Europe. One point was gained, however, when the invaders of the Zulu domain induced Cetewayo to submit the question of the disputed territory to arbitration.

The commissioners to whom was submitted the matter of adjusting the territorial dispute awarded Cetewayo more than he claimed; but to the British this would never do, and the announcement was delayed until his opponents could enforce additional demands upon him. This move was one of watchful waiting, for reenforcements were first promised and then denied the British, but later assured and finally refused. Forbearance and compromise were suggested instead, but even with limited forces Frere decided that the issue had to be met and the Zulus must be broken.

The next step was to present the award with a drastic ultimatum which the Zulu chief could not honorably accept. The Europeans required Cetewayo to disband his army, to institute a modern system of trial for offenders, to make reparation for carrying away two wives of Chief Sirawayo, to protect missionaries and natives proselyted by them, and to permit the rule of his actions by a British resident. This ultimatum Cetewayo ignored, and when the thirty days given for acceptance had expired British troops under Lord Chelmsford invaded Zululand. This was the beginning of serious trouble. The British, advancing in four columns on a two hundred mile front, hoped to keep Cetewayo too busy at home to have time for attacking the European settlements. The invaders, however, did not find all things according to their expectations. One of the columns crossed the Tugela near the coast, another entered the land of the Zulus near New Castle, and a third took a position at Rorke's Drift. Chelmsford himself led his division across the Buffalo River and pitched camp on the side of a steep hill called Isandhlwana, leaving himself exposed to a surprise attack in spite of advice to the contrary by Kruger and Joubert. Lured by an attacking native, Chelmsford rushed far away from base into a trap where he suddenly found himself surrounded by the bravest of the Zulu warriors on January 22, 1879. The Zulus attacked the British force with unwonted speed and excellent marksmanship with their assegais and annihilated the invading force, leaving 800 white and 500 of their native allies dead on that battlefield. This victory over the British caused great consternation in Europe.

Directly from this scene of great success three or four thousand Zulus commanded by Cetewayo's brother marched on to Rorke's Drift and besieged it. Barricaded behind improvised fortifications, however, the British force in charge fought off the attackers and prevented the much-feared invasion of Natal. Panic, nevertheless, reigned in Natal, for at the time no one could figure out how far the Zulus could advance in the face of diminished forces to oppose them.

Instead of following up the victory, the natives in keeping with their custom took up time in conforming to the ritual of purification after battle, and dissension broke out in the ranks of Zulus. This allowed time for every soldier available elsewhere in South Africa to come to the rescue. England, stirred by the news of the disaster at Isandhlwana, reversed its policy of compromise and economy and rushed 10,000 troops to the scene. In the meantime, one of the columns under Pearson had contrived to reach Eshowe in the center of Zululand but had lost their transport to the besiegers. The northern force succeeded in reaching and holding Kambula, but a detachment therefrom was defeated and their leader killed at Hlobane Mountain the following March. Chelmsford took the offensive again after relieving his beleagured soldiers by a victory over the Zulus at Ginginhlovo on the second of April.

Humiliating defeat, however, was still ahead. A reconnoitering party in which Prince Louis Napoleon, the only child of Emperor Napoleon III and Prince Eugénie, was serving to show his gratitude to the British nation, was surprised and defeated by the Zulus, who killed the Prince. Disraeli felt sufficiently moved to comment thus: ''A very remarkable people, the Zulus, they defeat our generals; they convert our bishops; they have settled the fate of a great European dynasty.''

And these reversals of the British soldiery all but wrecked Disraeli's Government, which rocked and reeled under the bitter criticism of his apparently failing colonial policy when in addition to the South African disaster the British had to face the possibility of Russian aggression in Afghanistan. Frere had to bear the blame of the troubles, and although temporarily spared, probably because he was popular among the British in South Africa, he had to give place in May, 1879, to Garnet Wolseley who, a general of the army, took over the administration of Natal. Before this change could be made effective, however, the forces led by Chelmsford had finally engaged and decisively defeated the Zulus at Ulundi on July 4, 1879. Cetewayo was taken prisoner. The power of the Zulus had actually been broken.

This victory enabled Wolseley to carry out the policy of Shepstone in dividing the Zulus into thirteen independent tribes or provinces with petty chiefs ruling under a British Resident rather than under a paramount chief. This British officer had no actual authority to enforce decrees inasmuch as the British had not gone so far as to annex Zululand. War broke out among the petty chieftains, and to maintain order the British had to restore Cetewayo with a much diminished jurisdiction and limited power. Cetewayo soon became involved in war with that part of the domain placed under a rival chief, Sibebu, at whose expense, contrary to the wishes of the British he desired to expand; and within a short while Cetewayo was defeated and driven to seek refuge. The British burned his capital at Ulundi and destroyed his means of support. He was finally captured by the British at Eshowe and died there in 1883.

Upon the death of Cetewayo the trekkers from the Transvaal into Zululand were glad to recognize Dinizulu as the paramount chief of the thirteen petty chiefs among whom the remaining portion of Zululand left to the natives had been apportioned. This proclamation of Dinizulu as paramount chief was followed by a grant of land to the Boers who in 1884 established a new republic with Vyrheid as the capital. Kruger, the Boer leader, had his eye on St. Lucia Bay as the possible outlet to the ocean in rivalry with those which led only from British ports where their imports were subject to unjust duties, as they contended. Thus aided, Dinizulu defeated his rival Sibebu (Usibepu) but he stirred up the British when he tried to expand too far. The Dutch had no love for the Zulus, but they might serve as useful means to an end. The Boers demanded more land. The British stepped in to extend "peace" and became involved in a war against Dinizulu. After a brave and stubborn resistance he had to surrender and was exiled in 1898 to St. Helena.

So much disturbance followed in Zululand, however, that

Dinizulu was brought back to restore peace. The colony of Natal, moreover, was having trouble with their East Indian subjects who, under Mahatma Gandhi, were fearlessly fighting disabilities imposed upon them by the Asiatic Law Amendment Act of 1907. The colonists were rapidly expanding into areas formerly reserved by the Zulus and in so crowding the natives were reducing them to pillage and war to find a subsistence. In the proportion as this encroachment progressed the number of raids on the cattle of the European settlers increased. The natives and the colonists grew farther and farther apart as these grievances multiplied, and signs of trouble everywhere could be seen.

As the immediate cause of an outbreak came the imposition of a poll tax of one pound on every European and every native who did not pay the hut tax of fourteen shillings. Two policemen, attempting to collect this tax in the Richmond district, were killed. Martial law was declared, a punitive force was hastily mobilized, and twelve natives were speedily rounded up and condemned to death. Fearing direful results from such a sweeping execution, the Earl of Elgin, secretary of state for the colonies, urged a stay of execution. Indignant at such an interference with measures taken to protect British subjects in a colony of responsible government, the Natal Government resigned. The Earl of Elgin receded from his position, however, and the natives were executed three days after the date first set for the purpose.

This drastic action did not immediately crush the rebellion. In four other districts, Mapumulo, Krantzkop, Umvoti, and Nkandhla, other natives resumed the warpath, although not in an organized way. The European forces entered the field in time to defeat these rising forces one by one before they could become a formidable army by uniting. Bambata went down to defeat and death in the battle in the Mome Gorge June 9-10, 1906, and Sigananda, leading others was soon forced to surrender. By that time the colonial forces

DINIZULU

had increased to 5,000, and McKenzie, the commander, easily defeated the two chiefs operating south of the Tugela River. The resistance thus broken degenerated into a guerilla warfare, marked by the killing of isolated Europeans and the destruction of their property. This resistance had been sustained without the open encouragement of Dinizulu who could have made matters worse. He started a rebellion the following year, but the insurrection was nipped in the bud, and Dinizulu had to surrender. He was tried for treason under a special act of Parliament late in 1908, and for defending his own native land was sentenced to imprisonment in Cape Town.

In 1910 Dinizulu was permitted to retire to a farm in the Transvaal, where he soon died. Solomon, the son of the deceased, was recognized in 1916 by General Botha, the Premier of the Union of South Africa, as chief of the Zulus. This did not please the natives, but their power of resistance had finally been destroyed. Solomon became a mere marionette in the hands of the imperialists, who paid him three hundred pounds a year. Out of this reconstruction of native control came the more clearly defined policy of restricting to demarcated areas all the natives whether living as those confined to reserves or granted individual ownership in a detribalized state.

MOSELIKATZE AND LOBENGUELA

Out of Chaka's regime developed another nation known as the Ama-Ndebele, Matabele, or Abakwa-Zulu. While not typically Zulus they had sufficient of the same blood and spirit of the Zulu to speak of this as their origin. About 1824, when Chaka had lost his balance and began to turn upon his own people, even upon his loyal supporters, Moselikatze (Moselekatse, or Umseligazi), one of Chaka's generals, escaped from that domain with 15,000 of the best soldiers of the tribe and led them far away across the Drakensberg Mountains into what is now a part of the Transvaal.[1]

The immediate occasion was that Moselikatze had refused to carry out certain orders of Chaka; and, according to the rules of war, this treason meant death to him and his followers. Despising the methods of Chaka, whom they considered too despotic to serve further, they nevertheless used the same system in dealing with others among whom they

MOSELIKATZE

had to fight on their way to a new home. In the course of this flight they had to contend with the Bechuana—represented by the Bakwena, the Bamangwato, the Bangwaketse, and the Barolong.

---

[1] The story of Moselikatze and Lobenguela may be gleaned in fragments from Green's *Rhodes Goes North*, Raphael's *The Cape to Cairo Dream*, and S. M. Molema's *The Bantu*. Other sources, of course, are valuable but not easily accessible. In the various works on Cecil Rhodes these and other natives appear in the picture.

The Matabele finally established themselves in the Marikwa valley with their capital at Mosega. The migrating Boers, however, were on the way to offer them further trouble. These voortrekkers had already reached the site of the present Orange Free State and had advanced beyond Thaba Ncho, where they met the Matabele. The natives commanded them to stop and return whence they came. This order the Boers refused to heed, and the Matabele gave them the battle of their lives. With the telling fire of grapeshot the Boers forced the Matabele to retire temporarily but in the possession of all the cattle, draught oxen and cows of the trekkers. With merely their wagons the Boers could go no further, and they were doomed to perish upon the spot of their partial victory; but, history again repeated itself. The Barolong at Thaba Ncho, hostile to the Matabele, came to the rescue of the Boers with supplies and cattle. With such help the Boers under Gerrit Maritz and a Griqua regiment, took the offensive against the Matabele and forced them to abandon Mosega, in the northwestern part of the Transvaal. The Matabele then went 400 miles northward to a position south of the Zambesi, now called Matabeleland. There, in order to fortify their position the Matabele waged destructive wars on the Bamangwato, the Makalaka subjects of the Monomatapa dynasty, and the Mashona, the former inhabitants of Matabeleland. Some of those attacked, like the Bamangwato under Khama, inflicted heavy losses on the Matabele. Once settled, however, they built a new nation of scattering fragments dislocated from other tribes. Moselikatze chose Buluwayo as his capital.

Trouble lay ahead, however, for the Boers were ever expanding toward the north and grabbing land. If the natives undertook to dislodge them they resorted to war on the grounds that they had some sort of claim the origin of which no one but themselves could ever determine. Under various pretexts but for the simple reason to get away from the British in the south and be independent to enslave the natives and use them only for their selfish purposes, the Boers under Hendrix Potgieter invaded Matabeleland in 1855. The Matabele, true to their record, met the invaders and forced them back to their frontier. This victory was sufficient to guarantee peace to the Matabele until 1870, when Moselikatze died. He was succeeded by his son Lobenguela. Lobenguela first had to deal with the ever troublesome Boers. These interlopers figured out that they needed not only sufficient land to satisfy present needs but to guarantee the future development of a modern republic able to cope with the British in South Africa. What they did not conquer the British would. When gold was discovered in Matabeleland the Boers had still another reason for invading that domain. The first method employed had been force, now it was a method of friendly approach. P. J. Joubert, therefore, speaking for the Boers, addressed to Lobenguela a most deceitful letter on March 9, 1882, and sent gifts for him and his wife.

Joubert expressed a desire to see Lobenguela, the son of his friend, the late Moselikatze. He wanted to tell him the truth about the state of things in the world since so many things circulated as the truth were false. He told him of the evil deeds of the British and especially of their taking away from the Boers their country, the Transvaal; but now the British were gone and the country was free, he said, and the Boers desired once more to live in friendship with Lobenguela as they had lived in friendship with Moselikatze. For this reason Joubert desired so much to see Lobenguela, and he planned to visit him when things became settled. Joubert referred to the fact that he was a child when Franz Joubert, Jann Joubert, and Pieter Joubert, thirty-two years prior to that time, returned after making with Moselikatze a peace which during these years the evil-doers (British) had not been able to disturb. Joubert referred to troublesome chiefs who had invaded the Boer lands and caused damage to property. Evidently Joubert wanted to secure Lobenguela's assistance in dealing with them or to prevent him from being alarmed should he hear that the Boers were striking back at such enemies.

Lobenguela's task was somewhat different from that of his father, who had fought his way through hostile tribes to the present site of the nation which he had nobly defended against the aggressive Boers. Lobenguela's task of dealing later with the expanding British as well as with the inevitable Boers, however, required nevertheless a man of steel. To this requirement he measured up in every detail. The European aggressors finally expropriated his land, but had Logenguela had the same equipment which they used against him they never could have invaded his territory.

At the time that Lobenguela began to rule over the Matabele a new problem was facing the natives in Africa. Europeans who had once looked upon the acquisition of territory in Africa as a questionable enterprise became gradually committed after 1885 to the policy of partitioning that continent according to the agreement reached that year at Berlin. After hard work by direct and indirect methods of the most questionable sort Cecil John Rhodes had secured the support of the forward looking British imperialists in favor of his Cape-to-Cairo dream. Chamberlain was his mainstay with the British Government. Concession after concession was obtained from the natives, telegraph lines were built, railroads constructed, mines opened, resources exploited; and about the only developments that tended to check the expropriation were the Mahdi's movement in the Egyptian Sudan and the Fashoda affair with the questions incident thereto. The French, hoping to connect their possession in West Africa with those in East Africa, conflicted with the British pushing their way from the Cape to Cairo. Rudd, Maguire, Rochford, Jameson and Thompson served as the efficient agents of Rhodes in most of the South African enterprises opening the way from the Cape.

In dealing with the Matabele natives they found their

LOBENGUELA

greatest opposition since the time they had to deal with Din-gaan in that celebrated battle on Blood River. In the first place, Lobenguela had too many of the qualities of Rhodes himself to be easily handled. Lobenguela was a clear thinker, a man of foresight, a leader who had a program for his people, and an indomitable will to make his dreams come true. His people had ceased to migrate and no longer made war on their neighbors except with cause. The Matabele desired to enjoy the fruits of their industry in peace. To maintain the peace Lobenguela believed that it was necessary to keep the Europeans as far away from him as possible. He had no objection to Europeanization from the point of view of accepting the best methods for the enlightenment of the people and development of his territory. To admit Europeans in large numbers he had learned from experience meant the loss of one's country in the end. Missionaries were finally admitted in limited numbers only after Lobenguela felt assured that they meant to work for the welfare of his people.

Yet it was difficult for Lobenguela to distinguish between the concession-hunter and some one seeking the good of the natives. They came from all quarters, Germans from the west, Portuguese from the east, and Boers and Englishmen from the south. Under pressure Lobenguela finally made a mistake in signing with Pieter Grobler, Kruger's emissary, a treaty upon which the Boers hoped to claim the land of the Matabele. The Rev. John S. Moffat, the Assistant Commissioner of the Bechuanaland Protectorate, however, visited Lobenguela at Bulawayo and persuaded him to repudiate the agreement. Nevertheless, in so doing, the chief was merely extricating himself from the claws of one hawk to fall into those of another. At that time Lobenguela signed an agreement with Moffat not to enter into any treaty with any other foreign state; and Hercules Robinson, the High Commissioner, not only ratified the agreement secured by Moffat but ordered troops northward to close to foreigners the route to Matabeleland. In the meanwhile the advance guard of British

concessionaires had worked their way peacefully into Matabeleland by professions of friendship. Lobenguela accordingly had restrained his soldiers ever eager to strike down the
exploiter.

Rhodes was wise in his generation. He saw that he must
act quickly. He had sent one agent after another into Lobenguela's territory to obtain some sort of concession, and they
were abruptly refused. The expansionists from the Cape
could not use force at that time, because the Home Government was committed to the policy of safeguarding the rights
of the natives. But if they could obtain some semblance of
right to do one thing in Matabeleland, they could easily find
some excuse for claiming an additional right and thereby
induce the Home Government to intervene to extend "the
peace of Britain." Once on the ground, they could report
that a missionary had been killed, or that a British agent
had been murdered while in the act of extending the trade
of the Empire. The Home Government, then, would be compelled to act in assuming more authority this time and still
more the next until the land would be declared a British
possession.

In order to secure a right of way and the claim to the mineral wealth of the country Rudd, Rhodes' agent, with the assistance of the Rev. C. D. Helm, finally succeeded in obtaining a concession "to dig" in one place, as Lobenguela
thought, just as he had seen the Europeans digging at Kim-
berley. Even in the very beginning Lobenguela had some
fears about the trap thus set, and he refused to receive the
1,500 stand of arms promised for this grant, and let them
rust on the spot where they were first deposited on his territory in Matabeleland. The capitalists interpreted the agreement as ceding to the exploiters the entire mineral wealth of
Matabeleland. Hearing this, Lobenguela wrote the Queen a
letter when the agents sent out by Rhodes began to occupy the
country.

In his letter Lobenguela showed that he, too, was not lacking in diplomacy. Addressing the Queen, he referred to the visit of a party desiring a concession to dig for gold. They left him under the impression that the operation was to be restricted to one spot. He expressed to the Queen his surprise to learn that these men and those whom they represented were interpreting the agreement to mean the mineral rights of the entire land. Lobenguela informed her that in re-examining the document he found that it contained neither his words nor those of the men who negotiated with him. He had endeavored to get back the original agreement to which he had affixed his mark, but they never brought it back. Thus he had been led into a trap not only by these agents, but at the suggestion of Moffat and Helm, missionaries who professed to be advising Lobenguela in the name of God.

The letter was sidetracked, in fact, purposely delayed, so as to reach the Home Government after things had gone so far that the matter could not be conveniently readjusted in favor of the Matabele. At once Lobenguela, having had no reply, called a meeting of his indunas and certain Europeans and disavowed his mark on the dotted line. The Matabele were summoned to arms to defend their native soil. Lobenguela pointed out the dangers facing them, the expropriation of their land, the dislocation of the people, and their ultimate extermination. Fight now even if you die, for die you must under the yoke of the European conqueror. Armed with the assegais and in native fashion they prepared to meet soldiers of Rhodes' company long since prepared for the coup. "Why do you kill us?" he asked the Europeans. "We have done you no harm."

Once in the land with the hope of military support to hold it on the basis of the concessions obtained, the British maneuvered next to get rid of the brave Matabele who stood ready to put down any invasion of their local rights except as provided in the concession as they understood it. The Chartered Company desired to recoup from the extensive investments in establishing its claim to the frontier and de-

LOBENGUELA BETRAYED

sired to assure the large rush of settlers desiring new homes and the hidden mineral wealth of Matabeleland. Lobenguela had long restrained his impis, but could not hold them in check in case of an effort to take over the whole territory. Yet for the final blow at native authority only an excuse was needed.

The desired pretext came when some of the impis of Matabeleland, sent to suppress a local chief, attacked at Victoria, it was claimed, some of the Mashona servants of the British. Jameson, still representing Rhodes, decided this was excuse enough to clear out every vestige of native authority. He was in a position to play off one native against the other, for along with one of the company's force of 200 went 225 Bechuana, and 2,000 natives led by Khama, the chief of the Bamangwato; and two columns of settlers advanced upon Bulawayo from the northeast. These forces joined on the western plateau, and on the Shangani River they met the Matabele October 25, 1893.

With their primitive weapons the Matabele fought like men and died like heroes in the last great stand of the African for his native land. With machine guns the invaders mowed down so many of the Africans that they had to withdraw. The Matabele attacked the invaders again at Imbembesi on the first of November, but there the machine guns had the same telling effect. Hearing of this disaster, Lobenguela burned his great kraal and abandoned Bulawayo. The British advanced into the city, and undertook to capture the chief, but they failed in the pursuit. A party of thirty men endeavoring to capture him were cut off by his rearguard and annihilated.

Chapter X

MOSHESH

The career of Moshesh, another distinguished South African, was also somewhat influenced by the career of Chaka. Moshesh was the builder of an African nation of comparatively recent formation. The nucleus for this development came out of the circumstances incident to the dislocation of tribes battled on one side by Chaka's forces and on the other by those of Moselikatze. The latter had broken away from Chaka and had led 15,000 of his soldiers to fight their way across the Drakensberg Mountains, encountering both Boers and hostile natives on their way through the Transvaal to what was later called Matabeleland. Battled on the right and the left, many of these hard-pressed tribes were exterminated or forced under their sub-chiefs into the areas to be merged with others. The Basuto nation under the guiding hand of Moshesh was one of the two exceptions of those who survived this disorder and internal strife.[1]

Moshesh was born about 1790. He was the son of Chief Monaheng, or Mokachane, a great hunter and village chief of the royal Bakwena line. Moshesh early came under the influence of his cousin, Mohlomi, a wise man who greatly influenced his life. One day in an interview with this seer the latter prophesied that some day Moshesh would rule men, and he cautioned the youth thus: "Learn then to know them. And when thou judgest, let thy judgments be just."

Moshesh, following this precept, developed into a man of vision. He saw the world from a point of view different

---

[1] Moshesh's life may be further studied in Dr. J. Stewart's *Dawn in the Dark Continent*, *The Encyclopedia Britannica*, Lagden's *The Basutos*, and S. M. Molema's *The Bantu*.

from that of most African chiefs. Moshesh was humane, truthful, sagacious, peaceful, and forward-looking in the hope of a better day for Africa. This millenium he thought would come, not in the continuation of self-exterminating wars, but in learning from others the best of their culture to unite with the best in that of Africa for a regeneration and growth unto a higher stature. His intellectual gifts and diplomacy placed him above most of the Europeans with whom he had to deal in later years. His character showed a rare combination of vigor and moderation. In his first contest with the Zulus he repulsed them but treated them so generously that they refrained from further raids. He tried later thus to deal with Europeans, but they reacted to the contrary.

Moshesh began his career during the troublous years of 1821-1825. He received as followers the remnant of decimated Bakwena tribes under subchiefs and those Zulus who had the courage to break away from Chaka and make haste to more settled quarters. Moshesh then emigrated to the all but impregnable mountain fastnesses to Thaba Bosigo, in what is now called Basutoland. He had been attacked in his first home at Butho-Buthe by Sekenyela and the Batlakoa and had led his people farther to a place secure from raids and forays. At Thaba Bosigo his problem of settlement was not difficult, for the country had as inhabitants only some small Becoana tribes and Bushmen clans; and when they were once established there no aggressor could easily dislocate them. The Matabele once tried to charge these heights and dispossess the Basuto, but Moshesh drove them back in defeat. To appease their hunger and to show his humanity he sent them cattle to feed them on their way home.

Other tribes repaired to this mountain stronghold, and Moshesh received them. Although many of them were Zulus, the majority were Bechuana and tended to conform more closely to the culture of the latter by whom the others

MOSHESH

were absorbed. Their language, for example, was a modification of the Bechuana tongue which became known as Sesotho or Sesuto. The people called themselves Basotho, or Basutho (Basuto); but, since their neighbors had to go north to reach them they were called the Makosie, or Northerners. Once united, the Basuto did not experience the internal strife which often developed in African nations. They were doubtless held together by the fear of being conquered or destroyed by their warlike neighbors from whom they had taken flight. From the founding of the nation there seemed to be the rule to bear the ills which they had rather than run the risk of plunging into greater troubles by rebellion. The Basuto had to look out always for the dangers from their disputes with the Barolongs, whose tribes centered around Thaba Ncho as their capital. Next there were the Boers ever ready to penetrate areas occupied by the tribes to take both land and cattle, and to enslave the natives. This policy became more pronounced after 1836, when the Great Trek took place north of the Orange River under Hendrik Potgieter. During the years of quietude, however, Moshesh had cultivated the arts of peace and built up an industrious, progressive, and loyal people. They finally attained a homogeneity far removed from the diversity of elements from which they sprang.

The migrating Boers offered the first test of this new nation. These interlopers after pushing their way into the native areas harassed the Basuto beyond the point of endurance. To justify their aggression the Boers concocted all sorts of fabrications which they published to the world as a vindication of their land-grabbing and man-stealing. Since these Boers were escaping from the domination of the British at the Cape and were their enemies, the Basuto asked the British for help against the attackers. The British, however, failed to respond favorably. At that time the settlers at the Cape and the colonial office in London saw no advantage for themselves in such an intervention.

In 1840 the Basuto and the Boers met in battle to settle their differences, but a decisive victory was not claimed for either party, and subsequent events complicated matters. Endeavoring to play one European element against the other, Moshesh concluded in 1841 a treaty with the British through Sir George Napier of the Cape, bringing his country under a sort of British protection. The agreement from the British point of view meant merely to exploit the country through the representative sent to the court of Moshesh. The troubles with the Baralongs of Thaba Ncho and with the Boers continued in spite of this arrangement, and the British actually betrayed the Basuto in giving no support. The Basuto, then, took up arms on their own behalf. This effort at self-defense set the British against the Basuto.

The justice of their cause, however, is shown by reports on the situation at this time issued by French missionaries whom Moshesh had invited to his country. Referring to Moshesh's enemies, especially the Boers, one of these missionaries mentioned ''an unwarranted disregard of their rights, the past history, the different habits, the relative position and the respective wants of the native population.'' ''This,'' he said, ''had led the natives to suspect the Government of a disposition to divide and rule. . . . Natural rights, past grievances, past benefits, past engagements and treaties, feudal allegiances, kindred ties, family bonds have been discarded and overlooked.''

Drawn into the dispute between the Basuto and Boers in 1851, the British proclaimed its sovereignty over Orange Free State; and, re-enforced· by the Baralong of Thaba Ncho in keeping with the custom of setting one tribe against another, the British attacked and defeated the Basuto under Moshesh at Vierfort. The Basuto, however, had not been conquered. This reverse had merely aggravated these natives, and they prepared for the British when they invaded their country again with another army under Sir George Cathcart in 1852. The British advanced in three columns.

One got into ambush and had to beat a hasty retreat, another the Basuto repulsed in attack, and the third had to hide in the rocks until retirement was possible the next morning. Moshesh had defeated the British humiliatingly and forced them to leave his country.

And so, the British discovered a new nation in Africa, a formidable type of African with whom they would have to reckon. In the negotiations which followed Cathcart said, ''Another advantage I gained was in the acquaintance with Chief Moshesh, whom I found to be not only the most enlightened but the most upright Chief in South Africa, and one in whose good faith I put the most perfect confidence, and for whom, therefore, I have a sincere respect and regard.''

Knowing that the Boers could secure arms through the British in Cape Colony and Natal, and in the final outcome would be better prepared for war than Africans, Moshesh sought to treat the British generously. He hoped they might follow the example of the Zulus who, appreciating the humanity of Moshesh when he had defeated them, refrained from further raids. Moshesh, therefore, advised the British to withdraw because, although defeated, their expedition had been sufficiently punitive in what they had taken and destroyed. Peace was made with the British in 1852 at the conclusion of the first Basuto war.

During these years of numerous troubles the British administration in South Africa was grappling with the problem of maintaining its authority over the trekker republics and the consequent matter of federation for economy in carrying out a native and foreign policy. The natives, facing dispersion to inhospitable parts where they were destined to die of starvation, could not be restrained from disputing authority in areas where they had long lived. The chief trouble in his case, however, was that of the Basuto with the Boers of the Orange Free State. The Boers could always find some complaint to justify their aggression; but as Moshesh once aptly said, the only sin he had committed

MOSHESH MAKES READY

was that he possessed a good and fertile country. The British had tried to wash their hands of frontier troubles by renouncing in 1854 their sovereignty over the Orange Free State, but this merely left the Boers free so to press upon the natives as to make them a menace to the British frontier. The Boer settlers had long since taken up the lands of the Basuto on the Caledon River and defied the natives to reclaim them. President Boshof, of the Orange Free State, undertook in February, 1858, to check the "intrusion" of the natives into what they considered their own territory. Charging the Basuto with stealing Boer cattle, he issued a proclamation that any further effort in this direction would be considered an act of war.

This was the very position into which Moshesh desired to force Boshof at the time that he felt that the Free State would not be able to defend the Boer claims. These Boers were allied with one of Moshesh's enemies, a chief named Jan Letele, but they could not expect encouragement from the British to whom they were hostile. Moshesh, therefore, urged further encroachment upon that territory rather than restrain his followers as the head of the Orange Free State proclaimed that he should do. War consequently broke out in 1858.

The Free Staters made the most of their precarious situation, but with their thinly settled frontier they were unable to repel attacks of the brave and formidable Basuto. The Free Staters, moreover, had practically no funds in the treasury with which to finance such a war and had no hope of income from import duties since those went to the British ports through which their goods came into the Orange Free State. Boshof thought as the last resort to effect an alliance with the Transvaal or the Cape; and, since the government at the Cape refused, his only resort was the Transvaal. Governor Grey, of Cape Colony, did not like any such union as it would be prejudicial to the interests of the Cape, and he succeeded in blocking that plan by threatening to modify

the Convention of Bloemfontein which was a conditional
withdrawal of British sovereignty over the Free State.
In the meantime, Moshesh was making headway against
the Free State, meeting raid with raid and attack with attack. Yet he realized at the same time that, should the
union with either the Cape or the Transvaal be effected,
he would be in the precarious position of losing all rather
than the particular territory which he contested. Moshesh
agreed, then, to yield to Sir George Grey's negotiation for
peace between his nation and the Orange Free State. This
settlement, however, worked out to the detriment or the actual victor in the war in the so-called Treaty of Aliwal. The
British authorities were not seeking to build up any great
native state. What they were trying to do was merely to
prevent their enemies, the Boers, from profiting unduly by
acquisition of territory which they hoped some day would
fall into the hands of the British. The Boers not only
had grabbed a large portion of Basutoland but had carried
away 40,000 cattle, 5,000 horses and 60,000 sheep as a war
indemnity. They took, moreover, two sons of Moshesh as
hostages and expelled from Basutoland the French missionaries who had espoused the cause of the natives.

Following the Basuto War of 1858, came other difficulties. The question of land occupied by the settlers and
claimed by the natives as theirs became a problem of great
concern. In his advancing years, moreover, Moshesh proved
to be less efficient in restraining his subchiefs and their
fighting men from rushing further across the so-called frontier to defend their claims. Yet the situation was so deplorable that the natives had to act in fighting extermination. The crowding of horses and cattle on an area inadequate for pasturing animals and feeding the natives left
them no other remedy but war. At the same time on the
Free State side there was an eagerness to enter upon land-
grabbing by furthering a scheme for the extension of that
frontier. Cattle stealing and raids of both sides character-

ized the prolonged dispute in this area as the ruthless traders and border chieftains disputed the territory between them.

The Basutos were great sufferers in this case, however, because the hostile chief, Jan Letele, was stealing the cattle of the Basutos and disposing of them to white thieves who rushed these animals across the frontier into the Free State and sold them. Both Pretorius, the head of the Free State at this time, and Moshesh, therefore, appealed again to the Cape to take measures to improve the situation. Governor Wodehouse refused to aid Moshesh. The Free State had effected a union with the Transvaal, but it did not at first prove to be of any consequence.

Finally, when Pretorius had passed out of the presidency and had been succeeded by Brand as head of the Orange Free State, Governor Wodehouse was called upon to arbitrate the Basuto Border dispute. The decision awarded to the Free State a large portion of the disputed land which the white pioneers had claimed. Instead of settling matters this unsettled everything. Hostility developed among the Basutos, and they could not be restrained from open war which broke out in June, 1865.

The economic condition of the Transvaal and even that at the Cape at that time was not such as to justify any aggressive policy against the natives. While the European settlers of various South African republics were very much stirred up to enter the war against the Basutos because of continuous raids, it was realized that at the same time the natives themselves both in Kaffraria and Basutoland were likewise moved. The trouble with the Zulus had not yet ended although their power apparently had been broken. Yet the High Commissioner, insisting on neutrality, prevented volunteers of the Cape and Natal from interfering in the Basuto war.

In the meantime the forces of the Free State were doing the best they could in trying to carry the Basuto strongholds of Berea and Vechtkop, but they had failed to gain possession of the key fortress of Thaba Bosigo. A Transvaal commando gave the Free Staters some assistance in helping the campaign against these positions. The best they could do, however, was to make the border uninhabitable for both the natives and the settlers. The Boers, nevertheless, continued their attacks north with increasing vigor and set themselves to dispossess the Basuto altogether or force Moshesh to agree to their overlordship.

Moshesh, however, well knew that he could not afford to fall into such cruel hands. Fearing that the Free Staters might triumph in the conflict and ultimately carry out their plan, Moshesh again appealed to the British Government to annex the territory. Governor Wodehouse referred the matter to the Secretary of State and offered at the same time his mediation in the combat. Because of an extensive destruction of the crops and of the cattle of the Free State at the border, the Basuto faced a menace of famine for the winter and therefore had to enter upon negotiations. The settlement, then, worked out disastrously to the Basuto in the Treaty of Thaba Bosigo in April, 1866. Moshesh lost half of the fertile land of his country and had to be content with accepting a smaller area into which his nation had to be crowded.

For this reason almost before the treaty could be signed the natives began to violate the agreement. The pangs of hunger and starvation faced them in their cramped quarters. The natives were driven out of the border territory again, but some provision had to be made in offering the Basutos land for reserves in that disputed area. The Basutos, moreover, repudiated the treaty and again appealed to the British for annexation, a thing that the British Government had repeatedly frowned down upon because of the increasing expense which the Government thought would be involved. Then, there was a dispute as to whether Basutoland should be annexed to Natal or to the Cape. Wodehouse finally proclaimed the annexation to the Cape on

March 12, 1868. The Free Staters protested and could be satisfied by the British only when they awarded the republic a large strip of Basutoland in the Convention of Aliwal in February, 1869. This, however, was dubbed by the missionaries such a robbery that, under fire also from the Aborigines Protection Society, Parliament came almost to the point of producing a crisis; but the Secretary of State ratified the agreement in March, 1870, the very month when Moshesh died. The British functionary did not want to extend these annexations but had to do so to keep ahead of the Boers.

The reduced area of the Basuto forced upon them a new economy. They no longer had sufficient land for pasturage and thereafter had to abandon cattle raising to some extent and devote more time to agriculture. Numbers of these natives had to leave their tribal areas and either work for wages on the farms of Europeans or serve them as laborers in industry. The discovery of gold on the Tati River in 1867 made it seem desirable to force natives into crowded areas from which they would be starved into industry.

Moshesh was succeeded by his son, Letsie. No disturbance of the peace marked his reign except the War of Guns which broke out in 1880. The trouble grew out of extending to Basuto the Disarmament Act of Cape Colony with the hope of annexing the remaining territory and depriving the chiefs of power. The immediate cause of this extension of the Disarmament Act was the formidable rising of the Quthing Chief, Morosi, in the southern district of Basutoland. It required Cape troops a long time to secure the strongholds and restore peace, for the application of this act was fraught with the greatest danger. The Basuto were like the liberty-loving Swiss of the mountains. They were very skeptical of any movement to encroach upon their natural rights. Basuto laborers, returning with guns from the diamond fields, moreover, had encouraged the nation to believe that they could repeat the demonstration of their military prowess

shown on the battlefields of Berea and Isandhlwana and drive
the whites out of that part of Africa. On this policy, too, the British were divided. The party of
the opposition of the Cape Government opposed the effort,
and the Aborigines Protection Society in London added a
firm protest. On the side of the Basuto spoke out friendly missionaries who urged the natives not to give up their
guns. Lord Kimberly, again in charge of the Colonial Office, repudiated all responsibility, but acquiesced in the use
of force to compel disarmament. To start the conflagration,
Spriggs, the Cape Premier, doubled the hut tax and proposed
to confiscate a part of the Quthing territory as an indemnity
for the expenses of the prolonged campaign against Morosi.
While Letsie, the Paramount Chief, was willing thus to agree
in order to keep the peace, Lerothodi, his son, led the masses
into rebellion in September, 1880. Unfortunately for the
British, moreover, the rebellion extended to Griqualand,
east to the Tembus, and other tribes south of the Drakensberg mountains.

Divided at home, the British did not present a bold front
in battle. In the mountain fastnesses the British met with
one reverse after another with their troops cut to pieces by
the Basuto. How to get out of the trap the British did not
know. Reverses which they had suffered at the hand of
the Basuto had struck a severe blow at white prestige in
South Africa. The British finally extricated themselves
from this position before the modern world and patched up
some kind of peace in April, 1881. The Basuto promised to
give up their guns. but only a few old, practically worn-
out muskets were turned over, and the British did not dare
exact any war indemnity. Sprigg's Government fell, and
Thomas Scanlen, his successor, denounced both the Disarmament Act and the Robinson Award which imposed a fine
of cattle on the Basuto.

The Cape Government now had succeeded to the position of the Boers in antagonizing the Basuto. After this trouble, however, the Basuto nation was placed under the domination of the Imperial Government which assured more liberty than when attached to the Cape. The British Government had thus reversed its decision not to extend its authority over the lands of the interior. If they had not the Boers would have acquired that territory. The European nations at that time, moreover, were on the eve of the rush into the interior of Africa.

That the Basuto contrived to exist in the midst of such harassing enemies on all sides was due to the foresight and statesmanship of their founder and leader. Moshesh was a wise ruler who adhered to the principles of equity and justice. He believed in sound laws, education, the advancement of trade, the protection of property, and the abolition of the liquor traffic imported from Europe. In all this he was unselfish. He labored not for personal aggrandizement but for the public good. All these things he accomplished as an animist. He welcomed missionaries to his country, but did not become a Christian until near the end of his career. He said that he would watch the introduction of Christianity as one does an egg until it hatches.

Letsie, Moshesh's successor, died in 1891 and was followed by his son, Lerothodi, under whom the people made permanent progress in peace. The Basuto were restrained by Great Britain from striking at their former enemies, the Boers, during the South African War. Nothing disturbed the peace thereafter until the death of Lerothodi in 1905. He was succeeded by his son, Letsie II, who reigned only eight years. In 1913 Griffiths, a Christian chief, became the ruler and showed in his administration of affairs some of those desirable qualities found in Moshesh. In the First World War the Basuto, through Griffiths, offered England men to fight her battles in Europe and contributed 52,000 pounds to the war fund.

CHAPTER XI

KHAMA II

Moshesh was the chief factor in the development of the Basuto nation. These people belonged to the first division of the Bantu stock in South Africa composed of both the Bechuana and the Basuto. The Bechuanas comprised the Bakalahari, Batlaping, Barolong, Bakwena, Bahurutse, Bamangwato, and Bangwaketse. These tribes succeeded each other in their migrations southwesterly into South Africa; but with the exception of the Batlapings' attack on the Transvaal and the Free State Boers in 1857 and the Basutos' stand against the interlopers these natives did not offer much resistance to the invader. They did little to stop the raids of the Zulus or the Matabele and the Mantatisi hordes.

The Bamangwato, however, offer a slight exception to this rule. They reached their highest development under Khama II. This leader and builder was the son of Sekhoma, who was the third son of Khari, a descendant of Ngwato, the founder of these people. Mathibe succeeded Ngwato, and then came Khama I when a part of his father's people went with his brother to found the Batauana. At the close of the reign of Khari Sekhoma, the third son undertook to obtain the entire inheritance by disposing of his brothers. After dispatching one he found an insurmountable obstacle in his brother Macheng, who took refuge among Moselikatze's warriors and returned with sufficient power to depose Sekhoma; but Macheng became so despotic that the people restored Sekhoma.

An epoch was reached when Khama II was born to Sekhoma about 1830. This young man came under the influence of missionaries and embraced their faith. He did not please his father in adhering to Christian living, which was considered an undesirable innovation. Khama was accordingly driven out of the country, but these differences were adjusted, and he contrived to return and succeed his father. Under Khama some power of resistance developed. When Macheng returned the second time to claim the throne the people were so well satisfied that they did not take his claim seriously.

The people prospered and developed one of the most progressive areas on the continent with their chief town of 30,-000. This was the largest purely African settlement on the continent. Khama's father could drive back the Matabele army and Khama himself inflicted heavy losses on their forces in 1862 and 1870. Other tribes unable to offer the invader such resistance came to the Bamangwato for protection. This made the nation still more powerful, for Khama, unlike the other Bechuana chiefs, welcomed these people as fellow-subjects and equals rather than as slaves. Moselikatze said of him, "Khama is a man. There is no other man among the Bechuana."[1]

Greater troubles came in the disputes with the land-grabbing Boers. After the discovery of gold at Tati in 1867 by Karl Mauch and of iron and copper in Mashona in 1868, the Boers had other reasons for expanding into that area. From 1865 to 1885 the Bamangwato were harassed by these invaders who were migrating from the British, whom they disliked. Khama, then, could play one European against the other. During these years the British had no definite policy of taking over the interior, and they uttered many protestations and sometimes came to the rescue of the natives. Yet Khama seemed to have had no thought of uniting Africans

---

[1] Khama is treated in most of the works of missionaries who served in his part of Africa. Hepburn has entitled his work *Twenty Years in Khama's Country*. Bent in his *The Ruined Cities of Mashonaland* pays Khama high tribute. Khama's record is interwoven in all comprehensive histories of South Africa.

KHAMA

for Africa. He was satisfied with keeping peace within his restricted area. At the time of Piet Grobler's venturing into disputed territory after having negotiated that infamous treaty with Lobenguela Khama's forces attacked and killed him, a deed for which Khama later had to compensate. Yet in the destruction of Lobenguela by the British Chartered Company's forces Khama assisted in leading 2,000 of his soldiers to make the attack.

When hard pressed by the Boers, Khama sent the British Government in 1876 an appeal to come to his rescue. These pioneering Boers intended to annex the Bamangwato to the Transvaal. Khama said in referring to the Boers, ' Their actions are cruel among us black people. We are like commodity to them. They sell us and our children. . . There are three things which distress me very much—war, selling people, and drink. All these things I shall find in the Boers, and it is these things which destroy people to make an end of them in the country. The custom of the Boers has always been to cause people to be sold, and today they are still selling people.''

This appeal from Khama, coming at about the same time that Montisioa, of the Baralong tribe was asking the British for similar aid against the Boers, doubtless helped to change the British African policy of non-intervention in native affairs. The politicians of Cape Colony, ever antagonistic to the Boers, supported the policy of intervention and the petitions were answered by the Warren Expedition in 1878 and 1885 into the heart of Bechuanaland. The country became British and in the end about what it would have been if the Boers had conquered it.

Khama had neither experience nor history to guide him in dealing with the Europeans. He finally accepted as the truth the words of the missionaries who preached a more intelligent manifestation of God than the fetishism of Africa. He did not know from history that these Christians professed Christ as their ideal only with their lips while substituting their program of racial autocracy as their supreme divinity, or god of gods. Khama's people and other Africans learned later by experience that in the final analysis one European master is about as undesirable as the other. The British granted him considerations not accorded any other African, chiefly for the reason that he preferred the domination of the British to that of the Boers. The British, however, had no special interest in the natives except so far as they could be used under Khama as a means to an end. A few missionaries established in that area schools and hospitals which showed what could be done to bring these people the benefits of modern culture, but the masses in this once most highly favored part of Africa have been left in a condition not far removed from that obtaining when the Boers prior to the establishment of the Union of South Africa had full sway in dealing with the natives. Since that time the expanding Boers have ever tried to enforce their policy as a national program for the natives in parts where they were once supposedly liberally treated by the British.

For thus turning his country over to the British and the exploiters approaching in the guise of Christians Khama has been highly praised by the economic imperialists who have thereby profited. Other chiefs who stood their ground like men were called rascals, thieves, and murderers while Khama passed as a sober ruler, an honest man, a Christian gentleman ruling over a people whom he had taught honesty, the security of property, temperance, the art of peace, law, and justice. Bent, in paying Khama a high tribute on pages 23 to 27 of his *"The Ruined Cities of Mashonaland,"* recorded this estimate:

"I must say I looked forward with great interest to seeing a man with so wide a reputation for integrity and enlightenment as Khama has in South Africa. Somehow, one's spirit of scepticism is on the alert on such occasions, especially when a Negro is the case in point; and I candidly admit that I advanced towards Palapwe fully prepared to find the chief of the Ba-Mangwato a rascal and a hypocrite, and I left his capital, after a week's stay there, one of his most fervent admirers.

"Not only has Khama himself established his reputation for honesty, but he is supposed to have inoculated all his people with the same virtue. No one is supposed to steal in Khama's country. He regulates the price of the goat you buy; and the milk vendor dare not ask more than the regulation price, nor can you get it for less. One evening, on our journey from Shoshong to Palapwe, we passed a loaded wagon by the roadside, with no one to guard it save a dog; and surely, we thought, such confidence as this implies a security for property rare enough in South Africa. . . .

"Everything in Khama's country is conducted with the rigour—one might almost say bigotry—of religious enthusiasm. The chief conducts in person native services, twice every Sunday, in his large round *kotla,* at which he expects a large attendance. He stands beneath the traditional tree of justice, and the canopy of heaven, quite in a patriarchal style. . . .

"The two acts, however, which more than anything else display the power of the man, and perhaps his intolerance, are these: Firstly, he forbids all his subjects to make or drink beer. Anyone who knows the love of a kaffir for his porridge-like beer, and his occasional orgies, will realise the power one man must have to stop this in a whole tribe. Even the missionaries have remonstrated with him on this point, representing the measure as too strong; but he replies, 'Beer is the source of all quarrels and disputes. I will stop it.' Secondly, he has put a stop altogether to the existence of witch doctors and their craft throughout all the Ba-Mangwato —another instance of his force of will, when one considers that the national religion of the Bechuana is merely a belief in the existence of good and bad spirits which haunt them and act on their lives. All members of other neighbouring tribes are uncomfortable if they are not charmed by their

witch doctor every two or three days. . . . On one occasion
he did what I doubt if every English gentleman would do.
He sold a horse for a high price, which died a few days
afterwards, whereupon Khama returned the purchase money,
considering that the illness had been acquired previous to
the purchase taking place. . . .

"There is something Teutonic in Khama's imperial discipline, but the Bechuana are made of different stuff to the
Germans. They are by nature peaceful and mild, a race
with strong pastoral habits, who have lived for years in dread
of Matabele raids; consequently their respect for a chief
like Khama—who has actually on one occasion repulsed the
foe, and who has established peace, prosperity, and justice
in all his borders—is unbounded, and his word is law.

"Khama pervades everything in his town. He is always
on horseback, visiting the fields, the stores, and the outlying
kraals. He has a word for everyone; he calls every woman
'my daughter' and every man 'my son'; he pats the little
children on the head. He is a veritable father of his people,
a curious and unaccountable outcrop of mental power and
integrity amongst a degraded and powerless race. . . . Perhaps he may be said to be the only Negro living whose
biography would repay the writing."

Khama's contribution was purely temporary—one growing
out of a misconception of the situation dominated by men
who had come to Africa in the name of God but served the
economic imperialists in expropriating the country. His life
offers the African little to inspire him toward regaining a
place among men. Khama may be duplicated many times in
the history of the Negro in contact with the ever aggressive
Caucasian.

Khama himself lived to see what could be expected from
the British to whom he had given his country. Although
lauded as the most famous and respected chief in South
Africa, when he was entertained at a luncheon by the Duke
of Westminster while on a visit to England in 1895 a wave

KHAMA IN THE ROLE OF THE GOOD

of indignation and disgust swept over South Africa. The thought of thus recognizing a Bantu ruler as the equal of an Englishman of rank was so revolting that the Caucasian claims of superiority as a necessity for race supremacy had to be asserted and reiterated.

Khama continued loyal to his superiors in spite of inclinations to honor him less. He declared his undying loyalty to the King of Great Britain during the First World War and sent one thousand pounds as a token of his appreciation. He doubtless had reason to be thankful that his country had not been overrun by the Boers who would have exterminated the Bamangwato or reduced them to serfdom. During these years his people had been able to live in comparative peace when they could make progress along agricultural and educational lines in the hope of a still better day. At the present time, however, this day does not seem to be dawning. The country, like other such protectorates, is now administered by the Imperial Government represented in South Africa by a High Commissioner.

Although the Bamangwato are not yet governed from Bloomfontein, the Boers now incorporated into the Union of South Africa and dominating the policy of that country toward the natives, still hope to see their plans carried out in that area. In our day the Boer and the British are one in reducing the natives to serfdom. Khama's intentions were good. He was permitted to see some advantage in the cooperation which he had given the exploiter, but his successors have felt the heel of oppression. Since Khama's day many changes have been made so as to reduce the sub-chiefs to marionettes under the representative of the British. No one in Bechuanaland is recognized there as paramount chief, a position of dignity which passed apparently with Khama when he died in February, 1923.

Chapter XII

IN EAST AFRICA

Into the area opened up by the defeat of Lobenguela went numerous European settlers and smaller trading corporations which were the forerunners of Rhodes' South African Company taking over the land and minerals of the Mashonas and the Matabeles. This part of the continent has been organized by the Imperial Government as Southern Rhodesia. Going north across the Zambesi one finds Northern Rhodesia, which Rhodes and his Company also once owned but later turned over to the British Empire. The natives of this area have been depopulated by sleeping sickness and forced labor on the plantations and in the mines, but the Barotse, founded by their distinguished Chief Lewanika, still exist on an area by themselves under a nominal paramount chief who is permitted to govern in local matters according to native customs under a system of so-called indirect rule. The Barotse have a national school at Mongu.

Running along the eastern border of Northern Rhodesia is Nyasaland, which on the east is bounded by Lake Nyasa. This is considered a protectorate under indirect rule, but in reality it is a crown colony. David Livingstone was the first missionary to reach these parts. For what he had done in opening up that part of the continent Scotchmen established a mission there in his honor in 1876. Around this as a nucleus they built up a center of economic and political importance in the region and called it Blantyre. Backed by British capital, traders from this center launched the African Lakes Company with sufficient missionary backing to justify the provision that some of the income from the enterprise would go to religious work. The saving of the natives' souls went along peaceably with robbing them of their property for awhile, but the infamous scheme incurred so much displeasure of both the Yao and the Arabs on the grounds that conflict with the Company followed, and one missionary was killed. This upset both evangelism and trade to the extent that the exploiting corporation suffered. The Portuguese, invading the territory about this time, decided to annex it, and only an ultimatum from the British Government in 1890 saved it for the Empire, and its "protection" was extended to the country the next year. The area was then pacified, with Sir Harry Johnston as High Commissioner. The African Lakes Company was absorbed by the South Africa Company, which acquired in the transaction almost three million acres of land in Nyasaland, of which the chiefs had been robbed.

Tanganyika and Uganda in the east constitute another area in which grave questions developed. The Germans took over that of Tanganyika against the most hostile manifestations of the natives to the contrary. Once in possession after five years of struggle culminating in the Maji-Maji Rebellion in 1905, the Germans reduced it to order in their characteristic fashion—expropriating the land, shooting down hostile Africans, and forcing the natives to labor as serfs.

Uganda, on the other hand, although handicapped by religious strife imported by Catholic and Protestant missionaries and an unjust allotment of land, is considered one of the most prosperous and advanced parts of Africa. It is made up of such African states as Baganda, Bunyoro, Ankole and Toro and inhabited by a prosperous Hamitic-Bantu people called the Japanese of Africa. Because of their romantic history and advanced culture these people could not be easily conquered.[1]

The Baganda nation was founded by Kintu, their first

---

[1] The German colonization in East Africa may be traced in the works on the partition of Africa already cited. George Padmore's *How Britain Rules Africa*, however, gives additional facts with respect to the natives in discussing Tanganyika and Uganda.

king. Under him and his successors the country grew by
conquest and was organized along feudal lines of a military
order. The king was known as the Kabaka, the lord of the
entire realm, and others held land under him. Six hundred
kings had sat on the throne, but the greatest of them was
Mutesa Mukebya, the strong man and great statesman who
organized the conquest and developed an efficient army for
its defense.

The country was first made known by the exploration of
J. A. Grant and John Speke from the expedition headed by
Richard Burton in 1862. Then came H. M. Stanley not long
thereafter. Protestant missionaries followed Stanley in two
years and soon came the Catholic missionaries. Trouble
along sectarian lines developed at once. One sect wanted the
country to be Protestantized and the other Catholicized; and
to complicate matters further the Arabs and their proselytes
set out to Mohammedanize it.

Mutesa, the king, refused to accept any of the three faiths
and remained loyal to his fetishism, as an animist would be
expected to do under the circumstances. The successor of
Mutesa, his son Muanga, distrusted Europeans who at that
time were grabbing all of Africa they could. To prevent invasion of his country he declared the frontiers closed and
ordered his soldiers not to let any European touch his soil.
Bishop Hannington, who ignored the order and crossed into
the country in 1885, was killed. The Christians in holy
horror, then, organized a revolt against the fearless Muanga,
who in turn ordered the slaughter of all Christians and the
suppression of all missionaries.

Open war broke out between the Christians and animists.
The Christians, when first defeated, retreated to Ankole,
where they were reenforced and from which they made an
attack on Muanga, now supported by the Mohammedans in
his land. The Christians, well supplied with modern military equipment and led by Charles Sokes, an Irish Catholic
to the manner born, captured Mengo, the capital of Uganda,

and divided the territory between the Catholics and Protestants.

The matter was not thereby settled, however, for the Christians failed to work in harmony. They had wrangled too long before. The Catholics started the next conflagration with a declaration of war. The Mohammedans, rallying in behalf of Muanga, pressed the missionaries so hard that they appealed to the British East Africa Company for help in a terrible crisis. This brought a military detachment under Sir Frederick Jackson, who later had the assistance of Lord Lugard. The Catholics were defeated. The situation then developed into a contest between the British East Africa Company and the German East Africa Company, represented by Karl Peters. The Catholics, angered because of defeat by the British, espoused the cause of the Germans. The slaughter of the Protestants was then possible, but Captain Lugard appeared with troops and prevented it. This action nevertheless angered the opponents to the extent that actual war broke out in 1892.

The Germans, however, did not press matters because of having had a friendly settlement with the British in the Treaty of Heligoland in 1890, and the Catholics were defeated. British Sudanese troops later pacified the factions. This was all being done by the British East Africa Company which found the situation too difficult, and the corporation appealed to the Imperial Government to intervene. In 1893 the Government took over the administration of the country and declared it a protectorate the following year.

Yet the matter had not thereby been adjusted from the natives' point of view. Muanga, who had taken refuge in German East Africa, returned in 1897, supported by those natives who had embraced Islam. He attacked the British military post at Luba in Bosoga and compelled them to retire. Next he proceeded to wage war upon his enemies in Bunyoro for about two years. In 1899, however, he was finally defeated, captured, and deported to the Seychelles.

Sir Harry Johnston, appointed as High Commissioner of the country, undertook its pacification by the usual promises to respect the rights of the natives. By the Uganda agreement in 1900 the native chiefs were to be recognized with specified legislative and judicial powers over their own people. The Kabaka of Baganda agreed to renounce duties or taxes paid him in return for an allowance of about $7,500 a year from the British who would thereafter use him as a sort of mouthpiece. And yet the ancient culture of the Baganda is preserved very much in its original form. The present Kabaka has been knighted by the British as Sir Daudi Chwa, the grandson of Mutesa. He is considered the highest authority among the natives. Chiefs under him exercise delegated authority and sub-chiefs act accordingly.

The nation still has also its legislative body called the Lukiko composed of eighty-nine members. The Kabaka has a cabinet composed of a prime minister, chief justice, chancellor of the exchequer, chamberlain and the like after the order of that of England. Either the King or the Prime Minister presides over this cabinet. Impressed with the exceptional advancement of these people, Lugard, the conqueror, had to say, "So far as we are aware, no purely pagan tribe in Africa, shut off from contact with surrounding peoples on a higher plane of civilization, has ever developed so extraordinary a social, political and even legal system as was found at the time of its discovery in Uganda."

In the position of Prime Minister Sir Apolo Kagawa served with distinction under three Kabakas, Mutesa, Muanga, and Sir Daudi Chwa. Sir Apolo Kagawa was enabled to render this service because of his knowledge of both the English and native customs. He was a well educated man and united the best afforded by the African and European civilizations. He inspired confidence by publishing in an official gazette the enactments of the parliament that every one might know and respect the law.

The native land question in Uganda has always been a difficult problem because of the collectivity ownership which implies that land belongs to the tribe and the chiefs cannot alienate it. The land question was further complicated by having also two other kinds of ownership—of private lands and of state lands held by the Kabaka as trustee of the nation as well as that held by the collectivity. In addition, time or custom brought into this already complicated system special areas controlled by the Kabaka as head of the nation, and lands held by monasteries and administered religiously. Land among the natives in Africa is not sold, but one parcel may be exchanged for another. The system looks feudal, but it is not exactly so, for the chiefs and subchiefs do not seem to have absolute right to the extent of alienation. The English have departed from this custom and granted lands in violation of what the natives considered their rights. Since land in Africa means the right or opportunity to earn a living, the life of the people being based upon the soil, it has been a source of much trouble, inconvenience, and injustice.

The efficient manner in which Sir Apolo Kagawa dealt with this and other difficult problems to the satisfaction of both natives and British won him the praise of all. This was accomplished in spite of the difficulty arising from the policy of Sir Harry H. Johnston. As High Commissioner of Uganda, he introduced private ownership of land to reward with holdings the native chiefs who helped to suppress the revolt of the Sudanese troops who were brought in in 1890 to stop the war between the religious factions. Some clarification and improvement of the land situation was effected by reformatory measures enacted in 1925 and 1927.

Kenya on the East Coast, long since touched by Asiatics who dominated almost that entire littoral, did not present much of a conflict between the natives and Europeans. The matter of obtaining standing ground in Kenya as well as in Tanganyika reduced itself mainly to the dispossession of the Arabs who had trading posts on the coast. The power of the Arabs had been recognized there from about 1820, when the British first began to trade in that quarter. A new stage in the development was reached about 1860, when as a result of the extinction of the slave trade through Europeans the traffic was reduced to what the Asiatics could do by overland routes to supply mainly Arabia, Persia and Turkey.[2]

The British Imperial East African Company conceded certain rights to the German Imperial East African Company in the Tanganyika area in 1886. The Germans agreed to respect the independence of Zanzibar and Pemba, organized and conducted at that time as sultanates which the British finally took over through the Company by paying the nominal functionary a stipulated amount. The Company gave up to the Imperial Government in 1895. The coastal region is called a protectorate but the inland, settled by such natives as the Masai, Kikuyu, and Kavirondo, has been made a colony.

This interior with fertile highlands of a mild climate which Europeans can endure has been made a white man's land. In violation of pledges made in the beginning the natives have been deprived of their lands and so dislocated as to be dependent upon the Europeans for whatever means of escape they may offer through serfdom or wage slavery. And at the same time the British who have expropriated these lands do not always develop them, but hold large areas for speculation. The natives have no means of existence except through the land, of which they do not have sufficient. Here, as Norman Leys has said, "Avarice allied with racial pride and domination showed least signs of shame, where common people were most despised and proved where the law was least regarded and loyalty least possible."

The natives started an agitation and sent memorial after

---

[2] Kenya has been the subject of numerous articles and books, but only a few of them like Norman Leys's *Kenya* and *The Last Chance in Kenya* show how the natives have been robbed of their lands. George Padmore's *How Britain Rules Africa* gives also the natives' point of view.

memorial to the British Government without avail. A revolt broke out, however, and the Colonial Office had to consider these complaints. As a result a revision of the land policy in 1924 allotted the natives additional land from the Crown domain. Another complaint that the law was being violated in taking the natives' lands was sent in 1926. The Kenya Legislative Council had to pass another land ordinance in 1930. And yet the natives are still being robbed and oppressed. Among the whites there is no public opinion to support the law requiring justice to the natives.

Harry Thuku, the leader of the revolt, incurred the ill will of the Empire for raising his voice too generally against such grievances as high taxes and forced labor in Kenya. The movement rapidly spread; the people stopped work. Thuku was arrested, and the people protested with an open revolt in a general strike in 1922. The soldiers fired upon the people and killed 150. Hundreds of others were apprehended, fined and imprisoned. The right to assemble and associate for their common good was abrogated, and Thuku was deported to Kismay on the Somali border. Since that time he has been permitted to return to pursue a more peaceful course along other lines, but the work which he started is being promoted by Jomo Kenyatta through the Kikuyu Central Association.

In the meantime Egypt and the smaller Barbary States had passed into European hands. Egypt, Mohammedanized long since and ruled by the Turks, had tended to become independent or autonomous under the Khedive; and what he could not effect personally toward deliverance from control of the Turks he did by international complications. Entangling Egypt by financial transactions, he made it necessary for the British to take over the country to protect the investments of their citizens who constituted the majority of the creditors of that once ancient land. The French, already dominant in certain Egyptian circles, were unwilling to concede the ascendancy of the British, and serious international problems grew out of the controversy. The English won the upper hand finally, however, by agreeing to the dominance of other European nations in North Africa and elsewhere on that continent. Morocco and Algeria, and even Tunis became in one way or another a zone in which French influence was paramount. Spain was able to hold only a small area. The Germans, challenging the right of France thus to retrieve by colonial expansion what she had lost in having to cede Alsace Lorraine to Germany in 1870, did not secure a firm foothold in North Africa, but did thereby force the French to recognize their right to dispossess the natives in Togoland, Cameroons, Southwest Africa, and Tanganyika.

Egypt was subdued, but Abyssinia, becoming more generally known after the reign of King Theodore, remained as an isolated area for which the imperialistic powers yearned. Menelik, who followed some years later, undertook to bring the Ethiopian centers into a sort of consolidation and to conquer others. Italy, hoping to gain influence at his court and to forestall both the English and the French, recognized his claims on Ethiopia, and signed with him a treaty in which the Italians contended he gave them a protectorate over Ethiopia. Disagreeing with this interpretation of the agreement, Menelik repudiated it altogether and met the indignant Italians at Adowa in 1896, when he decisively defeated them as the defender of his native land.

Italian influence was crushed in that quarter for two generations. Thereafter the English and French tended to influence the Ethiopian king, but mainly for commercial concessions, the most important of which was the right of the French to build a railroad from Djibouti to Addis Ababa. The English secured a recognition of their rights in the Lake Tana district where the white Nile takes its rise and gathers water for irrigation in Egypt. The influence of Italy showed some recovery in the international councils when in 1906 she was asked as one of a tripartite treaty to agree that neither France, nor England, nor Italy would invade

MENELIK

HAILE SELASSIE BEFORE THE LEAGUE OF NATIONS

Abyssinia without joint action. It was of some consequence that Italy could defeat Turkey in 1911 and expand
in Libya. Italy's influence rose again when in the First World
War she was secretly promised to be allowed to expand in
North East Africa. Since fortune brought the conflict to a
close with Ethiopia on the side of the allies they did not
have the audacity to carry out the secret agreement at the
expense of Ethiopia. Italy under Mussolini, however, in
defiance of the League of Nations, registered again his
claim by the conquest of Ethiopia in 1935-1936.[3]

---

[3] The international problems involved in the partition of Africa and
the effect of it on that continent may be adequately studied in such
works as Lamar Middleton's *Rape of Africa;* Sir Charles Lucas's *Partition of Africa;* Sir Edward Hertslet's *Map of Africa by Treaty;*
H. A. Gibbons' *New Map of Africa;* N. D. Harris's *Europe and Africa.*

Chapter XIII

HEROES IN OTHER ROLES

In the long era of so-called peace during which the conquerors have become drunk with the joys of exploitation, the native in his subordination has not been altogether without spokesmen. In South Africa where the situation has reached its worst stage Africans even there have registered their protest against the cruel regime. Native newspapers undertook to voice the sentiment of an oppressed people, but under such rigid censorship and with such a small clientele of natives educated according to modern standards these journals could not live long to tell the story. J. Tengo Jabavu with his long service as editor of the *Imvo Zaba Ntsundu* (*Opinions of the Brown People*) did not score any great victory for the lowly. Nor did the *Naledi ea Lesotho* (*The Star of Basutoland*), edited by A. Monyakuane, or the *Ilanga lase Natal* (*The Sun of Natal*) edited by John L. Dube in Zulu, or the *Abantu* or *Batho*, by Kuene and Soga at Johannesburg.

Another method sometimes productive of results was to send delegations to England to appeal directly to the Imperial Government, inasmuch as it was impossible to have the complaints of the natives transmitted intact through official colonial channels. These efforts tended to have diminishing success as the economic imperialists grew sufficiently influential to register their will at home with great force. Money talks now the language of the British Empire.

Still another device was that of publishing the truth to modern nations. The British who had professed to be going into Africa as the trustees of weaker peoples whose local rights they had promised to respect would be shamed, it was believed, to the extent of making some reforms in face of an indignant world. The extent of such achievement, however, is evident not by the results obtained, but rather by the more difficult method of estimating what the natives prevented from being enacted against them—a thing which cannot be accurately evaluated.

One of the first to use his talents to appeal to the reason of the oppressor was Casely Hayford of the Gold Coast. Educated in England as a barrister, he returned to the Gold Coast to cast his lot among his people. Learned in the law of the Empire and in that of the natives over whom it ruled, Hayford rendered his generation a great service. He settled at Sekondi, and as he developed in the law he extended his practice into other parts, thanks to the support received from both races. Never forgetting his people, however, he wrote considerably for the press on native affairs in West Africa until he became considerably known in liberal circles in both America and Europe.

Hoping to give his thought more force, Hayford entered upon the more serious task of producing books on the African situation. His *Gold Coast Native Institutions* and *Ethiopia Unbound* are well known for their brilliant style and informing presentation of the life and aspirations of the natives. These books at the same time, without being polemic, showed how necessary it is to understand the natives in order to deal properly with them. Hayford, above all, showed remarkable courage in exposing how the methods of the economic imperialists were destined to wreck rather than build up the loyalty of the natives. The author excoriated especially the capture and exile of former kings like Behanzin and Primpeh as productive of more harm than good.

Another African to choose the exposé method of improving the African situation was Solomon Plaatje, a Bantu. Under the heel of the exploiter in South Africa where the natives were deprived of their lands and forced into serfdom,

Plaatje tired of the appeal merely to the oppressor. He had little hope for believing that much could be accomplished even by resorting to the liberal circles in England. British statesmen had long since taken the position not to interfere in the affairs of the dominions of the Empire. This very thing, they said, caused the American Revolution. Plaatje believed, however, that by giving publicity to such an unjust law as the Native Land Act of 1910, the civilized world would rise up in holy horror as it had done in the case of the Belgian atrocities in the Congo and by public sentiment force a new policy. For a short period he published the *Tsala ea Batho* (*The People's Friend*). Plaatje next brought out in 1915 a book entitled *The Native Land Act*. He not only produced this work for this exposé but traveled and lectured toward this end both in Europe and America.

Plaatje was well received among friends of freedom, but no government took it upon itself to fight the battles of natives so far away. The United States scarcely remembered treating the Indians worse than the Bantu had been in South Africa, and the people of this country so love Great Britain from whom most of them sprang that they are not wont to oppose their former home country even when they know that it is wrong. The whites in the United States, busy segregating the Negroes at the same time, moreover, paid little attention to the appeal. The Negroes themselves did not see anything which they could do to relieve the natives in South Africa.

Of the African editors who did not yield to the pressure of the oppressor or the pangs of poverty H. Macaulay of the Gold Coast deserves honorable mention. Many times called into court and convicted of violating the law in his exposure of the inequalities and injustices daily imposed upon native Africans, he has been undaunted and unwavering. On emerging from a trouble of this sort, he would come out the next day with "God Save the King" at the top of his paper but under it a most scathing denunciation of the crimes of the conqueror and of the cowardice of those who would say nothing to the contrary. His paper gives a bold recital of the injustices of functionaries who misuse the law to bolster up a regime in defiance of their declaration of policies and laws which provide for fair play and equality for all. Macaulay's fearlessness and the courage shown by others like him have been the source of so much anxiety to the Europeans of the Gold Coast that they have sought to silence such voices with the law at hand; and, that having failed, they have endeavored to extend to West Africa the Sedition Law of South Africa. By this measure the natives have been deprived of free speech. Whatever their grievances there may be they have no means of voicing their sentiments to the contrary, and persons who might speak for them are not allowed to enter the country.

Ben N. Azikiwe, an African who recently felt the sting of this repression, is better known in the United States. He was educated at Howard University and at Columbia. For a while he taught history and political science at Lincoln University, but that conservative center, it has been said, could not stand his teachings. He left the United States, then, to work among his own people. His first service was to write a book, *Liberia*, to show that the great stir about slavery in that country was only a camouflage to justify interference in its affairs and probably the partition of the country. Other European nations operating in Africa were guilty of the same sort of forced labor; and the acts of enslavement charged to the account of Liberia were just as much the acts of Spain. Liberia had supplied laborers in good faith according to agreement, and Spain, instead of treating them as freemen, had reduced these Africans to forced labor in contravention of the agreement on which they were obtained.

The heroic service rendered by Azikiwe, however, has been his work as editor of the *African Morning Post* at Accra and of the *West African Pilot* at Lagos. In this effort he made a most favorable impression on the natives by his fearless championing of their cause. At the same time he struck terror to the hearts of the British minority in control, for natives of the Gold Coast and throughout West Africa exercise much more authority and enjoy more liberty than they can soon hope to have in South Africa. The British finally found what they considered a good case against Azikiwe. He was arrested and charged with sedition on the grounds that he had published in his paper an attack on the British in an article by a contributor entitled ''Has the African a God?'' The court convicted the editor and sentenced him to prison for six months. The case was appealed to a higher court, which reversed this conviction.

Later at his new post, editing the *West African Pilot* at Lagos, Azikiwe again incurred the displeasure of the British and was fined a hundred pounds for a similar act, but he is still editing his paper. The economic imperialist, therefore, has failed in this case. ‾In his own stronghold the oppressor has thereby advertised more extensively his injustice without strengthening himself in the defense of his policy. The British see now more need than ever for the extension of the Sedition Law, but the natives are more determined than ever to resist any further invasion of their much abridged rights.

In South Africa there are native editors in most of the large cities where the urban Bantu population is considerable and literacy somewhat advanced. Most of these editors, however, are negligible in the struggle against their oppressors. They restrict themselves to the channels of agreement and avoid those of conflict. In their columns they discuss matters of health, education, and religion. They dare not mention the intolerable industrial and commercial agencies which exploit the Bantu, for their papers would be promptly suppressed and the editors imprisoned under the Sedition Act. Some of the chartered companies developing the mines and plantations maintain certain native editors who are supposed to publish not the truth but what these capitalists desire the natives to believe to be the truth. Some of the truth, however, is inevitably being disseminated among the natives by observation and closer contacts resulting from the breaking up of the tribes and the concentration of members thereof in urban communities. The natives thereby lose their tribal respect for their distant chief who can no longer be employed to control them. Out of these masses in the cities may come organizers who will be the next heroes of Africa.

In this account we take no special notice of those ministers and teachers of African blood who have cooperated with European and American missionaries in inculcating a keener appreciation of things spiritual and have advanced both education and health in parts where those who impose taxes for such purposes confer none of these benefits upon the natives themselves. Certainly this philanthropic service under adverse circumstances, even in the face of war and disease, has been heroic. As one has said in praise of them, ''Every pain which has pierced their bodies and every drop of blood shed at their posts of duty constitute greater testimony to the worth of the religion taught by Jesus of Nazareth than all the eloquent sermons preached from the pulpits of the world. These heroes have followed the example of the Nazarene in inspiring a new religious enthusiasm and they have given the world a new meaning of what it is to die.''

One is hardly wrong in concluding that some of these missionaries who thus championed the cause of the oppressed served as an inspiration to a few of these Africans who were thereby emboldened to do something for themselves. To confine this story to the natives themselves is justifiable only on the grounds that he who would be free himself must strike the blow. And this history of Africa, as dark as it may seem, bears out a truth repeated in history. In those parts where the African has been most active in doing for himself he has acquired the largest domain of individual liberty.

Of these other workers many may be passed in review.

Bishop Adjai Crowther, who, trained for the missionary service in England, became an organizer, and at the same time an explorer and geographer of merit. Great praise has been given J. E. K. Aggrey for returning to Africa after being educated in America to do educational work at Achimota. Certainly Max Yergan, though not an African, but a Negro American casting his lot wholly with those people, deserves much credit for his recent decision. After working under the auspices of the Young Men's Christian Association in South Africa fifteen years he learned from experience that such Christian teaching as is permitted the natives in South Africa without any mention of their oppression is mere mockery. He has come out of Africa in protest against such an ineffective method, hoping in a more direct way to prepare and to arouse intelligent natives to work against this injustice and ultimately deliver themselves from serfdom.

In thus taking this stand Yergan will make it difficult for Negroes to enter South Africa even as missionaries. There is today considerable objection to the program of certain missionaries and only with extreme difficulty can Negroes enter the country. The Government of South Africa seriously objects to the teaching that all men are brothers and that a Negro before God is the equal of a white man. The Government has decreed that men are unequal, and the blacks must remain content to be the serfs and wage slaves of the whites. No law to bar evangelization has been enacted, but certain economic imperialists believe that it must be done ultimately if their program of exploitation is to continue with success.

Dissatisfaction has been expressed nevertheless through other channels. This has resulted from a nascent social organization along the lines of the protest of labor against capital through strikes where the natives have been detribalized by industry. These labor revolts have been in evidence some time in the older African colonies where the natives have felt the heel of the imperialist squeezing out what the unfortunate laborer once enjoyed or believes he should enjoy. In 1919 and 1926 there were railway strikes in Sierra Leone. In the latter year the strikers became emboldened to enforce their demands by tearing up the railroad tracks and cutting the telegraph lines. In 1929 a strike occurred in Gambia, and it could not be suppressed until drastic action had been taken and fifty strikers had been wounded under fire of the police. In 1931 came a more dangerous rising led by Hahilara, a Mohammedan convert, who united religious fanaticism with an economic grievance. He ordered the natives to refuse to pay taxes, he demanded the cession of Crown lands, and urged the expulsion of the British. Starting with a force of only fifty armed men, Hahilara maintained his position until his followers were dispersed by Captain H. J. Holmes in a battle in which both he and Hahilara were killed.

Another demonstration came in Nigeria in 1929 when the colony undertook to refill its coffers by taxing the native women. The women of Aba thereupon arose in protest, seized public buildings, and defied the local authorities. The white colonists precipitously fled for their lives. Martial law was proclaimed, however; and soldiers ordered to the scene shot down native women by the hundreds. The open rebellion was suppressed, but fearful agitation took place in mass meetings which forced the Government to appoint a commission on economic grievances with two Africans as members. These investigators recommended reform. The Governor saw fit to impose a fine of 850 pounds on Aba, but a second agitation forced him to abandon the idea.

Then there were religious revolts with nevertheless an economic significance. The first important one was the Chilembwe rising in Nyasaland in 1915. This upheaval developed from a long protest against the Scotch missionaries who while converting the souls of the natives enslaved their bodies for cheap labor on their coffee plantations. When these missionaries were succeeded in proprietorship by a syndicate the

natives received no humane consideration at all. Then
Chilembwe, a native, appeared upon the scene. After having
been educated in the United States he sought work at the
African mission stations, but he was refused. He set up
therefore a church of his own from which he preached revolt
against the Europeans. The workers flocked to his standard
and killed the five Europeans at the head of the estates, sparing and protecting nevertheless their wives and children. Just
after Chilembwe had finished a sermon with the head of one
of the white managers on the pulpit, however, the police,
supported by a detachment of soldiers, charged the natives'
stronghold, drove the rebels into the forest and shot them
and their leader as a hunter does game. Twenty of those
captured were hanged, and the remainder were given life
terms in prison.

In the Belgian Congo in 1921 another formidable religious
revolt took place. Kimbangu, a native carpenter converted
to Christianity, proclaimed himself a prophet, set up an independent church and drew off the natives from the European churches. The movement tended also to disorganize
labor, especially when Wednesday was proclaimed as the
weekly day of rest. Then followed minor prophets, more
anti-European than Kimbangu and more disastrous to the
general control of the natives. To stop the movement the
authorities arrested Kimbangu, convicted him by court martial, and sentenced him to death and his leading coworkers
to life imprisonment. Mandobe, a heroine in the rising, was
sentenced to serve only two years.

This drastic action, however, merely added fuel to the
flames. The natives threatened the Government with open
violence. Strikes became widespread and paralyzed industry
and agriculture. The aggrieved exploiters urged that Kimbangu be publicly hanged as a remedy. The natives coun-
tered, however, with the threat that the execution of their
leader would be avenged by a massacre of the whites. The
Home Government, therefore, calmed the water by commut-

ing Kimbangu's sentence to life imprisonment and deporting the other leaders.

Even in South Africa where the condition of the natives is more deplorable than in the Belgian Congo the spirit of resistance also still lives. Two recent outbreaks give evidence of such a survival of the invincible spirit of the African. In 1919 there was even a recurrence of the customary tribal rising in the Bondelwarts revolt. The Bondelwarts are a tribe of Hottentots whose leaders, Jacobus Christian and Abraham Morris, once expatriated by the Germans, returned to Southwest Africa after the dispossession of the Germans as a result of the First World War. The return of these native leaders was contrary to the orders of the Government. Trouble started when the police undertook to arrest them as dangerous characters. The people ceased work and assembled at the headquarters of Jacobus Christian at Haib, from which they threatened violence to the Europeans. The people armed themselves, and resisted the effort to arrest their leaders; but they had only four hundred men capable of bearing arms. The crisis came May 26, 1922, after the whites had failed to induce the natives to give up their arms. The Europeans, with artillery, machine guns and airplanes, charged the natives' settlement and shot them down in hiding in the mountains. So many of the natives were thus exterminated that the Government forbade the publication of the facts in the face of a "civilized" world.

The South African upheaval which was more typical of present tendencies was that of the Industrial Commercial Workers Union with Clements Kadalie, a Nyasaland native, as the moving spirit. The organization started with twenty-four members. The movement made itself felt at Port Elizabeth in 1920 when unskilled laborers struck for higher pay and obtained an increase of sixpence a day. They later demanded another increase and received an additional sixpence. Thus encouraged, these workers struck for a minimum daily wage of ten shillings for unskilled male workers and seven shillings sixpence for females. Agitation ran high with an opposing faction of natives led against Kadalie by the native Dr. Rubiusama, who narrowly escaped with his life from a clash which ensued.

The Government took steps at once and arrested Kadalie on October 22, 1920. His followers demanded his release. This was refused. The people then said that they themselves would release him and assembled for this purpose. The police and European volunteers thereupon fired upon the crowd. One European and 23 natives or colored males were killed; 45 colored and native males and one female were wounded. Four European women were wounded. The total casualties were 76. This attack increased the influence of the Industrial Commercial Workers Union instead of weakening it. Hertzog, trying to gain political prestige, sent a donation to Kadalie, although he punished the Workers' Union when he later became Prime Minister of the South African Union. In 1926 Kadalie had a following of 100,000 and professionally employed Africans were abandoning their posts to serve as agents of the order. Champion became Kadalie's ablest assistant.

This was the peak of the movement, however, for it was neither organized thoroughly nor conducted efficiently. There developed a division from the charge of misappropriation of funds. The natives, moreover, could not connect their order with that of the hostile union of the skilled white workers, and they were afraid to ally with the Third International. The Industrial Commercial Workers Union finally connected officially with the International Federation of Trades Unions and brought in a white man, one Ballinger, to assist Kadalie in organizing. The movement declined, however, and split into two rival sections which have no such influence as the original order.

Recently have occurred such dangerous developments as the organization of the Gold Coast and Ashanti cocoa farmers against the ''Pool'' set up by the corporations exploiting this trade in 1937. In 1938 the drivers struck against a fine imposed on one of their number and all but stopped the importation and consumption of European goods. The Rhodesian native miners revolted in 1935 because of rising taxes and could not be calmed until six natives had been killed and twenty-two wounded. As usual the natives are the sufferers. He pays the penalty for protesting or for revolting, but he does not cease to assert himself.

Chapter XIV

THE EVILS AGAINST WHICH
AFRICANS FIGHT

Only by keeping in mind the actual program brought by the economic imperialists to Africa and the methods employed in carrying out their policies can one understand the struggles made by these African heroes and heroines. Yet in discriminating between the policy pursued by one nation and that of another there arises much difficulty in grasping the situation. While methods of these conquerors have differed widely the results have tended to be the same with respect to the effect on the natives.

The student of colonization and economic imperialism, therefore, should not be misled by the large output of sentimental works in this field. When the Belgians were committing atrocities in the Congo writers on colonization branded them as the most cruel interlopers in Africa although England and France were committing the same atrocities in their colonies and hoped by the outcry to stop Leopold from taking territory which they desired. The United States Government was brought into the game through its imperialistic Sanford who was seeking the same sort of loot while serving as our minister to Belgium and a hireling of Leopold. When the Spaniards became so oppressive of their subjects as to cause uprisings in Cuba and the Philippines, the Americans, who succeeded the Iberians as economic imperialists, grew loud in their castigation of the Spaniards as heartless oppressors of weak peoples. When the Germans lost their African colonies to the Allies during the First World War the victors in taking over the spoils heralded a regime of mercy supplanting wanton murder and extermination by Huns—and this holier-than-thou attitude when the natives were to come under the rule of the South African Union where dominates the native policy of Boers who have annihilated more natives than the Germans have been able to reach.

The British professing to have their hands clean of such stains may be convicted on their record, nevertheless, in more than one colony. From the very beginning of their penetration of Africa they declared their policy as that of a stronger nation extending assistance and protection to weaker nations. Yet Great Britain has resorted to the use of cannon and rum just as the other nations in dispossessing and exterminating the natives. Of course, among the British the thing has been accomplished in such a subtle fashion that the deceit and hypocrisy have not always been apparent. Only by studying the development of the British policy over a long period of years can the record be clarified.

It is little known, moreover, that scarcely from any other of the economic imperialists can the natives expect less than from the British. While other European nations have annihilated natives to secure control of African territory they have since then welcomed in all spheres those natives who have become Europeanized and are willing to cooperate with the conquerors. The British, however, are so prejudiced against the blacks that they close in their faces the door to all the highest pursuits and avenues controlled by the Government. The French, for example, have had Negroes as generals in their armies, governors of their colonies, members of their parliament, and cabinet officers of the nation, but the intellectual bias of the British and their subtle policy of keeping the blacks in subordination would not tolerate such consideration. The discrimination against blacks in the British Empire, while deftly disguised, is worse than that in the United States.

All the European nations dominating Africa have their hands most shamefully stained. Their guilt differs only in

MAP SHOWING THE PARTITION OF AFRICA

extent and degree. In rushing to grab lands and claim the
mineral wealth of Africa they turned a deaf ear to the pleas
of suffering natives. All these European nations bribed the
natives with trinkets, made their chiefs drunk in order to
cheat them out of their lands, taxed the natives cruelly,
flogged them, forced them to labor, and murdered those who
would not yield. To the home government such crimes were
reported as "disciplinary measures;" and since the natives
could not speak for themselves, everything from the point of
view of the Colonial Office went well.

It is equally futile to accredit one class of European immi-
grants into Africa with higher motives than the others,
whether they be explorers, missionaries, traders, or public
functionaries. They all served the economic imperialists.
Stanley, who has been highly praised as carrying forward
the "glorious work" of Livingston in opening up heathen
Africa, was merely an advance capitalistic agent parading
his claims for sale before European chancelleries to forestall Pierre de Brazza who would establish the claims of
France. In 1884 Germany sent Gustav Nachtigal to the Cameroons on a "scientific mission" which resulted in negotiations and treaties annexing not only that territory but also
Togoland. About the same time Karl Peters, also an explorer with two other Germans disguised likewise in the
name of "science," penetrated East Africa and stealthily obtained, with the usual amount of gin and trinkets, treaties
granting his country a large area in East Africa. And so on
the records of other explorers may be given in extenso.

The missionaries with good intentions were not allowed to
extend their influences too far in Africa. Only those who
"could be squared," as Cecil John Rhodes once said, could
long proceed undisturbed. And some of the so-called sainted
apostles to Africa were in reality only economic imperialists.
Livingstone, as stated elsewhere, went first to Africa in the
name of God but returned later to serve the Empire. The
missionaries who took up the work of Livingstone at Blan-

tyre in Nyasaland joined with the English capitalists to rob the natives of their best lands and to cheat them out of the products from what soil was left them. The Reverend J. S. Moffat, and the Reverend C. D. Helm, consecrated to the service of God, betrayed the confidence of Lobenguela in advising the chief to sign with the British concessionaires treaties by which they finally expropriated Matabeleland. On account of the killing of Bishop Hannington for ignoring the order given by Muanga of Uganda not to cross the frontier, the Christian missionaries, both Protestants and Catholics, plunged into a war against the natives who with the support of the Mohammedans made the last stand fighting for that native land.

And even in the case of missionaries against whom no charges of insincerity can be sustained their work generally had the same result as those known to be to the contrary. The zealous missionary, for example, often innocently interfered with the sacred customs of the natives and in their applying to him the law of the land he lost his life. This news engendered in the public mind a holy horror, and with this as justification the military forces of the economic imperialists subdued the guilty natives, drove them from their homes, or annihilated them on the spot. In the expropriation of the territory the religious motive was lost, and the agents of the capitalists had another chance to proceed with their gin and rifles in having the chiefs make the usual marks on the dotted line. The trader either accompanied or followed the missionary. A most successful propagation of the gospel for the propagator, but a rather expensive one for the natives.

As to the colonial functionaries sent out to represent the Empire they had no choice but to serve the interests behind them. Theirs was not to reason against cruel outrages upon the natives. Those functionaries who undertook to pursue a human policy became too unpopular long to endure. Thus went Pierre de Brazza from the French Congo, when he hesitated for sentimental reasons. Dr. John Philip, the missionary who championed the natives' cause when Governor Durban, of the Cape, deprived them of their lands, became dangerously unpopular in the Cape Colony. His endeavors resulted in the Lord Glenelg's reversal of the expropriation of the natives' land in 1835. Only those colonial governors at the Cape who showed an attitude of aggression toward the natives could continue in power, for the public sentiment and the influence of the capitalists would not tolerate any other policy. Parliament and the British public might blame Frere, Hicks Beach, Chelmsford, and Sandhurst for the disaster at Isandhlwana, but such attacks were not prompted by sympathy for the natives. In this case the economic imperialists had failed to bag the game at low cost. Sir Garnet Wolseley, who more successfully dispossessed the natives pleased much better than his predecessors both the Cape and the Empire.

At present, therefore, the native Africans speak of the whites from Europe as interlopers who have no right on the continent. This was once the attitude toward the Arabs who traded along the Eastern and Northeastern coast of Africa at certain points from time immemorial and by the year 1000 A. D. gained a foothold in the interior. The Arabic invasion of Africa, however, differed widely from that of most Europeans. The Asiatics did not generally dispossess the natives of their lands and drive them to infertile areas and "reserves" inadequate to support the population. The Asiatics freely mingled with the natives to form a slightly different African stock. Europeans, professing to be penetrating the interior as the trustees of native rights and for the advancement of Christian civilization, have taken by force not only the lands wherever the climate is mild enough for them to live, but even that under the Equator; and they have expropriated from the natives by the same force the mineral wealth in all parts of the continent.

The dispossession of the native by the Europeans has

assumed three important aspects: (1) The extermination of the aborigines altogether in order to make room for the settlement of the conquerors, (2) the destruction of only a part of the natives and enslaving those remaining to exploit the country for the benefit of the economic imperialists, (3) and the mere extension of the foreign rule indirectly through the native chiefs coming under the "protection" of the Europeans. German Southwest Africa and the Boer Republics offer examples of areas from which the natives were murdered on the spot or driven out altogether. Almost any European colony in Africa may be taken as an example of the partial destruction of the cultural life of the natives and large numbers of the aborigines themselves in order to establish new authority and provide for European homeseekers. The British in Nigeria and in Tanganyika, as well as in other parts, have shown the way of what they designate as indirect rule. The French, while not espousing exactly indirect rule, control the natives by accepting on the basis of nominal equality a select few of the natives to rule the others by a system which some have designated as "cooperation."

While thus dispossessing the natives and driving them into restricted areas, where the making of a living is extremely difficult, the Europeans have closed up any loophole which may be left for the natives in the "reserves" to compete with European planters in Africa or with those engaged there in agriculture, mining, and trading. In the South African Union, where these conditions obtain in their worst form, the natives are prevented by law from doing skilled labor. This sphere is restricted to the whites and for unskilled labor the natives are paid barely enough to live, about $3.75 a week. The whites by law, however, must be paid on an average of from $4.00 to $6.00 a day to live according to European standards. In other parts, as in Kenya, the natives are not allowed to produce coffee because it was observed that their production of coffee competed with that raised by the Europeans.

While thus restricted, moreover, the rates on the imperialistically controlled railroads are kept so high that the native has almost nothing left from the proceeds after paying the cost of shipping his products to market. Practically throughout Africa, too, this low wage system and high taxation of the natives make it all but impossible for the majority of the natives on the reserves to earn enough to live and pay the required taxes; and taxes they must pay or be imprisoned. This forces the natives to leave the reserves to work for the Europeans on the plantations and in the mines. The whites thereby secure the natives' labor by force, or they enslave those who are nominally free.

The native has no way of escape. The law or his condition compels him to work for someone. In South Africa he must carry with him a pass or passes wherever he goes in order to show who he is, for whom he works, when he reported last for work, whether he is an efficient worker or "a loafer," why he is in transit, where he is going, and what he proposes to do there. Negro slavery in the United States never had so many checks and handicaps to afflict the Negroes once held in bondage.

At the same time these Europeans do practically nothing for the health and education of the natives while taxing them to provide such facilities for the whites. The missionaries do something through their schools and hospitals; and for this service they receive here and there a little aid from the government. What the missionaries do, however, is not sufficient to change materially the aspect of things; and there are some missionaries who do not believe in educating the natives. A native leaving the Belgian Congo for education is not allowed to return. He might spoil those wearing the yoke if he returned to teach them new ideas. Other European imperialists are working toward the same policy. This reminds one of a law in Virginia enacted in 1838 to prevent the return to the state of any free Negro who left there to secure an education.

To change these conditions the natives can do practically nothing themselves. Most natives dislocated from their tribal areas and without their former social organization cannot easily protest. Some of the tribes are supposedly left intact, and a few of them have what is called indirect rule through their chiefs. This, however, means control through marionettes set up by Europeans whom they serve in oppressing the natives more tyrannically than chiefs ever had the chance to do under native law.

To all intents and purposes the large majority of Africans have been enslaved to do the biddings of the Europeans settled on that continent, and where they cannot be thus used every measure possible under the pretext of war and maintaining the peace has been taken to work out their extermination. For the present the situation seems all but hopeless. Where these conditions obtain in their worst form the avenues for change through education, travel, and the introduction of liberal ideas have been purposely closed.

That such is the state to which Africa has come is considered evidence of the inferiority of the Negro although Asia, which has recently passed the same way is not thus challenged. Unfairly, moreover, what the natives did to defend their soil is omitted from history. The unusually fine record of their leaders for an heroic defense may be taken as evidence that some day the natives may learn from the Caucasian imperialist how to defeat him at his own game. Every conquered valley had a shrine which marked some heroic stand. Every tribal center could erect an altar on the spot where sons of Africa died for their fatherland.

These persons were the real makers of African history. To ignore them because their country has been conquered would be establishing a rule which, if applied elsewhere, would eliminate most of what our distinguished professors of history now teach the youth as the record of the progress of mankind. India, Mesopotamia, Egypt, Greece, Rome and Carthage would pass from the picture. Nations which rose and fell during ancient, medieval and modern times would cease to constitute any part of the history of the world. We would have to forget Boadicea and Caractacus in their sacrifice for ancient Britain, Leonidas at the pass of Thermopylae, Robert Bruce at Bannockburn, and Joan of Arc leading Charles VII to Rheims to crown him. The empires and their dynasties built and defended in these feats have failed or have given place to new regimes, but the heroism displayed on these occasions has been an inspiring record for others who have followed not altogether in imitation of the deeds of these heroes but in answering the call to duty with the same honesty of purpose and nobleness of soul. In the purposely neglected history of Africa are similar examples which when known will enrich our historical literature and serve as a proof of the universality of the innate trait of man to respond finally to the appeal of the good and beautiful and to die for high ideals.

The economic imperialists discredit the story of these and the more recent heroes. The Christian nations who have expropriated the natives' lands and reduced them to serfdom contend that there is practically nothing interesting in their history. These exploiters say that the African natives were ruled by despots, and the people were on the level of those who indulged in such practices as human sacrifice and cannibalism. This assertion is a general falsehood which has been so frequently repeated by traducers and pseudoscientists that it passes as the truth. It originated in making desire father to the thought. African chiefs, as a rule, were less despotic than primitive rulers in other parts of the world. In many of the tribes the chiefs were elected; and it was all but a general rule that the chief had no authority to alienate the land of the tribe. He had his own parcel of land as any other dweller, but the land as a whole was collectively held as the property of the community. The Europeans who went into Africa, then, forcing the chiefs to sign on the dotted line, or to make their mark on treaties ceding land, thereby obtained no right to land, for the chief could not alienate what belonged solely to the collectivity. This method of obtaining territory must be recorded as one of the greatest frauds in history—worse than that perpetrated in the treaties made between the Americans and the Indians. The chiefs of the American aborigines did have some semblance of authority in the matter of alienating land.

As to human sacrifice the writers of Europe would make it appear that many Africans found special delight in this performance. The outsider, however, even when trying to record the truth saw these practices from the European point of view only. Without sufficient knowledge of the culture of the people these observers simply misjudged the natives. In Dahomey, for example, where one hears so much about human sacrifice, history shows the observance of the custom of putting to death captives and criminals kept as state prisoners to be executed on such occasions as the death of a chief, a coronation, and a jubilee celebrating some great victory. These executions at the same time served to conform to religious rites, to terrify would-be opponents to the ruling regime and to inspire obedience to the strongly entrenched power. The record of so-called Christian nations shows practically the same custom. In the United States we publish beforehand dates of lynchings to give time for men, women, and children to come with refreshments as people go to picnics.

Americans shot down Filipinos in cold blood in the pacification of the Philippines. In similar way Hitler recently executed more than a hundred of his German enemies; Mussolini thus put to death thousands of Ethiopians immediately after the attempt to murder the Italian governor.

In the case of war in the early days in Africa the rule in many parts was not to take prisoners, and Africa was no exception to the others thus situated. Even in the Civil War most Confederate soldiers decreed no quarter to the Negroes

taking up arms in behalf of their own freedom and mas-
sacred them without mercy as was done at Fort Pillow. The
Spaniards on both sides of their conflict recently did this
in their own country.

It is unreasonable, then, to brand Africans with such terrible epithets for doing in their unenlightened state what
Europeans and Americans in spite of all their so-called
progress have done to others and to one another. The Africans merely developed along the line of most so-called primitive peoples. Their rulers killed off their opponents who
pretended to the thrones and vanquished in the same fashion
formidable enemies standing in the way. European nations
began in the same cruel way and continue thus even today.

As to cannibalism there is more exaggeration than probably any other aspect of African culture. Cannibalism is not
confined to any race. It results from lack of food or famine.
When one tribe was forced down upon another by a migration or by an immigration from Asia the social and economic
life thus suddenly upset often reduced the nation to starvation and as a last resort, to cannibalism. This has happened
in all parts of the world. Even during the early colonial
period of Virginia a man had to be put to death for killing
and eating his wife during the period of great starvation.
Europe reports similar cases among those reduced to straits
on the sea and distressed on land, and islanders other than
those of the Fiji group have descended to the same level.

The strong argument for the European conquest and development of Africa is that these economic imperialists have
removed these abuses and directed the activities of the natives
away from war and strife toward more peaceful pursuits.
In this respect, if this be admitted, they have been more successful in Africa than at home. Their assertion, however, is
only a half truth. What these apologists should say frankly
is that the conquerors of Africa have disrupted the old
social and economic and political order of the tribes, destroying the good as well as the undesirable in their culture,

while preventing these same natives from coming into the enjoyment of the good in the European culture. At present, therefore, the natives are worse off than they were in the tribal state. Whether this present undesirable state is a transition to a better one nobody can tell, but there appears nothing in the policy of the economic imperialists which offers the large majority of natives any status higher than serfdom or wage slavery.

These evils it was thought would be considerably mitigated by the conditions due to the Second World War. The Nazis overran Europe and seemed likely to subdue Africa. They established themselves on fighting ground in collaboration with the allied Italians and menaced West Africa where French colonials cooperating with the puppet Vichy Government seemed likely to turn French West Africa over to the Nazis. To provide for adequate defense every able-bodied person in Africa was called upon to play his part. Europeans had to go to war, and natives had to produce food and supplies and defend the home country. These new demands brought forward the advocates of the reconstruction of colonial system and of reform in the native policy. Many urged a new allotment of land in South Africa and in East Africa where the natives have been so starved out on inadequate reserves that they have to enter the employ of Europeans for wages amounting to a fifth or sixth of what the latter receive. This inadequate compensation, they insisted, must be remedied. Some urged the removal of restrictions within ghetto which have rendered the housing of non-Europeans miserable. A few thinkers even attacked the denial of representation to the Natives in the South African Parliament and contended for the extension of suffrage. Where Negroes are known to be efficient, some argued, they should be promoted to commanding positions rather than be kept on the level of assistants and subordinates. All these changes advocated, of course, were to be carried out within limitations in order to safeguard the interests of the Home Government. Hitherto, however, these dreams of the natives have not been realized.

These proposals most assuredly secured the loyalty of the natives, the end sought by the Europeans. African women as well as men answered the call to work and kept the continent's quota of men and supplies at the front and thus enabled the South Africans to do valorous fighting in North Africa and in Europe. The outstanding example of loyalty was the stand taken by Felix Eboué, the Governor of Chad in French Africa, in supporting De Gaulle's Committee for the Liberation of France in preference to following the French who desired to hold the West Coast of Africa for the puppet Vichy Government. With submarines the Nazis were making a desperate effort to get control there and thus eliminate Africa as a source of help for their European opponents or for a base for the United States Expeditionary Force. Eboué rallied the French and Natives in Chad and the adjoining French possessions in his capacity as governor. Because of his significant achievements in blocking the Nazis from that area and furnishing also troops and supplies to drive the Nazis out of North Africa he was acclaimed as a great factor in defense of democracy and was made Governor General of the French Equatorial Africa with his capital at Brazzaville. His duties were so strenuous, however, that he succumbed in 1944.

Another gesture toward improving the African situation was the restoration of Haile Selassie in Ethiopia from which British troops expelled the Italians who had subdued the land in 1937. In thus destroying the short-lived empire set up by Mussolini the British established their so-called right to these possessions themselves. The Atlantic Charter disclaims any thing like war for conquest, but the allies will hardly return Ethiopia to Italy. It will doubtless remain under the control of the British with Haile Selassie in the same position where he was in 1936 when the Italians, French and the British claimed joint supervision of the country. At that time the

Negus Negasti had three lords, but now he has only one. His last state may be worse than the first. Already Ethiopia is complaining that she has not obtained the much desired outlet to the sea through Eritrea. The economic imperialists find it to their advantage to control the egress and regress there by way of the railroad ending at Jibouti. In this way economic imperialism will be well served.

President Tubman, of Liberia, may be more fortunate than his contemporary in Ethiopia. Liberia, though attacked and reduced in extent by overpowering French and British imperialists for many years, is nevertheless an independent republic at least in name. In order to reach certain parts of Europe and the East to prevent the Nazis' encircling effort to bisect the British Empire, Liberia was sought as a strategic base to counteract what might be done by the Nazis operating from Dakar. Liberia reached an agreement with the allies, joined the effort to crush Hitler, and offered its facilities to the forces for the liberation of Europe. President Edwin Barclay, accompanied by President-elect Tubman, was warmly received as a visitor to the United States. He was entertained by President Roosevelt at the White House, was invited to visit and to address the House of Representatives and the Senate, and was conducted on a tour of the war industries of the country. It would seem, then, that if the allies have any sense of gratitude they will assure Liberia a sovereign and independent status after the war.

Despite the long list of heroes and heroines, Africa has been regarded by some people as the home of a "child race." Because there is little discussion and presentation of Africa in the schools and colleges this belief has persisted until it became traditional. However the tradition began to change in the period shortly after World War II. Then black and brown Africans undertook an organized interest and participation in their governments and their independence of foreign controls. They strove first to achieve unity among themselves for independence, but this proved to be very difficult to achieve. Foreign offices had always found a way "to divide and conquer." Nevertheless unity began to spread as it had not done prior to World War II.

Preceding these movements, Pan-African Conferences had directed attention, although they were small in attendance, to the new endeavors for independence. Six congresses of Africans were held. The first was in London in 1900. It was at this conference that DuBois first made the statement that "The Problems of the Twentieth Century is the color line." Three years later these words appeared in his *The Souls of Black Folks*. The movement was inactive until after World War I, which led to a revival of the idea resulting in a Pan-African Congress in Paris. The prime mover of these events was W. E. B. DuBois, February 19-21, 1919. This Congress representing fifteen countries asked for African representation on League of Nations Committees. Another Congress was held in 1921 with meetings in London, Brussels, and Paris.

The Third biennial sessions were held in 1923 in London and in Lisbon. Thirteen countries in Africa sent representatives. After four years, a Pan-African Congress met in New York City. There were thirteen countries represented by 208 delegates. It was not until 1945 that another Congress assembled in London. In the meantime, African independence marched on.

By April, 1958, the momentum became so great that eight independent states, Ethiopia, Ghana, Liberia, Libya, Morocco, the Sudan, Tunisia, and the Arab Republic, of West and North Africa assembled their representatives at Accra and called on France to withdraw its troops from Algeria and recognize its independence. They expressed concern over the non-announcement of definite dates of independence in Africa by all colonial powers and that assistance should be given to the remaining dependent peoples in their "struggle for self-determination and independence." They condemned the "practise of racial discrimination and segregation" as evil and inhuman. They declared that "racialism is a negation of the basic principles of human rights and dignity." They agreed to reconvene at least every ten years.

During the 1960's, the old colonial way of Africa continued to change as black nationalism spread over the continent giving rise to new independent governments. These governments became interested in their past and in recognizing their heroes, heroines, and significant events in history.

New acquaintance has come to the African through interest developed in African art. Museums and books have told of the artistic endeavors of Africans and it has become known that these black people were less barbarous and more talented than was known. Researches in archeology, ethnology, and material culture have opened new doors to Africa's unknown past. Dress and hair style have been indications of pride in the African past. To some observers this may appear to be superficial and trivial but they are major manifestations of pride in African styles and opposition to western dominance and assumed superiority. They and others now recognized that Africa has a history and civilizations as other people have had, and that black is not uncivilized and barbarian merely because of its color and difference.

Abderrahman Es-Sa'di, *Tarikh es-Soudân.* Paris, 1900.

Africa, Journal of the International Institute of African Languages and Cultures. London, 1928 and the following years.

Alberti, L., *De Kaffers aan de Zuidkust van Africa.* Amsterdam, 1810.

Aldridge, Thomas J., *A Transformed Colony: Sierra Leone.* London, 1916.

Alexander, A., *History of Colonization.* Philadelphia, 1846.

Alexander, J. E., *An Expedition of Discovery into the Interior of Africa.* 2 vols. 1838.

Andersson, C. J., *Lake Ngami.* 1856.

Ankermann, B., Ueber den gegenwärtigen Stand der Ethnographie der Südhälfte Afrikas. *Archiv f. Anthropologie,* N. F., Vol. IV (1906), pp. 241-86.

Arbousset, T., *Relation d'un Voyage d'Exploration au Nord-Est de la Colonie du Cap de Bonne-Espérance.* Paris, 1842.

Arcin, A., *Histoire de la Guinée Française,* Paris, 1911.

Autran, C., *Phéniciens, Essai de contribution à l'histoire antique de la Méditerranée,* Cairo, 1920.

Avelot, R., ''Les grands mouvements de peuples en Afrique: Jaga et Zimba,'' in *Bulletin de géographie historique et descriptive,* nos. 1 and 2. Paris, 1912.

Ayliff, J., and J. Whiteside, *History of the Aba-Mbo, generally known as ''Fingos.''* Butterworth, S. A., 1912.

Azikiwe, Nmandi, *Renascent Africa.* Accra, Gold Coast, West Africa, 1937.

Baines, T., *Explorations in South-West Africa.* 1864.

Bantu Studies. Johannesburg, 1921 and the following years.

Barbot, J., *Histoire de la Guinée.* Paris, 1660.

Barnard, Lady Anne, *South Africa a Century ago: letters written from the Cape of Good Hope, 1797-1801.* 1925.

Barnes, Leonard, *The Duty of Empire.* London, 1935.

Barrow, J., *Travels into the Interior of Southern Africa.* 2 vols. 1801-4. 2nd ed. 1806.

Barth, H., *Travels and Discoveries in Northern and Central Africa.* London, 1858.

Barthel, K., ''Völkerbewegungen auf der Südhälfte des afrikanischen Kontinents,'' *Mitt. d. Vereins f. Erdkunde,* Leipzig, 1893, pp. 1-90.

Bastian, A., *Ein Besuch in San-Salvador, der Hauptstadt des Königreichs Congo.* Bremen, 1859.

Beazley (Sir), C. Raymond, *The Dawn of Modern Geography.* 3 vols. 1897-1906.

Beer, G. L., *African Colonial Problems.* New York, 1923.

Bent, J. T., *The Ruined Cities of Mashonaland.* 1895.

Berger, H., *Geschichte der wissenschaftlichen Erdkunde der Griechen.* 2nd ed. Leipzig, 1887-93.

Berlioux, S. F., *Doctrine Ptolemoei ab injuria recentiorum vindicata, sive Nilus Superior et Niger versus, hodiernus Eghirren ab antiquis explorati.* Paris, 1874.

Binger, L. G., *Du Niger au Golfe de Guinée par le pays de Kong et le Mossi.* Paris, 1889.

————— *Esclavage, Islamisme et Christianisme.* Paris, 1891.

Bird, J., *The Annals of Natal.* 2 vols. Pietermaritzburg, 1888.

Blake, J. W., *Europeans Beginnings in West Africa,* 1454-1578, London, 1937.

Bleek, D. F., *Customs and Beliefs of the Xam Bushmen. Bantu Studies,* vols. V (1931), pp. 169 *sqq.;* VI (1932), pp. 47 *sqq.,* 233 *sqq.,* 323 *sqq.;* VII (1933), pp. 297 *sqq.,* 375 *sqq.*

————— *The Naron: a Bushman Tribe of the Central Kalahari.* Cambridge, 1928.

————— Bushmen of Central Angola. *Bantu Studies,* vol. III (1928), pp. 105-25.

Bleek, W. H. I., and Lucy C. Lloyd, *Specimens of Bushman Folklore.* 1911.

Blyden, E. W., *Islam, Christianity, and the Negro.* London, 1888.

Borelli, Jules, *Éthopie méridionale.* Paris, 1890.

Bowditch, T. E., *Mission from Cape-Coast Castle to Ashantee with a Statistical Account of that Kingdom.* London, 1819.

Brauer, E., *Züge aus der Religion der Herero.* Leipzig, 1925.

Breasted, J. H., *History of Egypt.* London, 1906.

Bricchetti-Robecchi, *Tradizioni storiche raccolte in Obbia.* Rome, 1891.

Brincker, P. H., *Unsere Ovambo-Mission.* Bremen, 1900.

Brookes, E. H., *The History of Native Policy in South Africa from 1830 to the Present Day.* 2nd ed. Pretoria, 1927.

————— *The Colour Problem of South Africa.* Lovedale, 1934.

Brown, J. T., *Among the Bantu Nomads.* 1926.

Brownlee, F., *The Transkeian Native Territories: Historical Records.* Lovedale, S. A., 1923.

Bruce, *Voyage aux sources du Nil, en Nubie et en Abyssinie pendant les années 1768 à 1772* (Castera translation). Paris, 1790-1792.

Bruel, G., *L'Afrique Equatoriale Française.* Paris, 1918.

Brunet, L. and G. L., *Dahomey et Dépendances.* Paris, 1910.

Bryant, A. T., *Olden times in Zululand and Natal, containing the earlier political history of the Eastern-Nguni clans.* 1929.

Bryce, J. (later Visct.), *Impressions of South Africa.* New ed. 1900.

Buell, Raymond Leslie, *Native Problem in Africa.* 2 volumes. New York, 1938.

Bullock, Charles, *Mashona Laws and Customs.* Salisbury, Rhodesia, 1913.

————— *The Mashona.* Cape Town, 1928.

Bunbury, E., *History of Ancient Geography.* 1879.

Burchell, W. J., *Travels in the Interior of South Africa.* 2 vols. 1822-4.

Burkitt, M. C., *South Africa's Past in Stone and Paint.* Cambridge, 1928.

Burton, R. F., *The lake regions of Central Africa.* London, 1860.

Cadamosto, *Relation des voyages à la Côte occidentale d'Afrique* (1455-1457), (Temporal translation, Schefer edition), Paris, 1895.

Caillé, René, *Journal d'un voyage à Timboctu et à Jenné dans l'Afrique centrale.* Paris, 1830.

Callaway, H., *The Religious System of the Amazulu*. Springvale, Natal, 1868-70; reprinted London, 1884.

Campbell, J., *Travels in South Africa . . . being a Narrative of a Second Journey into the Interior of that Country*. 2 vols. 1812.

Cana, F. R., *South Africa from the Great Trek to the Union*. 1909.

Cape of Good Hope. *Report and Proceedings, with Appendices, of the Government Commission on Native Laws and Customs*. (*Cape Parliamentary Papers*, G. 4, 1883.) Cape Town, 1883.

Capello, H. et R. Ivens, *De Benguella as terras de Iacca, Lisboa*, 1881.

———— *De Angola a Contra-Costa*. Lisboa, 1886.

Carbou, H., *La Région du Tchad et du Ouadaï*. Paris, 1912.

Carvajal, Marmol, *Descripción general de Africa, segunda parte; Tierra de los Negros*. Malaga, 1599.

Cary, M. and Warmington, E. H., *The Ancient Explorers*. 1929.

Casalis, E., *Les Bassoutos*. Paris, 1859, reprinted 1930. (English trans., 1861.)

Caton-Thompson, G., *The Zimbabwe Culture: Ruins and Reactions*. 1931.

Cavazzi de Montecuccolo, P. Gio, *Istorica descrizione de tre regni Congo, Matamba e Angola*. Bologna, 1687.

Chamberlain, D., *David Livingstone*. 1930.

Cherubini, S., *Nubie* (Vol. III of *l'Afrique*, in the collection *L'Univers Pittoresque*). Paris, 1878.

Chevalier, A., *L'Afrique centrale française*. Paris, 1907.

Cingo, W. D., *Ibali lama Mpondo*. Palmerston, S. A., 1925.

———— *Ibali laba Tembu*. Palmerston, S. A., 1927.

Cipriani, L., *Le Antiche Rovine e Miniere della Rhodesia*. Florence, 1932.

Clarkson, Thomas, *History of the Abolition of the Slave Trade*. London, 1808.

Clouzot, H. and A. Level, *L'art nègre et l'art océanien*. Paris, 1920.

Clozel and Villamur, *Coutumes indigènes de la Côte d'Ivoire*. Paris, 1902.

Coillard, F., *Sur le Haut-Zambèze*. Paris and Nancy, 1898.

Comte de Gobineau, *Essai sur l'inégalité des races humaines* (2nd edition). Paris, 1884.

Cook, P. A. W., *Social Organisation and Ceremonial Institutions of the Bomvana*. Cape Town, 1931.

Cornet, Cap., *Au Tchad*, Paris, 1911.

Cory, (Sir) G. E., *The rise of South Africa; a History of the Origin of South African Colonisation and of its Development towards the East from the Earliest Times to 1857*. 5 vols. New York, 1910-30.

Cultru, P., *Histoire de Sénègal du XVe siècle à 1870*. Paris, 1910.

Cunningham, J. F., *Uganda and its People*. London, 1905.

Cureau, (Dr.) Ad., *Les sociétés primitives de l'Afrique équatoriale*. Paris, 1912.

D'Albega, Alexandre L., *La France au Dahomey*. Paris, 1895.

D'Almada, Alvarez, *Traité succinct sur les rivières de Guinée et du Cap Vert*—(1594), (Diego Köpke edition). Porto, 1841.

Damberger, Fr., *Voyage dans l'intérieur de l'Afrique* (translated by Delamarre). Paris, 1801.

Dapper, O., *Description de l'Afrique*. Amsterdam, 1686.

———— *Naukeurige Beschrijvinge der Afrikaensche Gewesten*. Amsterdam, 1668.

Dehérain, H., *Le Cap de Bonne-Espérance au XVIIe Siècle*. Paris, 1909.

———— *L'expansion des Boers au XIXe Siècle*. Paris, 1905.

De Kiewiet, C. W., *The Imperial Factor in South Africa*. Cambridge, 1937.

Delafosse, M., ''Souffle vital et esprit dynamique chez les populations indigènes du Soudan occidental,'' in *Comptes-rendus des séances de l'Institut Français d'Anthropologie*, supplement to L'Anthropologie, no. 5, Paris, 1912.

———— *Haut-Sénégal-Niger (Soudan Français)*. Paris, 1912.

———— *Traditions historiques et légendaires du Soudan occidental traduites d'un manuscrit arabe inédit*. Paris, 1913.

———— ''Les Hamites de l'Afrique Orientale d'après les travaux les plus récents,'' in *L'Anthropologie*, Paris, 1894.

———— *Les frontières de la Côte d'Ivoire, de la Côte d'Or et du Soudan*. Paris, 1908.

———— ''Le peuple Sièna ou Sénoufo'' in *Revue des études ethnographiques et sociologiques*, Paris, 1908-1909.

———— ''Sur des traces probables de civilisation égyptienne et d'hommes des races blanches à la Côte d'Ivoire,'' in *L'Anthropologie*, Paris, 1901.

———— ''Les Agni,'' *L'Anthropologie*, 1843.

Delafosse, M. and H. Gaden, *Chroniques du Foûta sénégalais*. Paris, 1913.

Delegorgue, A., *Voyage dans l'Afrique australe*. 2 vols. Paris, 1847.

Denham, Clapperton and Oudney, *Narrative of Travels and Discoveries in Northern and Central Africa*, Philadelphia, 1826.

Dennett, R. E., *Nigerian studies or the religious and political system of the Yoruba*, London, 1910.

De Rochefort, Jeannequin, *Voyage au royaume de Senega*. Paris, 1643.

D'Escayrac de Lauture, *Mémoire sur le Soudan*. Paris, 1855-1856.

Desplagnes, L., *Le plateau central nigérien*. Paris, 1907.

Devis, L. M., *Le pays des Zendjs ou la Côte Orientale d'Afrique au Moyen Age d'après les écrivains arabes*. Paris, 1883.

Döhne, J. L., *Das Kafferland und seine Bewohner*. Berlin, 1843.

Donnan, Elizabeth, *Documents Illustrative of the History of the Slave to America*. Four volumes. Washington, 1930-1935.

Dornan, S. S., *Pygmies and Bushmen of the Kalahari*. London, 1925.

Dubois, F., *Timbouctou la Mysterieuse*. Paris, 1897.

Dubois, M., *Examen de la Géographie de Strabon*, Paris, 1891.

Du Bois, W. E. B., *The Suppression of the African Slave Trade*. New York, 1896.

Duggan-Cronin, A. M., *The Bantu Tribes of South Africa: Reproductions of Photographic Studies*. Cambridge, 1928.

Du Plessis, J., *A History of Christian Missions in South Africa*. London, 1911.

Dutton, E. A. T., *The Basuto of Basutoland*. London, 1923.

Earthy, E. Dora, *ValLenge Women: the Social and Economic Life of the VaLenge Women of Portuguese East Africa*. Oxford, 1933.

Einstein, Carl, *Afrikanische Plastik*. Munich, 1920.

Ellenberger, D. F., *History of the Basuto, Ancient and Modern*. London, 1912.

Ellis, A. B., *The Yoruba-speaking Peoples of the Slave Coast of West Africa.* London, 1894.
————— *The Tshi-speaking Peoples of the Gold Coast of West Africa.* London, 1887.
Ellis, George W., *Negro Culture in West Africa.* New York, 1914.
Endemann, K., Mitteilungen über die Sothoneger. *Zeits. f. Ethnologie,* vol. VI (1874), pp. 16-66.
Engelbrecht, S. P., *Geschiedenis van de Nederduits Hervormde Kerk in Zuid-Afrika.* 2 vols. Amsterdam and Pretoria, 1920-5.
Faidherbe, L., *Notice sur la colonie du Sénégal.* Paris, 1859.
Farrer, J. A., *Zululand.* London, 1879.
Field, M. J., *Religion and Medicine of the Ga People.* London, 1937.
Foa, Edouard, *Dahomey.* Paris, 1895.
Fourie, H. C. M., *Amandebele van Fene Mahlangu en hun religieus-sociaal leven.* Zwolle, 1921.
Fourie, L., "The Bushmen of South West Africa." In *The Native Tribes of South West Africa* (a *symposium*), pp. 79-105. Cape Town, 1928.
François, G. A. F. O., *Notre Colonie du Dahomey.* Paris, 1906.
François, H. von, *Nama und Damara: Deutsch-Süd-West-Afrika.* Magdeburg, 1896.
Fritsch, G., *Die Eingeborenen Süd-Afrikas ethnographisch und anatomisch beschrieben.* Breslau, 1872.
Frobenius, L., *Madzimu Dsangars: Südafrikanische Felsbilderchronik.* 2 vols. Berlin, 1931-2.
Gaffarel, P., *Eudoxe de Cyzique et le Periple de l'Afrique dans l'antiquité.* Paris, 1872.
Gardiner, A. F., *Narrative of a Journey to the Zoolu Country.* London, 1836.
Gastang, I. J., *Second Interim Report on the Excavations at Meroe in Ethiopia.* Liverpool, 1911.
Gentil, E., *La chute de l'empire de Rabah.* Paris, 1902.
Gibson, James Young, *The Story of the Zulus.* London, 1911.
Godée-Molsbergen, E. C. (Ed.) *Reizen in Zuid-Afrika in de Hollandse Tijd.* 4 vols. Gravenhage, 1916-32.
Golberry, S. M. X., *Fragments d'un voyage en Afrique* (1785-1787). Paris, 1802.
Goodwin, A. J. H., and Lowe, C. van R., *The Stone Age Cultures of South Africa.* Cape Town, 1929. (*Annals of the South African Museum,* vol. XXVII.)
Grevenbroek, J. G., *Elegans et accurata gentis Africanae circa Promontorium Capitis Bonae Spei vulgo Hottentotten nuncupatae descriptio espitolaris.* MS, 1695; printed in *The Early Cape Hottentots* (ed. I. Schapera).
Griggs, Earl Leslie, *Thomas Clarkson, the Friend of Slaves.* Ann Arbor, Michigan, 1938.
Grout, L., *Zulu-Land: or, Life among the Zulu-Kafirs.* New York, 1862.
Gsell, Stéphane, *Herodote.* Paris, 1916.
————— *Histoire ancienne de l'Afrique du Nord.* Paris, 1920.
Guillain, *Voyage à la Côte orientale d'Afrique.* Paris, 1846-1848.
————— *Documents sur l'histoire, la géographie et le commerce de l'Afrique Orientale.* Paris, 1856-1857.

Guillaume and Munro, *Primitive Negro Sculpture*. New York, 1926.
Hacquard, A., *Monographie de Tombouctou*. Paris, 1900.
Hahn, T., ''Die Buschmänner,'' *Globus*, vol. XVIII (1870), pp. 65 *sqq.*
—————— ''Die Nama-Hottentotten,'' *Globus*, vol. XII (1867), pp. 238 *sqq.*, etc.
—————— *Tusni-Goam: the Supreme Being of the Khoi-Khoi*. London, 1881.
—————— *Beitrage zur Kunde der Hottentotten*. Leipzig, 1869.
Hall, R. N., *Prehistoric Rhodesia*. London, 1909.
—————— *Great Zimbabwe, Mashonaland, Rhodesia*, London, 1905.
Hall, R. N. and Neal, W. G., *The Ancient Ruins of Rhodesia*. London, 1904.
Hardy, Georges, *La Politique Coloniale et le Partage de la Terre aux XIXe et XXe Siècles*. Paris, 1937.
—————— *Vue Generale de l'Histoire d'Afrique*. Paris, 1932.
—————— *L'Art Nègre*. Paris, 1927.
Harries, C. H. L., *The Laws and Customs of the BaPedi and Cognate Tribes of the Transvaal*. Johannesburg, 1929.
Harris, S., *Highlands of Ethiopia*. London, 1844.
Hartmann, R., *Die Nigritier*. Perlin, 1876.
—————— *Les peuples de l'Afrique*. Paris, 1880.
Hennig, R., *Von rätselhaften Ländern*. Munich, 1925.
Henry, J., *L'âme d'un peuple africain: les Bambara*. Münster (Wien), 1910. (Bibliothèque Anthropos).
Herodotus, *Histories*. Books I-III, ed. A. H. Sayce; Books IV-IX, ed R. W. Macan. 1883-1908.
Herrman, L., *A History of the Jews in South Africa from the earliest times to 1895*. London, 1930.
Historical Geography of the Colonies (The), London.
Hobley, C. W., *Romance of the Founding of Uganda and Kenya Colony*, East Africa Pamphlet, No. 90.
Hoefer, F., *Afrique Orientale et Afrique Centrale* (vol. V. of *l'Afrique* in the collection *L'Univers Pittoresque*. Paris, 1848.
Hoernlé, (Mrs.) A. W., ''Certain Rites of Transition and the Conception of !nau among the Hottentots.'' *Harvard African Studies* vol. II (1918), pp. 65-82.
—————— ''The Social Organization of the Nama Hottentots of South-West Africa.'' *American Anthropologist*, vol. XXVI (1925), pp. 1-24.
Hoffmann, C., ''Sotho-Texte aus dem Holzbuschgebirge in Transvaal.'' *Zeits. f. Eingeborenen-Sprachen*, vols. XVIII (1927-8), pp. 241 *sqq.*; XIX (1928-9), pp. 268 *sqq.*; XXI (1930-1), pp. 98 *sqq.*; XXII (1931-2), pp. 161 *sqq.*; XXIII (1932-33), pp. 59 *sqq.*; XXIV (1933-4), pp. 58 *sqq.*, 201 *sqq.* (In progress.)
Holden, W. C., *The Past, Present and Future of the Kafir Races*. London, 1866.
Holub, E., *Seven Years in South Africa*. 2 vols. London, 1881.
Houdas, O., *L'Islamisme*. Paris, 1904.
Hovelacque, A., *Les Nègres de l'Afrique sus-équatoriale*. Paris, 1889.
Hunt, D. R., ''An Account of the BaPedi.'' *Bantu Studies*, vol. V (1931), pp. 275-326.
Ibn-Omar El-Tounsy, *Voyage au Darfour* (Perron translation) Paris, 1845.

——— *Voyage au Ouaday* (Perron translation). Paris, 1851.

Ingram, T. K., *History of Slavery and Serfdom.*

Irle, I., *Die Herero.* Gütersloh, 1906.

Isaacs, N., *Travels and Adventures in Eastern Africa.* 2 vols. London, 1836.

Jabavu, D. D. T., *The life of John Tengo Jabavu, editor of Imovo Zabantsundu.* Lovedale, 1922.

Jacottet, E., "Mœurs, Coutumes, et Superstitions des Ba-Souto." *Neuchâtel Bull. Soc. Géog.* vol. IX (1896-7), pp. 107-51.

James, C. L. R., *A History of Negro Revolt.* London, 1938.

Jenkinson, T. B., *Amazulu, the Zulus.* London, 1882.

Johnson, J. P., *Some Implements of South Africa.* New York, 1908.

——— *The Prehistoric Period in South Africa.* New York, 1912.

Johnston, (Sir) H. H., *A History of the Colonization of Africa by Alien Races.* Cambridge, 1913.

——— *Liberia,* London, 1907.

——— *The Kilima-Njaro expedition,* London, 1886.

——— *British Central Africa,* London, 1897.

——— *The Uganda Protectorate,* London, 1902.

Jones, N., *The Stone Age in Rhodesia.* Oxford, 1926.

Jore, L., *La République de Libéria.* Paris, 1912.

Joseph, G., *La Côte d'Ivoire.* Paris, 1917.

Josephus, *Complete Works.* Paris, 1843.

Jouenne, Dr., "Les Monuments Megalathiques du Senegal," in *Annuaire et Memoires du Comité d'Etudes historiques et scientifiques de l'Afrique Occidentale Française,* Gorée, 1916-1917; and in the *Bulletin du Comité d'Etudes,* Paris, 1918.

——— "Les Roches gravés du Sénégal," in *Bulletin du Comité d'Etudes,* Paris, 1920.

Junod, Henri A., *Moeurs et Coutumes des Bantous, la Vie d'une Tribu Sud-Africaine.* Paris, 1936.

——— *The Life of a South African Tribe.* 2 vols., 2nd ed., revised and enlarged. New York, 1927.

——— *Condition of the Natives of Southeast Africa in the Sixteenth Century,* Capetown, 1914.

Kaufmann, H., "Die Auin: ein Beitrag zur Buschmannforschung." *Mitt. a.d. Deuts. Schutzgebieten,* vol. XXIII (1910), pp. 135-60.

Kawa, R. T., *Ibali lama-Mfengu.* Lovedale, S. A., 1929.

Kay, S., *Travels and Researches in Caffraria.* New York, 1833.

Keane, A. H., *The Gold of Ophir.* London, 1901.

Keith, Arthur, *The Belgian Congo and the Berlin Act.* Oxford, 1919.

Keltie, (Sir) John S., *Partition of Africa,* London, 1895.

Kidd, D., *The Essential Kafir.* London, 1904.

——— *Savage Childhood: a Study of Kafir Children.* London, 1906.

Kirby, Percival R., *The Musical Instruments of the Native Races of South Africa.* London, 1934.

Kohler, M., *Marriage Customs in Southern Natal.* Pretoria, 1933. (*Department of Native Affairs, Ethnological Publications,* vol. IV.)

Kolb[en], P., *Caput Bonae Spei Hodiernum, das ist, Vollständige Beschreibung des Afrikanischen Vorgebirges der Guten Hoffnung,* Nürnberg, 1719. (English translation, London, 1731.)

Kropf, A., *Das Volk der Xosa-Kaffern in östlichen Südafrika.* Berlin, 1889.

Labat, J. B., *Nouvelle relation de l'Afrique Occidentale.* Paris, 1728.

Labouret, Henri, *Le Royaume d'Arda et son Evangélisation au XVIIe Siècele.* Paris, 1929.

————— "Le mystere des ruines du Lobi," in *Revue d'ethnographie et des traditions populaires,* Paris, 1920.

————— "La terre dans ses rapports avec les croyances religieuses chez les populations du cercle de Gaouna," in *Annuaire et mémoires du Comité d'études historiques et scientifiques de l'Afrique Occidentale française,* Gorée, 1916.

La Roncière, C. Bourel de, *La Décourverte de l'Afrique au Moyen Age.* 2 vols. Cairo, 1924-5.

Lasnet, Dr., "Les races du Sénégal," in *Une mission au Sénégal,* Paris, 1900.

Leakey, L. S. B., *Stone Age of Africa.* London, 1936.

Lebzelter, V., *Eingeborenenkulturen in Südwest- und Südafrika.* Leipzig, 1934.

Lachaptois, Mgr., *Aux rives du Tanganika.* Maison-Carree (Alger), 1913.

Le Chatelier, A., *L'Islam en Afrique occidentale.* Paris, 1899.

Le Hérissé, A., *L'Ancien Royaume du Dahomey, Moeurs, Religion, Histoire.* Paris, 1911.

Leo the African, *Description of Africa, Three Parts of the World.* Paris, 1896-1898.

Le Roy, Mgr., *La religion des primitifs.* Paris, 1911.

Leslie, D., *Among the Zulus and Amatongas.* Glasgow, 1875.

Le Testu, G., *Notes sur les coutumes Bapounou,* Caen, s.d. (1920).

Le Vaillant, F., *Voyage dans l'Intérieur de l'Afrique.* 2 vols. Paris, 1790.

Lewin, Evans, *The Germans and Africa.* London, 1915.

Lichtenstein, M. H. C., *Reisen im südlichen Afrika.* 2 vols. Berlin 1811-12.

Lips, Julius E., *The Savage Hits Back, or the White Men through Native Eyes.* London, 1937.

Livingstone, D., *Missionary Travels and Researches in South Africa* London, 1857.

Ludolphus, Job, *A New History of Ethiopia.* London, 1682.

Lugard, F. D., *The Rise of Our East African Empire.* London, 1893.

————— *The Dual Mandate in British Tropical Africa.* London, 1923.

————— *The Story of the Uganda Protectorate.* London, 1900.

Mabille, H. E., "The Basuto of Basutoland." *Journal of the African Society,* vol. V (1905-6), pp. 233 *sqq.,* 351 *sqq.*

MacDonald, J., "Manners, Customs, Superstitions and Religions of South African Tribes." *Journal of the Anthropological Institute,* vols. XIX (1899), pp. 264-96; XX (1890), pp. 113-40.

MacGregor, J. C., *Basuto Traditions.* Cape Town, 1905.

MacIver, R. Randall, *Medieval Rhodesia.* London, 1906.

MacKenzie, J., *Ten Years North of the Orange River.* Edinburgh, 1871.

MacLean, J. (Ed.), *A Compendium of Kafir Laws and Customs.* Mount Coke, S. A., 1858.

MacMillian, W. M., *Bantu, Boer and Briton: the making of the South African native problem.* London, 1929.
———— *The Cape Colour Question: an historical survey.* London, 1927.
Complex South Africa: an economic footnote to history. London, 1930.
Mage, E., *Voyage dans le Soudan occidental* (1863-1866). Paris, 1868.
Mahmoud Kâti (or Kôti) Tarikh el-fettâch, 1913.
———— *Tedzkiret en-nisiân,* Paris, 1901.
Maingard, L. F., "The Lost Tribes of the Cape." *South African Journal of Science,* vol. XXVIII (1931), pp. 487-504.
———— "Studies in Korana History, Language and Customs." *Bantu Studies,* vol. VI (1932), pp. 103-62.
Malherbe, E. G., *Education in South Africa,* 1652-1922. Cape Town, 1925.
Marcus, Jacob R., *The Jew in the Medieval World, a Source Book,* 315-1791. Cincinnati, 1938.
Marquart, J., *Die Benin-Sammlung des Reichhmuseums für Volkerkunde in Leiden.* Leiden, 1913.
Martin, A. D., *Doctor Vanderkemp.* 1931.
Marty, P., *Les Mourides d'Amadou Bamba,* Paris, 1913.
Masudi (i) Meynard B., de et Pavet de Courteille, *Macoudi* (Masudi). *Les Prairies d'Or. Texte et Traduction. Société Asiatique.* Paris, 1861-77.
———— (ii) Sprenger, A., *El Masudi's Historical Encyclopaedia.* London, Oriental Translation Fund, 1841.
Maugham, R. C. F., *The Liberian Republic,* New York, 1919.
Meek, C. K., *Law and Authority in a Nigerian Tribe,* London, 1937.
Mentzel, O. F., *Vollständige. . . Beschreibung des Afrikanischen Vorgebirges der Guten Hoffnung.* 2 vols. Glogau, 1785-7. Translation in Van Riebeeck Society, *Publications,* Vol. IV, 1921-1925.
Mercier, E., *Histoire de l'Afrique Septentrionale depuis les temps les plus reculés jusqu's la Conquête Française.* Paris, 1888-1891, 3 vols.
Merensky, A., *Beiträge zur Kenntnis Süd-Afrikas.* Berlin, 1875.
———— *Erinnerungen aus dem Missionsleben in Südost-Afrika* (*Transvaal*). Berlin, 1889.
Mévil, A., *Samory.* Paris, 1899.
Meyer, F., *Wirtschaft und Recht der Herero.* Berlin, 1905.
Meynier, Cap. O., *L'Afrique noire.* Paris, 1911. (Chapter IV.)
Michon, L. A. J., *Quid Libycae Geographiae Auctore Plinio Romani Contulerint.* Lutetiae, 1859.
Mockford, J., *Khama, King of the Bamangwato.* 1931.
Modat, Cap., *Une tournée en pays Fertyt,* Paris, 1912. (Publication du Comité de l'Afrique Française).
Moffat, R., *Missionary Labours and Scenes in South Africa.* London, 1842.
Moffat, R. U., *J. S. Moffat.* London, 1921.
Mofolo, Thomas, *Chaka, an Historical Romance,* translated by F. H. Dutton. London, 1931.
Molema, S. M., *The Bantu, Past and Present.* 1920.
Monod, J. L., *Histoire de l'Afrique Occidentale Française.* Paris, 1931.
Monteil, Ch., *Monographie de Djénné.* Tulle, 1903.

—————— *Les Khassonké.* Paris, 1915.

Moritz, E. (Ed.). Die ältesten Reiseberichte über Deusch-Südwesta-frika. *Mitteilungen aus den Deutschen Schutzgebieten,* vols. XXVIII (1915), pp. 161-268; XXIX (1916), pp. 135--253; XXXI (1918), pp. 17-143.

Moszeik, O., *Die Malereien der Buschmänner in Südafrika.* Berlin, 1910.

Müller, C., *Geographi Graeci Minores.* Vol. I (contains Hanno's "Periplus," "Scylax," and the anonymous "Periplus") and vol. III (Tabulae). Paris, 1855.

Müller, W., *Die Umsegelung Afrikas.* Rathenau, 1889.

Mumford, W. Bryant, *Africans Learn to be French.* London, 1937.

Nachtigal, G., *Sahara und Sudan.* Berlin, 1879-1882.

Nicolas, Victor, *L'Expedition au Dahomey en* 1890, Paris, 1892.

Niebuhr, Reinold, *Moral Man and Immoral Society,* New York, 1932.

Nogueria, A. F., *A raça negra sob o ponto de vista da civil-isação da Africa.* Lisboa, 1881.

Obermaier, H. and Kühn, M., *Buschmannkunst: Felsmalereien aus Süd-west-Afrika.* Berlin, 1930. (English trans., Oxford, 1930.)

O'Neil, H. C., *The War in Africa and the Far East.* London, 1919.

Oordt, P. F. van, *Who were the Builders of Great Zimbabwe? A Study.* Cape Town, 1906.

Oepen, J. M., "A Glimpse into the Mythology of the Maluti Bush-men." *Cape Monthly Mag.* 2nd ser., vol. IX (1874), pp. 1-13; re-printed in *Folk-Lore* (London), vol. XXX (1919) pp. 139-56.

Osorius, J., "Lopex Castagnede and Others." *Histoire de Portugal,* Paris, 1587.

Park, Mungo, *Travels in the interior of Africa.* London, 1799.

Passarge, S., "Das Okawangosumpfland und seine Bewohner." *Zeits. f. Ethnologie,* vol. XXVII (1905), pp. 649-716.

—————— *Die Buschmänner der Kalahari.* Berlin, 1907.

—————— *Südafrika: eine Landes-, Volks-, und Wirtschaftskunde.* Leipzig, 1908.

Paulitschke, Ph., *Beiträge zur Ethnographie und Anthropologie der Somal, Galla und Harari.* Leipzig, 1886.

—————— *Ethnographie Nordost-Afrikas.* Berlin, 1893.

Peters, C., *King Solomon's Golden Ophir.* New York, 1899.

—————— *Ophir nach den neuesten Forschungen.* Berlin, 1908.

—————— *Im Goldland des Altertums, Forschungen zwischen Zambesi und Sabi.* Berlin, 1902.

Petrie, Flinders, *History of Egypt.*

Pliny the Elder, *Natural History.* Paris, 1860.

Polo, Marco, *The Book of Ser Marco Polo.* Trans. and ed. H. Yule. 2 vols. London, 1903.

—————— *The Travels of Marco Polo.* Translated from the Text of L. F. Benedetto by A. Ricci. London, 1931.

Pomponius, Mela, *De Chorographia.* Ed. C. Frick. Leipzig, 1880.

Posselt, F., *Survey of the Native Tribes of Southern Rhodesia.* Salis-bury, S. Rhodesia, 1927.

—————— *Ethnographical Sketch of the Natives of Southern Rho-desia. Official Year-Book of the Colony of S. Rhodesia,* No. 2 (1930) pp. 750-61,

Poto Ndamase, Victor, *Ama-Mpondo: Ibali ne-Ntlalo*. Lovedale, S. A., 1927.

Poutrin, Dr., "Contribution a l'Etude des Negrilles," in *L'Anthropologie*, vol. XXI, Paris, 1910.

—————— "Les Negrilles du Centre Africain," in *L'Anthropologie*, XXII and XXIII, Paris, 1911-1912.

Proyart, *Histoire de Loango et Kakongo et autres royaumes d'Afrique*, Paris, 1776.

Ptolemy, *Geography*. Ed. O. Müller. Paris, 1883-1901.

Rattray, R. S., *Ashanti*. Oxford, 1923.

—————— *Ashanti Law and Constitution*. London, 1929.

—————— "Arts and Crafts of the Ashanti," *Journal of the Royal African Society*, XXIII, 265.

Reindorf, C. C., *History of the Gold Coast and Asante*. Basel, 1895.

Rennell, J., *The Geographical System of Herodotus*. 2nd ed. 1830.

Richards, Audrey I., *Hunger and Work in a Savage Tribe: a Functional Study of Nutrition among the Southern Bantu*. London, 1932.

Richter, M., *Das Wirtschaftsleben der Südafrikanischen Bantu-neger*. *Dissertation*. Drenden, 1912.

Riegner, G., *Das Sachenrecht der Herero Dissertation*. Borna-Leipzig, 1911.

Rivers, Pitt, *Antique Works of Art from Benin*. London, 1900.

Robinson, C. H., *Hausaland*. London, 1896.

Rorke, Melina, *The Story of Melina Roke*. New York, 1938.

Roscher, A., *Ptolemeus und die Handelstrassen in Central-Afrika*. Gotha, 1857.

Roscoe, John, *The Bagesu and Other Tribes of the Uganda Protectorate*. Cambridge, 1924.

Sadler, Michael E., *Arts of West Africa*. London, 1935.

Samuelson, L. H., *Zululand: its Traditions, Legends, Customs and Folk-Lore*. Marianhill, S. A., 1930.

Samuelson, R. C. A., *Long, Long, Ago*. Durban, 1929.

Sauvage, Marcel, *Les Secrets de L'Afrique Noire*. Paris, 1937.

Schapera, I., "The Old Bantu Culture." In *Western Civilization and the Natives of South Africa* (ed. I. Schapera), pp. 3-36. 1934.

—————— *The Early Cape Hottentots, described in the Writings of Dapper, Grevenbroek and Ten Rhyne*. Cape Town, 1933.

—————— *The Khoisan Peoples of South Africa: Bushmen and Hottentots*. 1930.

Schinz, H., *Deutsch-Südwest-Afrika*. Oldenburg and Leipzig, 1891.

Schmidt, M., "Die Nama, Bergdama, und Namib-Buschleute." In *Das Eingeborenenrecht* (ed E. Schultz-Ewerth and L. Adam), vol. II, pp. 269-397. Stuttgart, 1930.

Schmidt, W., *Die Religionen der Urvölker Afrikas*. Münster i.W., 1933.

Schreyer, J., *Neue Ost-Indianische Reisz-Beschreibung*. Leipzig, 1681.

Schultze, A. Dr., *The Sultanate of Bornu* (translated by Benton, P. A.). London, 1913.

Schultze, L., *Zur Kenntnis des Körpers der Hottentotten und Buschmänner*. Jena, 1928.

—————— *Aus Namaland und Kalahari*. Jena, 1907.

Segoete, E., *Raphepheng: Bophelo ba BaSotho ba Khale.* Morija, Basutoland, 1913.

Seiner, F., ''Ergenbnisse einer Bereisung der Omaheke.'' *Mitt. a.d. Deuts. Schutzgebieten,* vol. XXVI (1913), pp. 225-316.

———— ''Die Buschmänner des Okawango- und Sambesigibietes.'' *Globus,* vol. XCVII (1910), pp. 341 *sqq.,* 357 *sqq.*

Sekese, A., *Mekhoa le Maele a Basotho.* 3rd ed. Morija, 1931.

Shaw, W., *The Story of my Mission in South Eastern Africa.* 1860.

Shooter, J., *The Kafirs of Natal and the Zulu Country.* London, 1857.

Slatin-Pacha, R. C., *Fire and sword in the Soudan* (translated by F. R. Wingate, 5th edition). London, 1897.

Soga, J. H., *The Ama-Xosa: Life and Customs.* Lovedale, S. A., 1932.

———— *The South-Eastern Bantu.* Johannesburg, 1930.

Soga, T. B., *Intlalo ka Xosa.* 2nd ed. Butterworth, S. A., 1917.

South African Journal of Science. Report of the South African Association for the Advancement of Science. First published in Cape Town, then Johannesburg, 1903-.

Sparrman, A., *A Voyage to the Cape of Good Hope.* 2 vols. 1785.

Spears, John R., *The American Slave Trade,* New York, 1907.

Speckmann, F., *Die Hermannsburger Mission in Afrika.* Hermannsburg, 1876.

Spratlin, Valaurez B., *Juan Latino, Slave and Humanist,* New York, 1938.

Starr, Frederick, *Liberia after the World War,* New York, 1925.

Stayt, H. A., *The BaVenda.* Oxford, 1931.

Stephen-Chauvet, *Musique nègre,* Paris, 1929.

Stow, G. W., *The Native Races of South Africa.* London, 1905.

Stow, G. W., and Bleek, D. F., *Rock Paintings, in South Africa.* 1930.

Strabo, *Geographica.* Ed. and trans. H. L. Jones. 1927-32.

Tardieu, A., *Sénégambie et Guinée* (vol. III of *L'Afrique,* in collection *L'Univers Pittoresque*). Paris, 1878.

Tauxier, L., *Le Noir du Soudan (pays mossi et gourounsi).* Paris, 1912.

———— *Le Noir du Yatenga (Mossis, Nioniossés, Samos, Yarsés, Silmi-Mossis, Peuls).* Paris, 1917.

Ten Rhyne, W., *Schediasma de Promontorio Bonae Spei ejusve tractus incolis Hottentottis.* Schaffhausen, 1686.

Theal, G. M., *Ethnography and condition of South Africa before A. D. 1505.* London, 1919.

———— *Records of South-Eastern Africa.* Vol. I. Cape Town, 1898.

———— *The beginning of South African history.* London, 1889.

———— *History of South Africa.* London, 1902.

Thevet, A., *Cosmographie universelle.* Paris, 1575.

Thomas, N. W., *Anthropological Report of the Edo-speaking Peoples of Nigeria.* Part I. *Law and Custom.* London, 1910.

———— *Anthropological Report on the Ibo-speaking People of Nigeria.* Parts I and IV. London, 1913 and 1914.

———— *Anthropological Report on Sierra-Leone.* Part I, *Law and custom of the Timne and other tribes.* London, 1916.

———— *Sierra Leone Studies.* Freetown, 1918-1925.

Thomas, T. M., *Eleven years in Central South Africa.* 1872.

Thompson, F. W. B., *Sierra Leone in History and Tradition*. London, 1926.

Thompson, G., *Travels and Adventures in Southern Africa*. 2 vols. 1827.

Thomson, J., *Through Masai Land*. London, 1885.

Thunberg, C. P., *Travels in Europe, Africa and Asia*. 4 vols. 1795.

Tongue, M. Helen, *Bushman Paintings*. Oxford, 1909.

Tönjes, H., *Ovamboland: Land, Leute, Mission*. Berlin, 1911.

Tozer, H. F., *History of Ancient Geography*. 2nd ed. Cambridge, 1935.

Transvaal Native Affairs Department. *Short History of the Native Tribes of the Transvaal*. Pretoria, 1905.

Trenk, P., "Die Buschleute der Namib." *Mitt. a. d. Deuts. Schutzgebieten*, vol. XXIII (1910), pp. 166-70.

Van Linschoten, J. H., *Descriptio totius Guineæ tractus, Congi, Angolæ et Monomotapæ Hagæ Comitis (The Hague)*. 1599.

Vedder, H., *Das alte Südwestafrika. Südwestafrikas Geschichte bis zum Tode Mahareros 1890*. Berlin, 1934.

Vergiat, A. M., *Les Rites Secrets des Primitifs de l'Oubangui*. Paris, 1936.

———— *Moeurs et Coutumes des Manjas*. Paris, 1936.

Verneau, R., "La Pretendue Parenté des Negroides Européens et des Boschmans," in *L'Anthropologie*. Paris, 1899.

———— "Les migrations des Ethiopiens," in *L'Anthropologie*. Paris, 1899.

Vignon, L., *Un Programme de politique coloniale*. Paris, 1919.

Von Luschan, Felix, *Die Altertümer von Benin*. Berlin, 1912.

Walckenaer, C. A., *Collection des relations de voyage par mer et par terre en différentes parties de l'Afrique depuis 1400 jusqu'à nos jours*. Paris, 1842.

Walker, E. A., *Historical Atlas of South Africa*. Oxford, 1922.

———— *A History of South Africa (to 1935)*. 1935.

———— *The Great Trek*. 1934.

Wandres, C., "Die Khoi-Khoin oder Naman," in *Rechtsverhältnisse von Eingeborenen Völkern* (ed. S. R. Steinmetz), pp. 313-25. Berlin, 1903.

———— "Ueber das Recht der Naman und Bergdaman," *Zeits. f. Kolonial-Politik*, vol. XI (1909), pp. 657-86.

Wangemann, T., *Die Berliner Mission in Bassuto-Lande (Transvaal-Republik)*. Berlin, 1877.

———— *Die Geschichte der Berliner Mission im Zulu-Lande*. Berlin, 1875.

Warmelo, N. J. van, *Contributions towards Venda History, Religion, Tribal Ritual*. Pretoria, 1932. (Department of Native Affairs, Ethnological Publications, vol. III.)

———— *Transvaal Ndebele Texts*. Pretoria, 1930. (Department of Native Affairs, Ethnological Publications, vol. I.)

Werner, Alice, *The Natives of British Central Africa*. London, 1906.

———— *Myths and Legends of the Bantu*. London, 1933.

Werner, H., "Beobachtungen über die Heikum- und Kungbaschleute," *Zeits. f. Ethnologie*, vol. XXXVIII (1906), pp. 241-68.

Wheeler, J., *The Geography of Herodotus*. 1854.

Whiteway, R. S., *The Portuguese Expedition to Abyssinia*. London.

Whitfield, G. M. B., *South African Native Law.* Cape Town, 1929.
Wilbois, J., *Le Cameroun.* Paris, 1934.
Williams, J. J., *Africa's God.* Boston, 1933-1938.
Willoughby, W. C., *The Soul of the Bantu.* Oxford, 1928.
——————— *Nature-Worship and Taboo.* Hartford, Conn., 1932.
——————— *Race problems in the New Africa.* Oxford, 1923.
Wilman, M., *The Rock Engravings of Griqualand West and Bechuana-land, South Africa.* Cambridge, 1933.
Wilmot, A., *Monomotapa (Rhodesia), its monuments and its history* London, 1896.
Woodson, Carter G., *The African Background Outlined, or Handbook for the Study of the Negro.* Washington, D. C., 1936.
Wookey, A. J., *Dico tsa Secwana.* Tigerkloof, S. A., 1913, 1929.
Wuras, C. F., "An Account of the Korana," MS, 1858; printed in *Bantu Studies,* vol. III (1929), pp. 287-96.
Yergan, Max, *Gold and Poverty in South Africa.* New York, 1938.
Zastrow, B. von, "Die Herero," in *Das Eingeborenenrecht* (ed. E. Schultz-Ewerth and L. Adam), vol. II, pp. 213-68. Stuttgart, 1930.
Zastrow, B. von, and H. Vedder, "Die Buschmänner," in *Das Einge-borenenrecht* (ed. E. Schultz-Ewerth and L. Adam), vol. II, pp. 399-435. Stuttgart, 1930.
Zelízko, J. V., *Felsgravierungen der Sudafrikanischen Buschmänner.* Leipzig, 1925.